GHOST HUNTING

TRUE TALES OF POLTERGEIST INVESTIGATIONS

MICHAEL CLARKSON

ROSEN PUBLISHING

New York

This edition published in 2016 by:
The Rosen Publishing Group, Inc.
29 East 21st Street
New York, NY 10010

Library of Congress Cataloging-in-Publication Data

Clarkson, Michael, 1948–
Ghost hunting: true tales of poltergeist investigations/Michael Clarkson.
   pages cm.—(True tales of terror)
First published as The Poltergeist Phenomenon.
Pompton Plains, NJ: New Page Books, c2011.
Includes bibliographical references and index.
ISBN 978-1-4994-6158-9 (library bound)
1. Poltergeists. I. Title.
BF1483.C54 2015
133.1'42—dc23

                        2014050346

Manufactured in the United States of America

First published as *The Poltergeist Phenomenon: An In-Depth Investigation into
Floating Beds, Smashing Glass, and Other Unexplained Disturbances* by New
Page Books/Career Press, copyright © 2011 Michael Clarkson.

To John Rossiter, who dared to dream.

Acknowledgments

I would like to thank all of those people who helped me with this book, including my publisher, New Page Books, and my literary agent, Robert Mackwood.

Special thanks to Dr. William Roll, a researcher's dream with his kindness and help, and to other parapsychologists such as Stephen Mera, Andrew Nichols, Malcolm Robinson, and the late Maurice Grosse.

Thank you to Sarah S. for opening up her life to these pages in Chapter 20.

For the St. Catharines case, thanks to the Niagara Regional Police, to my former employer the St. Catharines Standard, and to the subject, John Mulvey.

Other thanks go to the Toronto Public Library system, the Bridgeport (Connecticut) Public Library in helping find articles and sources, and to the many authors of books, periodicals, Websites, associations, and interviews given in the bibliography and notes.

Finally, a big hug to my family for putting up with the ups and downs of life with a writer.

Michael Clarkson,
winter 2010–11

Contents

Introduction

"Poltergeist activity is something that really scares the crap out of me."
Donovan van Wyngaard, South African producer and director

A book about the supernatural might seem like merely a diversion for a writer who has been heavily into police, investigative, and sports reporting for four decades—as I have. And yet, I have also studied fear and its energies for many years, and authored six books, based largely on psychology. The topic of poltergeists has intrigued me for a long time, even before 1980 when a young man who had been the center of a poltergeist case came to my house to talk. Since then, I have been following with added interest such cases as they pop up from time to time in the media and in scholarly publications, and some of them seem worthy of further examination. During the past five years, I have been closely examining the cases that appear in this book.

I am not an expert in poltergeists or paranormal phenomena, but as a journalist, I'm always looking for *reasonable* proof for things like extrasensory perception, UFOs, or ghosts. As a fear researcher, I believe we are just beginning to understand some of the amazing capabilities of the fight-or-flight system, which is hardwired into each of us by nature to allow us to adapt our physical response to mental and emotional tasks.

For this book, I have reviewed 75 poltergeist cases and interviewed more than 100 witnesses, parapsychologists, psychologists, university professors, magicians, and skeptics. Some of the cases may raise as many questions as they provide answers, and others may seem to have holes in them, or be completely the result of trickery. But if we are too quick to toss out everything, we might miss some intriguing stories, and theories on the edge of science.

Poltergeists are difficult to prove for a number of reasons. Reportedly, the phenomenon often involves adolescents or teenagers, who may be prone to trickery or at least to manufacturing attention for themselves, and families involved in reported poltergeist activity are often embarrassed, and reluctant to let investigators into their homes.

Reports of poltergeists have fascinated people, from ancient times to the Amityville Horror case on Long Island in 1974, and beyond, to the Harry Potter books and movies and a family in Ireland abandoning their home in 2010. Poltergeists were reported as early as 858 BC in a farmhouse in Rhine, Germany, where an unseen force reportedly threw stones, shook the walls, moved objects, and produced loud banging noises. Other cases were reported in AD 530 in Roman Italy and AD 900 in China. The Spiritualism movement in the United States began in 1848 when it was reported that sisters Kate and Margaret Fox were creating disruptive, noisy energy in their Hydesville, New York home. (Spiritualist belief is in the continued existence of the human soul, and it remains be popular in places around the world, particularly in Brazil.)

Many people are skeptical about early poltergeist investigations, which were sometimes done by superstitious researchers who might have too easily jumped to conclusions. Even the famous murder and poltergeist/haunting case in a house in Amityville (made into the book and two movies called *The Amityville Horror*) was said by many people to be fraudulent.

In ancient times, many people believed that demons were behind such activity, but then the theory turned to the idea that they were actually ghosts of the dead. Beginning in the 20th century, parapsychologists such as Sir William Barrett, Federic Myers, Nandor Fodor, and William Roll started to believe that the activity revolved around young people, that the loud bumps and moving objects were the types of things mischievous or angry youths might attempt; in these cases, it was believed the adolescents did it subconsciously through a type of kinetic energy in which they moved objects with their mind and emotions, possibly without even knowing they were doing it.

After reviewing many cases for this book, I have narrowed the description of a poltergeist, taking direction from what the contemporary investigators believe: The poltergeist is an unusual form of energy produced most often by a young person. However, others believe that ghosts or demon possession is responsible. Although each case has its own characteristics and idiosyncrasies, here are the trends I have found. The cases generally encompass:

- Dramatic events, such as unexplained knocking, electrical malfunctions, and movement of objects and furniture. Occasionally reported are levitation of objects, electrical appliances working without power, and stones falling apparently from nowhere. Infrequently reported are strange voices, apparitions, strange odors, cold spots, and water formings.

- A poltergeist agent, usually an adolescent entering puberty, immediately around whom the strange activities occur. He or she is usually quite intelligent.

- Some sort of repression or frustration of the poltergeist agent by others in a home.

- A high level of stress in the household, prior to the start of the poltergeist activity and continuing through the case.

- A mischievous or destructive intent on the part of the agent, rather than a downright malevolent intent (although about a dozen people have been injured, none seriously, in the cases in this book).

- A lifespan for a case of one week to several months.

Probably hundreds of millions of people in America believe in some form of the supernatural. A 2003 Harris Poll of more than 2,000 Americans revealed that 90 percent believed in God, 89 percent in miracles, 68 percent in the devil, 51 percent in ghosts, 31 percent in astrology, and 27 percent in reincarnation. In 2005, a Gallup poll showed that belief in haunted houses declined with age; 56 percent of people between the ages of 18 and 29 believed, while only 26 percent of those

65 and over did. In Britain, a 2004 survey showed that 42 percent of people believed in ghosts.

Are you one of these people?

Author's Note: Unless otherwise specified in the Notes section at the back of this book, all quotes have come from my personal interviews with those quoted.

⊚ PART I ⊚

THE EVIDENCE

"So many people have seen so many things;
we can't all be going mad."

*Adrian Payton, after seeing strange happenings in
a house in Cork City, Ireland, in 2010*

In this section we examine the evidence for the existence of poltergeists—eyewitnesses, the tests, photographs, and videos. Chapter 1 sets the stage with these issues, and the other six chapters examine North American cases with startling accounts from police and other investigators. In Chapters 2 and 3, we look in detail at a fascinating case in St. Catharines, Ontario, which has been under-publicized throughout the years. Chapter 4 involves a detective puzzler on Long Island, followed by chapters based in New England, Florida, and Canada.

CHAPTER 1

A Sampling of Eyewitnesses

"You stay around here, you get hit by a lot of stuff."

Mrs. Charles Daughtery, to a police officer who had been struck in the leg by a flying "poltergeist object" in her home in Portsmouth, Virginia

It's quite abnormal for the paranormal to come *to* investigators, and yet that is what happened in the fall of 2007 in Ahmedabad, India. There, at the Ramol police station, about a dozen officers claimed that they saw the effects of a poltergeist, and some officers claimed they were victims of it.

According to Constable Batuksinh Darbar, an unseen force terrorized the police station for more than a month, overturning furniture, moving chairs, and even assaulting police officers. "It pushed police officials off tables and chairs," Darbar said. "Some police officials even complained of chest pain in the middle of the night. They felt as if someone had jumped on their chests. Then there were others who felt someone was strangling them."[1]

Usually confident and skeptical police were even timid about working inside the station, where the poltergeist was said to wreak most of its havoc. "Almost all the cops working in the night shift noticed strange activity inside the police station. We were all so scared that we decided to park ourselves near the entrance after sundown," Darbar said. Some of the officers prayed to Meldi Mata, a Hindu goddess, when entering the station.[2]

Strangely, the poltergeist seemed to target police officers sitting on tables and chairs.

A team of paranormal investigators did some limited investigating and theorized that it was the work of a female poltergeist, perhaps the ghost of a girl who had died while working in a mill that had been on the site of the police station. A religious tantric, similar to an exorcist, was summoned to perform some rituals at the station, and the poltergeist activity gradually ceased. But questions remained whether the genesis was really a spirit related to someone in the building or an elaborate prank.

Police testifying to invisible ghosts and poltergeists? *Afraid* of poltergeists? What is going on here? Actually, although this story is unusual, it is not unheard of. In fact, at least 51 police officers around the world—in 17 cases since 1952—claim to have seen poltergeist activity up close. More than a dozen of them were assaulted by what they said was a poltergeist, but none were seriously injured, and no one was charged. One officer even pulled a gun on an "unseen force." Although there is no scientific proof that poltergeists exist, the eyewitness accounts of these officers, taken from published reports and from interviews I conducted, seem compelling. Gathering scientific proof is difficult because of the fleeting nature of poltergeists' alleged existence—by the time a family suspects that they may have something paranormal on their hands, it is often too late for anyone to study it, or the family may suppress it for fear of appearing crazy.

But if we go simply by eyewitness accounts of first-line responders, the police officers, even some skeptics may start to suspect there is something paranormal at work here; at least something that science cannot digest. Generally, police tend to be solid witnesses, trained and experienced in focusing when something is happening fast. As witnesses, they should be more accurate than the average person because they are trained to be observant, tend to be skeptical, and are sometimes cynical when a trickster is potentially at work. And if they are wrong about such a contentious subject, they have much to lose in credibility among their peers as well as the general public.

Having been a police reporter for daily newspapers for 13 years, I tend to listen when police officers speak. I think I know how to read them and how to interpret what they say. In this book, we have at least 51 cops who believe they saw—and had the courage to report to their superiors—what they believed to be poltergeist, or at least unexplained activity, right in front of their eyes.

Examples to be fully examined later this book include:

- In a middle-class home on Long Island, New York, in 1958, Detective Joseph Tozzi, one of the brightest gumshoes in the Nassau County Police Department, said he was hit in the back of the legs by a flying bronze horse, weighing nearly 100 pounds, while he was walking down basement steps with a 13-year-old boy. Many other witnesses claimed to see startling events, which lasted more than four weeks. (Chapter 4)

- In a Miami warehouse in 1967, police officers, newspaper reporters, television crews, and insurance agents claimed they saw cowbells, ashtrays, key chains, and rubber daggers fly or fall off shelves, sometimes at unusual angles, and always while a 19-year-old shipping clerk was nearby. (Chapter 6)

- An entire shift of police officers said they believed in poltergeists after watching furniture move strangely around an 11-year-old boy in his apartment in 1970 in St. Catharines, Ontario. (Chapters 2 and 3)

- In 1974 in the home of a factory worker in Bridgeport, Connecticut, Officer John Holsworth swore he saw a heavy refrigerator lift slowly off the floor, turn, and then set down again. (Chapter 5)

- In a house in London, England, in 1977, Constable Carolyn Keeps said she became a witness to a chair moving 3 or 4 feet, apparently without the help of human hands. (Chapters 15 and 16)

- Also in England, in 1952, police say they were witnesses, and also the victims, of strange incidents in Runcorn, in which a quiet, 17-year-old apprentice draftsman was said to cause dressing tables and other things to move with his mind throughout a 10-week period. (Chapter 18)

- In the Netherlands in 1995, two police officers investigating poltergeist-like activities in a house say they had sand thrown in their faces. (Chapter 18)

17

As well as police officers, teachers, doctors, and parapsychologists are often good witnesses. Examples of these that will be studied later on in this book include:

◉ At her home in Scotland and at primary school in 1960, 11-year-old Virginia Campbell was said to move objects with her mind, including a heavy desk. During class, her teacher said she observed Virginia trying to hold down her desk lid, which several times raised itself to an angle of 45 to 50 degrees. (Chapter 17)

◉ Late in the 19th century in Amherst, Nova Scotia, physician Dr. Gene Carritte said he saw potatoes hurl themselves across a room and a thundering noise come from the roof of a house. (Chapter 8)

◉ There are numerous accounts of parapsychologists claiming to see poltergeist activity. Dr. William Roll, then at Duke University, and psychology student/paranormal researcher John P. Stump said they both saw amazing occurrences at a home in Olive Hill, Kentucky, in 1968, while in the presence of a 12-year-old boy. (Chapter 10)

Of course, most scientists will not accept eyewitness accounts or anecdotal evidence as proof that poltergeists exist. Why should they? People sometimes can be fooled, or can hallucinate.

Although it is hard to prove that poltergeists are part of our universe, a respected scientist, Professor Robert Jahn, Dean Emeritus of the School of Engineering and Applied Sciences at Princeton University, believes they do. He says he has proven in laboratory experiments that psychokinesis exists, at least on a small scale. Professor Jahn told me, "The [poltergeist] cases are so rare and happen under such awkward circumstances, it is hard to set up research to investigate them. There's no doubt, however, that they do exist. William Roll has investigated them and I trust his work. The effects seen in his cases are substantial. You can't dismiss it."

One piece of evidence that poltergeists may exist is the fact that cases around the world share many common features (such as moving objects, rappings, and youthful agents), despite the fact that they are reported independently of each other.

testing the poltergeist agents

Some youths suspected to be the center or *agent* of poltergeist activity have been tested under scientific conditions in laboratories, but the results have not been spectacular, or even conclusive.

However, perhaps the laboratory is the wrong place for testing. Most poltergeist incidents are reported in homes, possibly as a partial result of family tension, and removing the poltergeist agent from the home may dissipate the unusual energy needed for such a paranormal event. Or, in some cases, perhaps the unusual energy has run its course by the time the agent is shipped off for testing.

In the Miami warehouse case, detailed in Chapter 6, shipping clerk Julio Vasquez was persuaded by William Roll to go with him to a psychical research foundation in Durham, North Carolina. Under controlled conditions, researchers say they saw a bottle fall off a table while Vasquez was nearby, and in another instance, a vase allegedly moved while he was standing with researchers. He was also tested with a dice-throwing machine and apparently showed better-than-chance averages, Roll said.

Otherwise, poltergeist events are "the most elusive and problematic to access for controlled research, despite their severe anomalous effects," Jahn told me. As mentioned earlier, he believes that, from 1979 until the facility closed in 2007, he and his colleagues at the Princeton Anomalies Research (PEAR) Laboratory produced good experimental data to support the existence of psychokinesis, or PK (also known as "mind over matter"). They say that some people have been able to influence small balls and pendulums through the force of their mind.

Possibly the most compelling evidence for PK was Nina Kulagina of Russia, who was given the pseudonym Nelya Mikhailova by the government of the Soviet Union in the Cold War years of the 1950s and '60s because they believed she possessed a new and powerful mental force. Initially, poltergeist activity was reported around her in her apartment—objects moving and lights flickering on and off. For three decades, she was probed by respected Soviet scientists, including two Nobel laureates, often in closely-controlled laboratory conditions, and they claimed that she could move things by focusing tightly with her mind. Kulagina was sometimes put in a cage to prevent trickery, or forced to move things placed in a Plexiglas cube with videocameras rolling. Apparently, no one ever caught her cheating. The chairman of theoretical physics at Moscow University, Dr. Ya. Terletsky, said that Kulagina "displays a new and unknown form of energy."[3]

In Poland in 1985, a biophysicist, a metallurgist, a psychologist, and other scientists studied 15-year-old Joasia Gajewski, whom two years earlier was reportedly at the epicenter of poltergeist activity in her home, in which police Sergeant Tadeusz Slowik was a witness. In the laboratory tests, the scientists said they saw an armchair start to move with Joasia sitting in it, cross-legged. The chair continued to move when she got out of it, they said, and it took a sharp turn in the air and rotated. Three of them reportedly could not hold the chair down.

Photos and videos

These days, the Internet, and particularly YouTube, is filled with video clips claiming to show poltergeist phenomena, but they cannot be verified.

Throughout the years, there has not been a lot of photographic evidence, partly because the events are so unpredictable, and partly because those who try to record them say they often have mysterious electrical problems while trying to document the cases. Electrical malfunctions and power failures are said to be common in poltergeist cases.

However, parapsychologist Dr. Hans Bender said he got videotapes of pictures rotating on the walls after 19-year-old Annemarie Schneider had breezed into an office in 1967 in Bavaria. He also got a photograph of a swaying lamp, which is reproduced in the book *Poltergeists* by A.D. Cornell and Alan Gauld. Throughout a period of several weeks, many electrical disturbances were reported, mostly revolving around Schneider.

In 1955, photographer Gerrard Lestienne of the newspaper *Semedi Soir* snapped a stunning picture of what appears to be several household items swirling in the air in the kitchen of the Costa family in the French village of St. Jean-de-Maurienne on the France/Italy border. Lestienne and reporter Michel Agallet were sent to the home on reports of a poltergeist. At first, they say they examined the home without finding any evidence, but after 90 minutes, they say that pots and cutlery started floating around the kitchen under their own power. The photographer said he saw the objects "slide from their places, make a semi-circle in the air and fall in different locations." This occurred throughout a prolonged period of time, he added. In Lestienne's photo, the woman of the house, Madame Teresa Costa, is looking concerned while protecting her baby in a blanket, and watching a saucepan, a pot lid, a pair of scissors and what seems to be a box of matches float in the air. The photograph depicts one of three things:

1. An elaborate hoax.

2. An incredible freak of nature.

3. A true poltergeist event.

Perhaps the most famous poltergeist photograph was taken on March 5, 1984, in a home in Columbus, Ohio. After several weeks of reported incidents, photographer Fred Shannon of the *Columbus Dispatch* took a series of shots of a telephone moving across the lap of 14-year-old Tina Resch, suspected of making many objects move or break in the home, either by trickery or with her mind. One of the photos, which appeared on the front page of the *Dispatch* the following day, and has subsequently been reproduced in periodicals around the world, shows the Princess phone in flight, either by sleight of hand or recurrent spontaneous psychokinesis.

In West Australia in 1998, a television camera crew from the *Today Tonight* show on TVW Channel 7 set up in a house in the town of Humpty Doo, where a family had reported flying steak knives, gravel, and babies' bottles. They used a thermal imaging camera to detect strange heat signatures left on the objects, which apparently were not made by human hands. In the same case, a freelance cameraman claimed he photographed a flying ball. Among the witnesses to report flying objects were a priest, a security guard, and a maintenance man.[4]

In 1975 in Buffalo, New York, a poltergeist may have been on live radio. Program host Tom Donahue reported on the air on WGR Radio from a home of strange occurrences with a woman and her daughter: "I was standing near a utility room, phoning in my report, when, my God, a bunch of dried flowers just flew out of my hand as if someone had grabbed them and they fell hard to the floor, 3 or 4 feet away," he said. The women earlier reported that boxes had moved under their own accord, their dog had been "knocked around the room," and a radio kept going on and off by itself. "I went in there a skeptic, but since then I'm more open-minded to the possibility of telekinesis," Donahue told me.

Audio recordings of alleged poltergeist rappings have different characteristics than normal sounds, according to British scientist Dr. Barrie Colvin, BSc, PhD. In 2010, Colvin analyzed the recordings of 10 poltergeist investigations, from the Sauchie case in 1960 to a case in Euston Square, London, in 2000, and including the Enfield case. Colvin reported that the sound of a normal rap, which often lasts only a few milliseconds, starts loudly and diminishes over a short period of time, whereas rappings from poltergeist cases start relatively quietly and work up to the maximum sound before the sound starts to diminish.

Colvin has been interested in such cases since 1974 when he investigated an alleged poltergeist haunting in Andover, Hampshire, England, involving a 12-year-old girl and strange rapping noises. "It was absolutely clear that no normal explanation could account for the observed phenomena," he said.[5] He added that there is some evidence suggesting a poltergeist rapping arises from *within* a structure of a material rather than from the surface of it.

Although there is as yet no solid evidence that poltergeists absolutely exist, the circumstantial evidence seems quite suggestive. In the following five chapters, we will examine some of the most compelling cases.

CHAPTER 2

'House Phenomena', in St. Catharines

"At first, I thought the family must be mental, but, believe me, what I saw was not done by human hands."

Constable Robert "Scotty" Crawford

I t's spring 2010 and the cherry blossoms are out in St. Catharines, the garden city of Canada's Niagara region. Life is pretty sweet for John Mulvey (a pseudonym), a successful 51-year-old businessman, father of two, and a national award winner in his profession. Mulvey has a solid support network of family, friends, and colleagues to ease his pain and remind him what a successful and traditional life he is leading. Just look at the comments from his many friends on Facebook, congratulating him, encouraging him, challenging him, and exchanging baby photos with him.

Surely he is a role model; Mr. Straight Laced. Or is he? On the surface, there is nothing to suggest to those friends and colleagues who do not know his past that four decades earlier, Mulvey had been called a freak and a monster by some people in a poltergeist case that garnered international headlines. As the 40th anniversary of that weird story is relived in the city's newspaper, the *St. Catharines Standard*, Mulvey has kept his true identity, and his very dark secret, intact. And yet I have known about him—about *it*—for 30 years. The following is his story from 1970.

the winter of 1970

It had all started in late January of 1970, approaching the final part of a long winter that had kept everyone cooped up indoors. Reportedly, there were bizarre goings-on in the Mulvey apartment, one of four units in an old downtown building above a little cleaning store, where John Mulvey, Sr., an immigrant who worked with his hands and had moved up the ladder at his company to become a supervisor, lived with his wife, Barbara, and their two sons, 11-year-old John and his 8-year-old brother Jeff (all pseudonyms).

The family was puzzled and scared as furniture started to shift and paintings came crashing down, seemingly under their own power. The Mulveys, who had lived there for many years without such problems, summoned the city's engineering department to check for structural failings, or perhaps wood groaning from fluctuation in temperatures. Engineers went over the place with a fine-tooth comb, but found nothing. "There was a problem with certain noises and items of furniture which appeared to be moving around," said Mel Holenski, assistant city engineer. "But, after checking, we satisfied ourselves that there were no problems with the building."[1] Yet the occurrences continued, and so the provincial gas company got involved, but there were no faults to be found in the gas furnace. Next came the fire department and the public utilities commission. They found nothing.

John Sr. and Barbara were embarrassed about having strangers walk through their apartment, but they soon found the presence of two Roman Catholic priests to be somewhat soothing. It was only as a last resort that they summoned the St. Catharines Police Department, and even then it only happened by chance—officers were in the apartment building for another matter and Mrs. Mulvey took the opportunity to call one of them inside her unit.

As soon as police started to investigate, the Mulveys asked for a media ban on the story, but leaks within the police department allowed bits and pieces of the strange tale to get out and into the *St. Catharines Standard* as well as the local radio stations. What media outlet could resist these details: a chair allegedly sliding across a room to the boy's bedside, a footstool turning upside down, a framed photo of young John and his parents becoming a *moving* picture. In another occurrence, a police officer was sitting in a chair when an unseen force flipped him onto his behind. Other alleged phenomena included the pinning of the boy, John, against a wall by a chair too heavy for one man to move, and the raising of a heavy bed 6 inches off the floor. All of the strange events occurred while little John was in the vicinity.

"At first, I thought the family must be mental, but, believe me, what I saw was not done by human hands," Constable Robert "Scotty" Crawford said to me. He was a salty cop who spoke with a thick Scottish brogue and was already a veteran of containing bar brawls. As he sent other officers to the Mulvey home, dispatcher Bob Little shook his head in disbelief: "You get a lot of funny calls in this business, and this seemed like a really funny one," he said.

Four of the first five officers submitted reports to their superiors. A fifth refused to hand one in because he worried they would have thought him crazy. In fact, some officers thought it was a United Kingdom joke concocted by the first three constables to reach the scene—two Scots and an Irishman. "Our superiors thought we were pulling a joke on them," Constable Mike McMenamin said to me. He was quite sobered by the experience. Other witnesses included two doctors, two priests, and two pinstriped lawyers. To this day, some of the officials refuse to speak to the media or even to be identified concerning what they saw.

The following is a sampling of some of the reported occurrences by witnesses in the Mulvey apartment.

Wednesday, February 4, 7 p.m. A bed reportedly moved away from a wall, was pushed back by Father Melvin Stevens, an assistant at the St. Catharines (Roman Catholic) Cathedral, and almost immediately moved away again by itself. Witnesses were Father Stevens and Barbara Mulvey.

Friday, February 6, evening. Mrs. Mulvey showed Constable Crawford a heavy chest of drawers lying on its side in the kitchen. She explained that in the past 10 days or so, many pieces of furniture had been moved by an unseen force. "She was starting to think both her and her husband were mental," Crawford told me. Father Stevens verified some of the strange occurrences, which he had witnessed. After interviewing Mrs. Mulvey and Father Stevens, Constable Crawford told them to go into the living room and he would join them. On his way out, the officer put a chair under the kitchen table and walked into the living room. He said he had just succeeded in calming down an upset Mrs. Mulvey when he heard what sounded like footsteps moving from the living room towards the kitchen, even though no one was walking in that direction. When the officer and the priest went back into the kitchen, they found that the chair was mysteriously out in the middle of the room. There was no one around. Father Stevens said this was typical of the occurrences he had witnessed throughout 10 days. Crawford logged all of this information in an official police report, which he entitled "House Phenomena."

Friday, February 7, 10 p.m. Crawford found that a heavy bed had been raised two feet off the floor by an unseen force. The incident was reported by Mrs. Baines, who told police she had seen it rise off the floor in the boys' bedroom. Crawford said he rushed into the room and saw the bed approximately 2 feet off the floor at one end—unsupported. "Not believing my eyes, I summoned Constable [Dick] Colledge, who was outside the apartment," Crawford said. "On our return, the bed was in the same position, but it was now supported by two chairs. At this time, there were two other ladies present [one was Shirley McKinnon, 32, manager of a hair salon]."[2] In addition, Colledge said he saw a picture in the bedroom forcefully come off the wall and arch in the air across a bed and fall to the floor. "With its trajectory, there was no way it could have simply fallen off a nail or it would have dropped onto the bed," Colledge told me. "It was as if someone or something had ripped it off the wall and thrown it, but there was no one in the room...very strange."

Saturday, February 7, evening. Shirley McKinnon said she saw a heavy rocking chair move from one side of a room to another and tip onto its back. At the same time, a knocking sound came from the children's bedroom, as though something had fallen. Crawford went into the bedroom and turned on the light to find that a doll he had earlier seen hanging on a wall about six feet from a bed was on the floor, not far from John Mulvey, who was still in bed. His younger brother, Jeff, was asleep nearby. Mrs. Mulvey entered the room and became very upset and was shaking, thinking, *How could this happen to one of her children? Was the family being punished for something? Was it the work of the devil? How long would this go on? And what will friends and family think?*

Constable McMenamin arrived, along with local residents Lorne and Janet Asher, who were visiting the apartment. Most of the people in the house went into the living room, along with Crawford, who watched through a door into the adjoining children's bedroom. He was keeping an eye on John Mulvey when a small picture frame fell from a wall onto John's head, the officer said in his report.

Several minutes later, there was a rapid succession of events in the bedroom, Crawford told me: A table lamp in the bedroom fell over, a large, heavy chest of drawers moved from a wall—and then back again—a chair was heaved up in the air and slammed forcefully to the floor, and numerous objects on a dressing table were hurled to the floor. All of the objects on the dressing table moved in the same direction, except for an alarm clock, which flew in the opposite direction. "I remember the boy was sitting on a chair and it rose off the floor, then started bouncing up and down...plaques and a painting on the wall started moving and falling and a bookcase toppled." Needless to say, the people in the house, which also included Monsignor M. Herbert Delaney of the St. Catharines Cathedral, and a Mr. Baines, were upset and puzzled.

Sunday, February 8, afternoon. Furniture was said to have moved about the apartment on its own accord. Witnesses: Monsignor Delaney, Mrs. McKinnon, and Father Stevens.

Tuesday, February 10. For about the 12th time in almost two weeks, Constable Bill Weir said he saw John Mulvey thrown off a chair. Weir wrote in his report:

> "I attended in the morning and was assisted by Constable Eddie Batorski. While I was there, I witnessed some phenomenal occurrences which I have attached to this report. At 9 p.m., I proceeded to the residence again with Constable Crawford, where we again witnessed some very unusual things taking place. Between the time of the two calls, I contacted Mr. Bradley, the city building inspector. We both agreed that the causes of these weird occurrences were in no way connected to the building structure itself. My only solution to these occurrences is that the boy [John], whom all the occurrences surround, has been inhabited by a spirit of a poltergeist.

This is the spirit which inhabits the body of a young child that does not generally seriously harm anyone. People who have witnessed these occurrences are Constables Weir, Crawford, McMenamin, and Colledge, and other officers. Briefly, this boy can't sit on a chair without being thrown off, and items are hitting him for no apparent reason. I the writer witnessed the boy being thrown on at least a dozen occasions, including while I was there with Constable Crawford."[3]

Weir's report was later signed and authorized by his commanding officer, Sergeant Buck Taylor.

Weir said he got "the treatment" from the unseen force. Although he did not write it on his police report, Weir told Constable Harry Fox, who then told me, that the poltergeist force picked up a chair he was sitting in and, according to Fox, "tipped him on his ass." Now, if little John Mulvey had really done that physically, that would be a tough one to explain to the boys back at the station: burly cop overpowered over by an 11-year-old!

Wednesday, Feb. 11, suppertime. A chair containing John Mulvey lifted itself 6 inches off the floor and slammed down. Constable Robert "Nobby" Richardson said he was sitting in the living room with John and his younger brother, Mrs. and Mrs. Mulvey, Constable Crawford, Detective Sandy Sandison, two physicians, and Monsignor Delaney. According to Richardson, at about 5 p.m., as several people walked into the boys' bedroom, the chair that John Mulvey was sitting in lifted abruptly about six inches off the floor, then slammed down. The casters that had been under the legs of the chair fell away onto the floor, the officer said, but there was no natural explanation.

Another witness was Andrew McQuilken of the law firm Ross-McQuilken, acting on behalf of the owner of the building and also as a liason between the Mulvey family and the public. Later that evening, McQuilken reported to police that he saw incidents at the apartment similar to the one at suppertime.

Date unknown. John Mulvey was sitting on his bed in his night-clothes, watched by Crawford. Because of the stress in the house and the disturbances, police asked the boy's father to make arrangements for the two boys to stay with friends for the night. When the boys began to dress in the living room, a bookcase suddenly tipped over and fell from the wall and onto the floor. The witnesses were Constables Crawford, Colledge, McMenamin, and Weir, along with Mr. and Mrs. Asher, Father Stevens, Mrs. Baines, and Mrs. McKinnon.

Early February. Constable Fox was talking to Mrs. Mulvey while sitting in an easy chair. "[The poltergeist] must like you," Mrs. Mulvey said, referring to the fact that the chair was the favorite of the poltergeist, and that it had not tried to throw Fox off. But the action was just to Fox's left, where John Mulvey was lying on a couch about 7 feet long, when the couch suddenly flipped the boy onto the floor, the officer said. "The back legs of the chesterfield came a foot or more off the ground; there was no way the boy could have done it. I had no idea what did that," Fox told me.

The police officers stood by the reports they handed in to their superiors, even though some people at the police station remained skeptical. "Some of the guys didn't even write reports on what they saw," Colledge told me. "They didn't want to be called nuts." But Crawford and others did sign their reports. "All persons interviewed were sober and responsible people," he wrote. Later, the crusty, no-nonsense Weir told me: "These occurrences were phenomenal."

"It was goddamn scary," Fox told me. "And yet [Mulvey] didn't seem scared. Of course, I got there [about two weeks] after it started, and by this time the lad was probably taking everything for granted."

However, McMenamin had a different observation to give me of Mulvey, and saw him more often than Fox did: "[John] seemed okay at the start [in January], but then he got scared and was crying. Overall, the whole family was very upset."

Fox added during his interview with me, "It was one of the scariest things I've ever been involved with. At least in your normal work, if you're confronted with a big man, you can defend yourself. But this was different, unpredictable. I think it was some sort of invisible energy which you couldn't see." Later, the mild-mannered, level-headed Fox would openly lecture about the case to his supervisors as the Ontario Police College: "As it turned out, I think the spirit was playful, not harmful," Fox told me.

One of the few officers who went to the apartment and did not see anything unusual was Batorski. "I can't figure out why nothing happened when I went there, but all the other guys swore things were moving," he told me. "I don't doubt they could have happened," he continued. "I liked the family. They were clean-living."

Some of the details of the Mulvey case made it into the three local papers and some radio stations, and eventually the wire services carried them to Toronto and around Canada, and then into the United States and around the world via the Associated Press. That's apparently how the producers of *The Tonight Show* heard about it, and it became part of Johnny Carson's monologue.

To try to appease the family, who shuddered at the thought of publicity, the police brass issued an executive order on February 12 to ensure that officers who had been in the apartment would not give comments to the media. By the mid-1990s, the official police reports had somehow made it onto the Internet.

During the course of the investigation, some parapsychologists were kept away from the Mulvey apartment, but theories abounded. A parapsychologist in nearby Hamilton, Nellie Nielson, speculated that John Mulvey had unleashed a type of psychic energy because he was entering puberty and was feeling frustrated, perhaps by his family. "These youngsters, when they are reaching puberty have a lot of emotion and energy, which may vent itself on the surroundings if the child is under pressure or frustrated," she said. "Frustrations can only aggravate the situation." Nielson suggested that Mulvey had taken on a secondary, psychic personality "and he's probably unaware of it, and I don't believe his family is aware of it, either. The longer he's bothered, the longer it will last."[5]

Many others had their own theories about what was responsible, from the devil to ghosts to John Mulvey himself, because some of the events were similar to pranks a young boy might try. But the police had kept a close eye on him and they contended that a boy could not have fooled such observant and cynical folks as they. "To me, he just seemed like an average boy," Colledge told me.

John's elementary school principal, who did not wish to be identified, told me John was "an above-average student, who didn't cause any problems and was not unusual in any way. What happened came as a surprise to us."

Apparently, no events occurred at school—only when Mulvey was in the apartment with his parents. When the family left the apartment, nothing happened to them. And nothing seemed to involve the boy's younger brother. The Mulvey family was reportedly close, although it was said the children were taught to be seen and not heard, as in many families of that era with a European background.

Altogether, the events in St. Catharines lasted several weeks, until the family took a vacation to Montreal to get away from it all. Apparently nothing out of the ordinary happened there, and when they returned, all remained quiet. A short time later, Constable Fox met the mother on the street and she nearly broke down in tears. "Thank God it's finally over," she said to him. "It went away."

In his later years in high school, John seemed to be a smart, popular teenager with a broad smile, sometimes flashy clothes, and perhaps an eye toward politics in the future. He was known for speaking his mind and standing up for his beliefs. He won an achievement award for his work outside school just five years after the mysterious occurrences.

To this day, no one has been able to shake the credibility of this compelling story or that of John Mulvey. "We were all skeptical at first," Fox told me. "After all, we were all adult police officers. But, after those weeks and all those incidents, not one of us thought it was trickery."

But the case remained a sensitive topic to some people. "I made a solemn promise to the family that I would never speak about it, and I intend to keep it. I'm a man of my word," Officer Weir told me. "Some of my friends from the media have been angry with me about this." Weir was shaken by the things he saw and slept at night with his police service revolver close to his pillow, and a glass of liquor on a small table.

CHAPTER 3

A Visitor on Halloween

"Why do I have to lie about who I am?"
John Mulvey

The only visitor we had on Halloween in 1980 came at midnight. He had no mask, and he didn't need one. It was John Mulvey, and his story seems a good case for the existence of the supernatural. We had never met, but he knew that I was a newspaper reporter interested in his story.

Mulvey's family had been so paranoid about publicity, they had managed to keep their identities secret for a decade after the incidents. And now he was coming over to my house at midnight. As his sleek, black sports car slowly crushed the brittle leaves down our long, narrow driveway, I peered through a small window and started to shake a little. Why had I invited him to our house as my wife and two young children slept? It had always seemed safe, out here in the country on the edge of Niagara Falls, removed from the tourists and the neon lights of the wax museums. There was no hiding now, on the last naked night of October.

I had talked to Mulvey briefly over the phone several days earlier, to get a quote for a 10-year anniversary story in my daily newspaper, the *St. Catharines Standard*. His name, of course, had been omitted, and I was one of the few people in the Niagara area who knew who he *was*. "You asked me to call you when I was ready to give you the story..." he had said. Prior to his phone call, I had been sitting in the kitchen at 10:30 p.m., toying with wrapped candy and wondering why no kids had come trick-or-treating.

And then the doorbell rang. There is something about a doorbell after midnight that rocks the framing of a house. I should have simply opened the door, but I kind of froze.

A broad-shouldered frame filled the doorway. He was no boy anymore. His hand reached for mine in the yellow of the porch light. "Sorry for bothering you this time of night," he said in a calm voice as he stepped inside. A smile broke over his face, and then he made a sudden move. I thought he was reaching for something, but he simply quietly removed his shoes, looked around for somewhere to put them, and settled on a corner. He was the most polite person in our house in a month—big, and yet trying to keep himself small.

Without speaking, my wife Jennifer appeared at the top of the stairs in a nightgown and a guarded smile. She shuffled down the steps and shook John Mulvey's hand. It broke the ice for me, and I felt safer. As John and I walked up the stairs to my office, the details of his 1970 ordeal raced through my head...

I ushered him into my office, across the hall from where my two sons were sleeping, corn candies in their tummies from Halloween night. John eased into a cushy rocking chair in the corner of the room while I sat by my desk, a couple of steps away. "Nice place," he said. Right from the beginning, this guy seemed inoffensive and obliging—boy, was I relieved. In fact, he was very clean-cut, from his round face (boyish by 21-year-old standards) to his neat leather jacket, football shirt, and high school ring. I cracked a meaningless joke. He laughed. He was cheerful. There seemed nothing frightening about him; here I was, expecting Rosemary's Baby, and who shows up but a chap from *Leave it to Beaver*, rocking quietly in the night.

I offered him tea and cookies, but he didn't need them, thanks to the wall of sweetness surrounding his personality; he talked pleasantly with his hands about things that other people might speak in anger. "Why did you print the article in today's paper?" he asked, referring to my 10-year-anniversary story. "It caused me problems at home." He was still living with his parents in St. Catharines. (My managing editor at the *Standard*, Murray Thomson, liked stories on the supernatural from time to time. "Anybody who doesn't believe in ghosts is foolish," he once said.)

I explained to John that his experience of 1970 had fascinated a continent. "I suppose people want to know how this could happen in a quiet city, and if the situation completely went away. They want to know about you."

"They wouldn't understand," he said. "Boy, oh boy, I thought this was all over. I wanted it to just die." Suddenly, his wide hands became more animated, and his brows darkened. "Today, after your article appeared, somebody put a ghost on my locker at work. People are starting to get close again. Ten years later and it's starting all over again! Hardly anybody knows. My neighbors don't know who I am. My friends at high school never knew who I was."

In my view, the people of St. Catharines tended to be conservative by politics and lifestyle, reserved, and slow to change. The world's ships passed through on the Welland Canal, part of the St. Lawrence Seaway, but who really knew its residents? In some ways, it was as though there was a bubble over the city, protecting it and keeping it from the rest of the world. The residents' poor record of voting in elections seemed to reflect apathy and they rarely reacted to anything—unless the English clock above the old courthouse forgot to chime on the hour. As a reporter, I became frustrated at the *Standard*'s readers for their lack of response to anything creative or different. To get their attention, it seemed, you had to bang on their door. In my articles throughout the years, I revealed a lot of well-kept secrets in St. Catharines, including one in which a man described as a cornerstone of the community, a successful salesman, father of two young children, a Sunday School teacher, soccer coach, and "perfect neighbor," set himself ablaze and died in his station wagon because he would not face the shame of being charged in a washroom sex scandal involving other men at a local shopping mall.

Now Mulvey sat in my rocking chair and said he wanted to stay home and blend in. "I want a normal life. My life now is what's important. I don't want to do anything to jeopardize it. I have a good job. I earn more than my father."

"Yes, that makes sense," I said. There was no easy way for me to back into what had happened in that tormented apartment in 1970. "I understand from the old press reports that the occurrences went away after two or three weeks." I did not use the word *poltergeist* or even *paranormal*.

"I'm no different now than I was then," he snapped. "I haven't changed, but in people's eyes, I'm a human being again. I don't want to be different. When I got home from work tonight [after the anniversary story had appeared], my father pulled the phone out of the wall. He's having it disconnected. When I called you, it was from a phone booth. Can you imagine that? This year, for the first time [since 1970], our telephone was listed in the phone book, and look what happens! It's like waving a red flag: 'Here I am!'" The rocking chair was moving quicker now, slightly towards me. "I've had ulcers," he sighed, looking down at the floor.

How many times had I heard that type of thing lately? Stories about ulcers and high blood pressure and anxiety and stress-related conditions were seemingly becoming common in society. "Since the day it happened, I'm not allowed to discuss it at home," John said. "You have no idea. My father gets upset...my parents can get emotional. We never talk about it. We're not allowed. We haven't talked about it since it happened."

He kept looking down at the floor, then up at me. His voice started to shake through quivering lips and I was afraid he was about to clam up, so I decided to mention something about my own family: When I had been a youth in the 1960s, I had penned several unpublished books and short stories that I had hoped my father would want to see and to share. He never did. Prior to his death in 2003, my father still had not bothered to read them. The papers ended up under a mound somewhere at a city dump. My tale seemed to get him going again. "Why did you allow me to come here in the middle of the night?" he said. "I could have come with a knife."

"Maybe we have a little bit in common," I said.

"Well, since it happened, very few people have known I was involved. But some people who know me have become suspicious over the years. I've had to lie to them about who I am. Why do I have to lie about who I am? Some people found out I had lived in that [apartment] building, so I told them yes, but that I actually lived in one of the other apartments."

Out of nowhere, something happened in the rocking chair: Mulvey broke down crying. One moment he was talking with a wry smile, and the next second he was sobbing like a child. The tears burst out through a leaky dam. It was almost as though another person inside him had emerged. He cried long and hard, and it was a bit discomforting to see a big man sob so much.

I offered him a Kleenex, but he found a hankie in his pocket and tried to mop up in a jerky motion, hampered by his breathing, which had taken on a haltering pace. The sweetness surrounding him melted, and, perhaps it was my imagination, but the room seemed to crackle with electricity. I expected framed photos of my family and a map of downtown St. Catharines to come crashing off the walls, or that my desk would move. But in reality, the only thing that jumped was my heart.

I wanted to reach out and be emotional with him. I recalled the times I had wanted to let the emotional other person out of me, just for a few minutes and do something to move my father (I had always wanted to make people move, but John Mulvey wanted things to *stop* moving). But my dad always had to go into the cellar, when moments like that came up. I never found out what was in the cellar that was so important, except for a few cigarette butts, hidden from my mother.

Once his tears had subsided, John started talking to me again. In recent years he had become a factory worker and he had also found a business organization where he could work with young people to help them reach their potential.

"I was just thinking," I said. "Of all people, you chose to open up to a reporter!"

But he was not ready to reveal everything. In fact, he asked if our conversation was being recorded. He got up from the chair and checked under my desk and in other areas of the office to see if there was a tape recorder. "I don't want to take the chance you're going to write a story for the *Standard* again tomorrow," he said. "Everything today is for a buck." In 1970, some authors, museum officials, and even some of his old neighbors had tried to make money on the strange happenings, he said. "I thought about telling my story, but it's not worth the price." He looked upon Halloween stories as hokey and "just stories for children."

John did not give me details of the 1970 occurrences, although he said he remembered them well. "I was an intelligent kid; I could read when I was 5. The papers didn't get the story right—they were guessing." For the record, the papers had inferred that a ghost or demonic possession was to blame. "Since then, I've done some reading, some investigating of my own. I have my own theories, but it's nobody's business."

"There was a rumor that you were into magic, and that you went to California to become a professional magician," I said.

"I don't know anything about magic," he said sternly.

Finally, after nearly two hours of conversation, Mulvey got out of the rocking chair and said he was feeling better. I offered him a bed for the night, but he shrugged, "No, I'll be okay. I'm going home." He apologized for "acting like a baby," but I told him he should be thankful he could let go.

☺☺☺

People continued to talk about the case.

Rich in military history, the Niagara region has its share of ghost and paranormal stories, as well as many mediums and psychics. One of them, self-proclaimed white witch Joanna Honsberger, believed that as a boy, Mulvey had been affected by restless spirits of the dead in his apartment. The apartment is gone now, the victim of a wrecker's ball, and has been replaced by a pizzeria, but John Mulvey still lives in St. Catharines, and now has a family and a son of his own.

One day in the early 1980s, I accidentally ran into him walking downtown. He was holding hands with an attractive woman. As we approached one another on the sidewalk, his eyes met mine, but he looked quickly away from me, as though he had glanced into the hot sun. The couple blended in nicely with the crowds strolling in the sunshine, peering into store windows. He was a little older and his hair a little shorter. Otherwise, he hadn't changed. And, like his shirt, his emotions were tucked in.

☺☺☺

Let us fast-forward 25 years. From 1980 to 2005, I had written nothing about the Mulvey case. It appears in *this* book because I think it is a compelling story that might help us better understanding our complex human species.

Since I saw John Mulvey in 1980, it appears as though he has lived a relatively normal life, raising a family, living a middle-class lifestyle, and doing his best for his community. He has found an outlet for his passion to help others. (I would love to fill you in on the joys and pains of his life into his 30s and 40s, but I must hold back most of the details because I do not want to identify him. Those are his wishes. I realize that by publishing the information that I am, people around him who did not know he was that poltergeist boy from 1970 might put two and two together. But I think he will be okay. The people who are close to him will understand. They know that he did nothing wrong, and that perhaps something paranormal transpired, but it does not mean that he is antisocial or a danger to anyone.)

In 1995, the radio show the X-Zone aired a program on the case and interviewed several of the police officers, who had retired from the force. Producers of the show put some of the police reports on the Internet, blanking out the family names to protect their privacy.

By 2005, Mulvey had moved up the ladder at his workplace (the same place he worked when he came to my house in 1980) and had been honored with several awards for his work throughout the years, particularly while working with young people. And his superiors now referred to him as a role model.

As the years have gone by, his name and picture have appeared in local papers for a variety of business and community events, and photographs have shown him smiling and enjoying himself with others. In 2004, I contacted him to ask him if he wanted to meet in relation to this book, which I had begun writing at the time. His response was swift: "I would not be interested in meeting at this time."

When I told parapsychologist Maurice Grosse of London, England, about the Mulvey case, he was sad. "Society…" he sighed. "There is so much to know and find out, but we can't study these phenomena properly, because of the stigma."

I'm sure that I will monitor how John is doing through the years. For now I can happily report that, in 2010, his life seems to have turned out well. Ask his many Facebook friends.

CHAPTER 4

The House of Flying Objects

"When the statuettes struck objects, they did so with
an almost explosive sound. It's unlikely that [a 12-year-
old boy] could have thrown them with such force."

David Kahn, Newsday *reporter*

In the 1950s, nearly 20 years before *The Amityville Horror*, the big
paranormal news on Long Island was Popper the Poltergeist. This
decade heralded the birth, or at least the rise, of the middle class in
America. The Nice People were assuming power in the suburbs as more
and more of them had a home and a car, and even a television set. And
in many areas, people were starting to blend in behind the rows of bun-
galows, pretty public parks and tree-lined avenues.

James Herrmann and his family, tenants of the 'burbs in Seaford
on Long Island, New York, seemed to fit this model, living in their six-
room, green-and-white, ranch-style home.

James was a representative for Air France in New York City and his
wife, Lucille, was a registered nurse. Their two children, Lucille, 13,
and James Junior (Jimmy), 12, seemed normal.

The extraordinary, however, reportedly started to become the norm
in the afternoon of February 3, 1958, when Mrs. Herrmann, who was
home with her two children, said she heard popping noises at about 4
o'clock. A quick check revealed that a small bottle of holy water on her
bedroom dresser had its top off and had fallen onto its side; its contents
had spilled. In the adjacent bedroom, her son's, she found that a plastic

ship model and a ceramic doll were broken. In a bathroom cabinet, two bottles had their caps unscrewed and their contents spilled. In addition, a bottle of starch in the kitchen and a gallon bottle of bleach in the cellar were spilled.

The children denied having done this, and Mrs. Herrmann was at a loss for what was responsible. In the next two days, other bottles had their caps popped off while the children were at home alone.

Although no one in the family saw what happened, they heard unusual popping noises. This was puzzling, because most of the bottles were fitted with twist-off caps, which needed to be turned three or four times to come off. If someone had simply unscrewed them in the usual manner, it would not create a popping sound. Was this something to do with air pressure or chemicals in the bottles, or too much carbonation?

The occurrences continued for nearly a week, in bottles of rubbing alcohol, nail polish, and detergent. Mr. Herrmann's initial theory was that his son, Jimmy, who liked science, was behind it all, perhaps with a liquid mix to set off mini-explosions. Although the seventh-grade honor student denied any involvement, his father closely, discreetly watched him. On February 9, three bottles popped and rocked back and forth on shelves in various rooms while James was keeping his son under observation. The father said it had been impossible for the boy to have rigged the bottles to pop at different times because he had been monitoring him intensely.

Also that day, Mr. Herrmann claimed he saw other phenomena: In a bathroom, with Jimmy standing nearby brushing his teeth, a bottle of medicine moved across the top of the basin and dropped into the sink. A few seconds later, a bottle of shampoo reportedly moved on its own power across the sink and crashed to the floor. "One moved straight ahead, slowly, while the other spun to the right for a 45-degree angle," the father said. The perplexed man went throughout the bathroom, looking for strings or wires that could have tripped the bottles, but found nothing. People who knew Mr. Herrmann tended to believe his account because they described him as a straightforward man who did not embellish things.[1]

Convinced that no one in the house was pulling pranks, Mrs. Herrmann called police on February 9. At first, Patrolman James Hughes of the Nassau County Police Department, Seventh Precinct, was skeptical, and suspected Mrs. Herrmann of heavy drinking, but the family had a good reputation in the community.

Hughes got a taste of the action on his first visit when he heard several bottles in the bathroom pop their lids. He found that medicine and shampoo bottles in the bathroom had spilled. Five of the bottles were sent to a police laboratory in Mineola, New York, and were found to contain no unusual chemicals or components.

The case became serious enough for the police department to assign it full time to Detective Joseph Tozzi, age 32. He was one of the force's best, having come out of the U.S. Navy in 1949, and if anyone could get to the bottom of this case, it was Tozzi, described as having a sharp and pleasantly cynical mind.

The first entry in Tozzi's police log came on February 11, when he noted that a bottle of perfume opened in 12-year-old Lucille's bedroom and spilled. No one was in the room at the time, Tozzi said. Then a bottle of holy water took center stage for a few days, reportedly popping its lid on several occasions. On one occasion when James Herrmann picked it up, the bottle felt warm. This was upsetting for the family, devout Catholics, and particularly for Mrs. Herrmann, who had put the holy water out to keep away potential evil spirits.

During Tozzi's second day at the house, the detective and Jimmy were walking down the basement steps when a bronze figurine of a horse, weighing nearly 100 pounds, reportedly flew across the basement and hit the officer in the back of the legs. Suddenly, Tozzi was fearful for the safety of the people in the house, and he decided to step up his questioning. Tozzi let his police instincts take over and went by the book—he accused Jimmy of throwing the horse, even though the officer had not seen him do it. With his compassionate eyes and strong jaw, Tozzi intensely questioned Jimmy, who denied wrongdoing in any of the occurrences. Even the sight of Tozzi's police badge didn't break him. Meanwhile, the family was in such hysteria, they went to a friend's home for the night, as they did several times during the occurences.

On February 15, a visitor reported a different type of disturbance. Marie Murtha, a middle-aged cousin of James Herrmann, said she was watching the black-and-white television in the living room with the two Herrmann children when she saw a porcelain figurine rise up off a coffee table and hover in the air. It reportedly moved several inches and dropped to the carpet.

Then the Herrmanns reached out to the Church for help. Father William McLeod of the Church of Saint William the Abbott sprinkled holy water in all six of the rooms and blessed the house, and yet the disturbances continued when the priest left.

By this time, the family was making news. When *Newsday* reporter David Kahn came to work on february 10, he was intrigued by a headline in his paper: "Balmy Bouncing Bottles Jar Long Islanders' Home," and he went to investigate. other media began contacting the Herrmanns or coming to their home. Television was a novelty in 1958, and news and updates of Popper the Poltergeist, as he was known, became popular on nightly newscasts across America, and was featured on the popular series *Armstrong Circle Theatre*. No paranormal phenomena were picked up by the camera, but only the aftermath, such as dents in the walls.

But reporter Kahn said that on February 24, he was sitting on a living room couch in the Herrmann home when a 10-inch cardboard globe moved seemingly on its own power and bounced into a corner of the living room. "I jumped up, ran into Jimmy's room and snapped on the light," Kahn said. "He was sitting up in bed, the covers on his legs. Could he have thrown it? I thought it was possible, but improbable." To have done some of the things suspected of Jimmy, Kahn said, he would have had to have been extraordinarily strong and agile, because when the statuettes struck objects, they made an almost explosive sound. Kahn did not suspect anyone else in the family, least of all Jimmy's sister, Lucille, who "didn't seem the type."[2]

Meanwhile, about 250 phone calls and letters poured in from a fascinated public; everybody, it seemed, had a theory about what was going on in Seaford: It was the Martians who were landing, or Satan, or perhaps just boring electromagnetic fields or sun spots. In fact, some people theorized that, as a Cold War tactic, the Russians had sent a submarine offshore and it was causing magnetic-field disruption. Many, if not most people believed the Herrmanns to be innocent, as they were well-liked by their neighbors, and because police could find no prankster.

Some people believed that spirits were responsible, due to the damage to the holy water and a figurine of the Virgin Mary. Religious groups tried to help, and some people thought the Herrmanns needed to repent for something they had done; some ministers conducted rituals on their front lawn.

Robert Zider, a physicist from Brookhaven National Laboratory, examined the property with dowsing rods. He believed that underground streams below the property were causing strange things to happen, perhaps creating an unusual magnetic field, yet a geological survey found nothing unusual. Neither did visits to the house by a structural engineer, a professor of engineering from Cooper Union College in New York, a civil engineer, and an electrical engineer from the Nassau Country Society of Professional Engineers.

During his eight-week investigation, Detective Tozzi did not rule anything out. Were sonic booms from airplanes causing vibrations in the house? Tozzi checked with the Air Force, which said its flight plans did not correspond with the area. And officials at the local Mitchell Air Field said none of their equipment could produce the effects occurring in the home. How about disturbances from radio waves? The Radio Corporation of America sent a test truck and found nothing unusual. Tozzi also brought in the Long Island Lighting Company, which put an oscilloscope in the cellar to try to pick up underground vibrations. There were none. Also, all the wiring in the house, along with the fuse panels, functioned properly.

The Seaford Fire Department and the Town of Hempstead Building Department checked the house and surrounding area: No drafts, nothing. And yet, the occurrences continued: Objects moved seemingly under their own power, a bottle of ink opened and made a mess on a wall, and a sugar bowl fell off a table as Tozzi watched. Young Jimmy was in the room, but Tozzi said he was not close enough to have touched the bowl.

When the family left home briefly, nothing occurred there. Also, many of the incidents took place in Jimmy's room or other rooms he was in: A record player moved 15 feet, a large bookcase fell to the floor, and the Virgin Mary statue "flew" about 12 feet and banged into a mirror, Tozzi said. Sometimes Tozzi nearly got dinged—a globe of the world came down a hallway and just missed him. Other neutral observers reported unusual things as well: John Gold, a photographer from the *London Evening News* in England, said his flashbulbs moved by themselves off a table and flew into the air, hitting a wall.

After more than a month of bizarre happenings, members of the Parapsychology Laboratory at Duke University in Durham, North Carolina, came to the home on March 10. They were Dr. Gaither Pratt and William Roll, who had been studying the possibility that, in rare situations, people, especially adolescents going through puberty, were able to move things unconsciously with their emotions or their mind. By the time they arrived, the disturbances were beginning to wane. They grilled Detective Tozzi, who said he had been closely watching Jimmy for weeks and was sure the boy was innocent. However, Roll and Pratt suspected that Jimmy was *unconsciously* causing the events through the phenomenon of mind over matter, partly because he was going into puberty and partly because of his attitude toward his father. After interviewing family members, Roll came to the conclusion that Jimmy was angry with his father, and that he vented this feeling through his unusual mental powers on objects, particularly those he associated with his parents. Because many of the incidents involved bottles that might be associated with a woman, they may have reflected "unmet dependency needs" that Jimmy had with both his parents, Roll told me.

At first, Roll considered the possibility that more than one person was involved in a prank, but he soon ruled it out because "the family was much too shaken for it to be a colossal hoax. And why would they fake things in front of all the people who came into their home?" Roll said that Mr. and Mrs. Herrmann had impeccable credentials—James with the airlines and also as a volunteer member of the auxiliary police in Seaford, and Lucille as a former supervisor at a large hospital.

The unexplained activity finally ended on March 2, 1958, with the breaking of a dish and the falling of a table and bookcase.

Altogether, 67 incidents were recorded. Duke University put together a 45-page report on the Herrmanns, entitled "The House of Flying Objects." The investigators said they could not prove something paranormal had occurred, but they suspected it had, because, despite all the attention paid by neutral observers in the house, including police, electricians, plumbers, firemen, and building inspectors, no one was caught faking anything.

The family remained puzzled years after the events. Mrs. Herrmann said there was a physical force behind it, although she did not know what it was. She became sympathetic to reports of other families who had suspected paranormal activity in their homes. When she saw news reports of a poltergeist case in Newark, New Jersey, in 1961, Mrs. Herrmann telephoned the family to offer her emotional support and to tell them of her experiences.

In the years following the Popper case, the family fell out of the limelight, and it is not known what became of them. Detective Tozzi went on to a successful career, arresting many Mafia members, and was police chief of Colleyville, Texas, from 1976 to 1984.

CHAPTER 5

Police Controversy in New England

"We're investigating. We would hope to find out what's causing this. I think we might come up with some logical explanation."

Police Captain John O'Leary

I ndeed, the Bridgeport, Connecticut, Police Department *did* come up with a logical explanation as to what caused strange goings-on in a small house at 966 Lindley Street on a late November weekend in 1974.

After furniture moved, plaster-of-Paris cherubs fell off the wall to the floor, and ashtrays flew, Police Superintendent Joseph A. Walsh scoffed at the testimonies of eight of his own officers: "Everything has a rational explanation," he announced. "This is the work of human powers. I don't believe in that supernatural stuff...there are not ghosts in Bridgeport."[1]

The following day, Walsh announced at a Board of Police Commissioners meeting that the case was closed. He said that a 10-year-old girl in the house, Marcia Goodin, had confessed to staging a series of incidents. "Oh, really?" many officers on his force asked behind his back—and in the newspapers. How about the testimony, Supt. Walsh, of your Patrolman John Holsworth, who said he saw a 450-pound refrigerator lift slowly off the floor, turn, and then set down again? Later, a large TV set seemed to float in the air and then crash to the floor, Holsworth said, but he could find no explanation for it.

And then there was Patrolman Joseph Tomek, who told the *Bridgeport Sunday Post*, "I just couldn't believe what I saw. Shelves fixed to the wall began to vibrate until they were loose, then flew through the air. I looked for evidence that someone was making it happen, but I couldn't find anything—no wires, nothing. Then I watched as the big TV fell over."[2]

There was a suspect nearby: Marcia Goodin, all 4-feet, 6 inches, and 70 pounds of her, soaking wet.

Not only did this highly publicized case cause a rift in the police department, but it was also championed by a number of people to show either that paranormal events truly exist, or that people will go to any lengths in order to get attention.

Gerald and Laura Goodin, the owners of 966 Lindley Stree, in a lower middle-class area of town, had bought the four-room bungalow 14 years earlier. It was modest and box-like, yet quaint. The house had been built in 1915 for a shirt manufacturer, and none of the previous occupants had even reported anything unusual. The heavy-set Gerald was a factory worker at the Harvey Hubbell Company, and Laura was described as a high-strung, devout Roman Catholic. After their 7-year-old son had died of an illness, the Goodins adopted Marcia, a Canadian from the Iroquois tribe, in 1970. She was described as being intelligent, attractive, and shy, yet friendly, but she was having problems at school, where she had been teased, and even beaten because of her Native heritage.

Gerald and Laura apparently became overprotective of Marcia, not allowing her to leave the house alone and walking her to school every day. When the occurrences began on November 22, Marcia had been home from school for about five weeks, partly to recuperate from the beating she had taken. On that day began loud poundings on the walls, objects dropping from shelves, tables overturning, and chairs levitating.

The following day, Laura Goodin was injured when a television set, which allegedly moved under its own power, fell on her, said Special Constable Jack Bracken, an emergency ambulance driver, who took her to St. Vincent's Hospital. She suffered injuries to two toes (one of them suspected as being broken) on her right foot, he said.

November 24 was the most hectic day. Mrs. Goodin said that at dawn, several easy chairs mysteriously moved, and a kitchen table flipped over. Her husband, Gerald, said he saw another table lift itself up and turn over and a knife holder fly off a wall. He said Marcia was with him, and she could not have done it.

The Goodins called for help to their friends, Harold and Mary Hofmann. Harold recalled to me in 1975 his entering the Goodin home: "The place was a real mess...there were tables overturned and knives, forks, and dishes all over. The big TV was on its side. When I put it back, a smaller TV began rocking back and forth by itself." Hofmann said there was no one in the room except for him.

Another neighbor, off-duty police officer Holsworth, ran into the home, and that is when he said he saw the refrigerator rise off the floor, turn at right angles, and then set itself down, bumping into his right elbow but not injuring him. He said he also saw three reclining chairs start to shake. After checking the house, including the cellar, for possible answers, he found none. "There has got to be a logical explanation for the things I saw, but whatever it is, I don't have it," he said. "I doubt that the Goodins could have caused these things to move. They weren't near them when they moved."[3] Tomek arrived with three other officers and made his observation about the flying shelves, noted earlier in this chapter. Almost immediately, several officers saw a lamp start to shake inexplicably. "When we got there, we thought we were investigating a burglary, the way [the house] was messed up," Tomek said. "Only later did we find out [it was an alleged case of the paranormal]. What we saw there was totally unexpected and some of the policemen were really frightened. I was told I would see a lot of things in the police force, but I never expected this."[4]

Shelves were reportedly shaking with high-pitched sounds, and Patrolman Leroy Lawson said he was nearly struck by a picture falling off the wall. Patrolman George F. Wilson, Jr., told me he saw the refrigerator move a few feet along the kitchen floor towards him, and then a brass crucifix on a wall reportedly vibrated, rattled, and fell to the floor. Wilson said he also saw a 21-inch portable television turn itself around and face the wall, and a bureau fall to the floor and bounce several times. Three chairs also bounced around and incredibly changed their positions in the room, he added.

"It was unreal in the house," Patrolman Cal Leonzi told me in 1976. "A picture fell off the wall and the TV set shook; it seemed like everything was moving." At one juncture, a tearful Mrs. Goodin was wearing a crucifix around her neck and clutching rosary beads.

Leonzi had been watching Marcia and was certain she was not moving anything. And yet, Leonzi said he saw pictures flying off the walls and a heavy wooden table moving. Leonzi also said he saw Marcia fly backwards three times in a heavy armchair. "Later on, we tried to get the chair to do the same thing, but even a guy 235 pounds couldn't make it move like that." Holsworth said that, apart from the kitchen, there were rugs in every room in the house, making it difficult to move chairs and objects through sleight of hand without getting caught.

The puzzled officers called in the Bridgeport Fire Department to check the foundations of the house and for malfunctioning gas lines or electric lines. Nothing was found, although Deputy Fire Chief of Operations Fred Zwerlein said he saw a kitchen chair jump several inches into the air, and fall over backwards. A short time later, when he was in the living room, Zwerlein said he saw a large recliner floating a couple of inches off the ground.

In addition, Fire Chief John Gleason told me that his men saw dinner plates "rattling, pictures jumping off the wall, a television set falling over, and a heavy leather chair jumping at least 6 inches off the floor." A crucifix was said to have fallen off a wall. Later, Professor John Nicholas, head of the geology department at the University of Bridgeport, ruled out earthquakes or tremors as the cause of the events. But firemen offered no theories as to the cause. "I guess you could say we're are not very good at chasing devils," Gleason told me.

Three firemen and a radio newsman said they saw an overstuffed reclining chair somersault, a television set spin, and chairs levitate, all without the help of human hands.

Tim Quinn, a newsman for WNAB Radio, said he saw little Marcia slammed into a wall five feet away as if someone had a rope on her and pulled her into the wall. She suffered a bump to her head. Quinn said he also saw a leather chair sitting on a thin rug—the sort that leaves a mark when you step on it. "I saw the back go down and the chair move a few feet," he said. "But there was no mark on the carpet from the runners underneath the chair."[5]

If little Marcia was causing this havoc, she was doing it with a tender back, which had been in a brace after she had been beaten and kicked at school.

Reverend William Charbonneau, an assistant pastor of St. John of the Cross Roman Catholic Church in Middlebury, who taught a course in the occult at St. Joseph College in West Hartford, Connecticut, said that during the 10 hours he was at the home on Sunday and early Monday, he saw a TV and a chest of drawers fall over. "This is no hoax," he told me. Rev. Charbonneau checked for evidence of fraud, such as strings or wires, but found nothing. He kept a close eye on Marcia, who was holding the family's white-and-orange calico cat, Sam, for comfort during some of the occurrences. "At one point, [Marcia] was next to me, showing me a bracelet, when a heavy dresser moved off a table and whizzed by," he said. Rev. Charbonneau also told me he saw several other strange occurrences, including a bureau crashing to the floor behind the girl. "I would say this was a classic case of a poltergeist. It came from a type of psychic energy, but what causes that energy, I don't know."

Also on Sunday, Rev. Edward Doyle of St. Patrick's Church, the fire department chaplain, blessed all the rooms in the Goodin home with holy water, but he saw nothing to suggest that evil spirits were present. As the weekend dragged on, requests for interviews became so intense that the family stopped media from entering the house. To add to the carnival atmosphere, the family called in two demonologists, Ed and Lorraine Warren of Monroe, Connecticut—members of the New England Society for Paranormal Research, who had seen 36 exorcisms throughout the years and had investigated everything from werewolves to ghosts. Lorraine said that police officers were humbled by what they saw. "Never in my life did I see so many police officers get down on their knees and ask for a priest's blessing as in that house."[6] An exorcism should have been performed in the house to learn what was causing the happenings, Ed Warren said, but no exorcism was done.

the hoax theory

On November 25, Barbara Carter, Marcia's tutor, said she saw a television set fall over and chairs move, but such occurrences were now becoming few and far between.

It was the following day that Supt. Walsh declared it all a hoax at a press conference.

50

He said Marcia was responsible for moving all the objects while people were distracted and that she had confessed to police. As was reported by the Associated Press and *The Bridgeport Post*, Walsh said, "She had been the one who had done the banging on the walls and floors, knocked a crucifix to the floor, threw pictures down, and caused other unusual things to happen." One of the incidents Marcia allegedly confessed to was throwing her voice as a ventriloquist through her pet cat, Sam, making it appear that the animal was talking. "There are no ghosts in Bridgeport," Walsh said. But Marcia told the media she did not fake anything, although she did not give extensive interviews.

Walsh did not investigate at the Goodin house, but one of his officers, Patrolman Michael Costello, believed that some of his fellow officers might have been tricked by 10-year-old Marcia, perhaps because they had been expecting to see something supernatural, and therefore quickly became believers. But Costello admitted he had not seen anyone in the house fake an incident.

Despite skepticism from many of their superiors back at the police department, most of the officers stood by their earlier claims that what they saw was a poltergeist, a ghost, or some other type of paranormal event. Sergeant Bernard Mangiamele, with 22 years' experience on the force, absolved Marcia of any blame: "I stood and watched a heavy wooden bureau slowly start to vibrate," he said. "Then it lifted itself up and moved around. If I hadn't seen it with my own eyes, I wouldn't have believed it...what I saw amazed me."[7]

Lieutenant Leonard Cocco trusted the reports of his four patrolman and a sergeant, who said they saw phenomena including a moving refrigerator, flying ashtrays and a slamming door. "Together, they have more than 100 years of experience," Cocco said. "If they said they saw something, they saw something. I just don't know what it was."[8]

Gerald Goodin refuted Walsh's claim about a hoax and said police officials wanted to get the case over with and for the commotion to go away. (At one point, the crowd outside the home swelled to about 1,500 people, including journalists, causing a major traffic tie-up. One man was arrested for disorderly conduct as armed police and guard dogs surrounded the home.) Goodin and others said that no one had caught

Marcia cheating and there had been more than 40 witnesses to the events. Gerald and Laura Goodin said they did not believe in a supernatural explanation, and that there had to be a logical one, although they did not know what it was.

The Warrens said the police brass officially called the case a hoax because it was getting too hot to handle in the community and in the media, and many officers were looking silly in some people's eyes because of their comments. "If the whole thing is a hoax, it's one of the biggest hoaxes I've ever seen," said Ed Warren, who claimed to have seen a number of unusual events in the home, including a mirror smash and a large chest of drawers fall down. "No 10-year-old child, who weighs 70 pounds, could create a hoax in full view of police, firemen, and investigators for that length of time."[9] Walsh refuted this statement, believing that the Warrens were out to make money on the case. The Warrens said they were not charging the Goodins for their services, but that they made money lecturing on the paranormal.

If the case was not a hoax, what was possibly behind it? A psychic investigator, Boyce Batey, of Bloomfield, Connecticut, said he was in the Goodin home for some of the occurrences and interviewed many witnesses. He concluded that some of incidents were poltergeist phenomenon, but he suspected that other incidents might have been simulated by Marcia or other family members. Batey believed the paranormal activity was caused by "unresolved and unexpressed tensions and emotions, especially the feelings of hostility and fear." He believed the tensions that accompany the pre-adolescent phase of development (in Marcia) were also an issue. "If one cannot find expression and resolution normally, then the tensions are released paranormally, although subconsciously," he said.[10] Another parapsychologist, Jerry Sawyer, of Fairfield, Connecticut, said he saw a television fall while Marcia was on the opposite side of the room. He also leaned toward the poltergeist theory, and he believed it was caused by intense stress in the Goodin house.

Long after the occurrences had ceased, the Goodin family continued to live in the house on Lindley Street, and by 1976, Marcia was reportedly doing well in school. A real estate company tried to sell the house for them for $21,500. Ten families were taken through the home, but no one bought it.

It is not known what became of Marcia. Her adoptive mother, Laura, died in a car crash in 1994. In 1995, Gerald Goodin was still living in the small house, and he died several years later. The house had a weathered look, with peeling paint, an American flag, a Catholic symbol on the door, and a whole lot of stories.

CHAPTER 6

Fire Sale at the Souvenir Place

"From then on, everything seemed to happen—boxes came down, a box of about 100 back scratchers turned over and fell with a terrific clatter over on the other side of the room, and then we realized that there was something definitely wrong around here."

Alvin Laubheim, warehouse owner

The winter of 1966–67 was not a booming time for the souvenir business—at least not at Tropication Arts, Inc., a novelty warehouse on 54th Street in Miami, Florida. Throughout the course of six weeks, novelties were being smashed at an alarming rate—back scratchers, mugs bearing Elvis Presley's likeness, alligator ashtrays, and imported cocktail glasses. No one knew who the vandal was, or perhaps who among the nine employees was incredibly sloppy. Or was the southern humidity getting to everyone? The co-owners, Alvin Laubheim and Glen Lewis, came to a stunning conclusion: A ghost was responsible. Laubheim had earlier suspected clumsiness on the part of his employees, and he had talked to them about it, but the breakage had continued.

On January 12, Laubheim instructed 19-year-old shipping clerk Julio Vasquez to lay mugs flat on the shelves with the handles facing out to prevent them from rolling, but almost immediately, Laubheim said, a mug went flying onto the floor, and boxes fell down. "For three days, we picked things up off the floor as fast as they would fall down," said Laubheim, described as a big, gregarious, easygoing man. "It was going on all day—quite violently but not hurting anyone...we tried to keep it quiet because we knew it would hurt our business, because we were right in the middle of a season and it would draw a bunch of curiosity-seekers."[1]

On the night of January 12, one of Tropication's employees, Bea Rambisz, was listening to a radio talk show on which a ghost researcher, Suzy Smith, was plugging her new book on the paranormal, *Prominent American Ghosts*. Rambisz phoned Smith to alert her about the goings-on at the warehouse. The next day, Friday the 13th, Smith was on the scene and claimed she saw strange movements of souvenirs. Insurance agent William Drucker checked all the warehouse shelves for vibrations, but found them to be solid.

On Saturday, the owners had had enough and called the cops. At first, Patrolman William Killin was wary of the call, fearing it to be a joke, but after checking with the police complaint's officer, Killin got into his cruiser and drove to the warehouse. There, he found two employees: Laubheim and Vasquez. While Laubheim and the likeable, good-looking shipping clerk stood at the back of the 30-by-40-foot warehouse, the officer patrolled the aisles. At one point, he turned around just in time to see a highball glass from a nearby shelf mysteriously shatter on the floor. A short time later, Killin reportedly saw two boxes flip over by themselves. Vasquez was not nearly close enough to affect the boxes, Killin said. The mystified officer said he would personally deliver an official report on the occurrence to his superior, Sergeant William McLaughlin, because he feared the officer would think he was nuts if he heard about this secondhand.

Also arriving Saturday morning were newspaper reporters, a magician, CBS television cameras, and other investigators. They were not disappointed; some of them reported seeing objects move mysteriously about the warehouse—ashtrays, mugs, key chains, rubber alligators, and rubber daggers. Some objects reportedly fell not straight down, but at unusual angles.

The magician present was Howard Brooks, a friend of Laubheim's, working at a nearby ice show. With at least eight men keeping a close eye for spooks or vandals, and on Vasquez, who was becoming a suspect in some people's eyes, two more events occurred, including a box of address books falling from a shelf. At first Brooks laughed it off as a cheap trick, and he tossed an item across the room, just to show how easily it could be done. But then, after he and a police officer, D.J. Sackett, saw highball glasses and beer mugs take apparent levitation, and several cartons drop to the floor, the magician was dumbfounded. After checking for wires or secret mechanisms and finding none, Brooks said he tended to believe something supernatural was at work.

Also that day, Airman Second Class Robert Gugino, home on leave from Mather Air Force Base in California, said he saw a souvenir rise in the air from one of the shelves, then fall to the floor. Another witness was Rev. Richard A. Seymour, a Baptist minister, who said he saw a box of plastic pencil sharpeners in motion.

On January 16, Tropication employee Ruth May, an artist who decorated the souvenirs with flamingoes and Florida scenes, said she saw a plastic tray become airborne off a shelf, then take an unusual trajectory to another shelf before returning through the air to the original area.

The following day, a visitor to the warehouse, Eastern Airlines pilot Sinclair Buntin, said he was about 15 feet from a box and could clearly see it when it fell at a 30-degree angle and could not have been pushed off. No one was near the box in either case, Buntin said.

Another witness was Laubheim's sister, Joyce George, who was watching a mug when it moved. She said it "sort of scooted off" the shelf, moving into the air, then dropped straight down. Parapsychologists say it is common for poltergeist projectiles to move erratically.

On January 19, parapsychologist William Roll came to the warehouse. The focus of Roll and other investigators quickly became Vasquez, a Cuban refugee, as the events seemed to occur only when he was nearby. As the days went by, Roll tried to make himself inconspicuous in the warehouse as the employees and investigators walked about. Whenever something fell, Roll ordered everyone to hold their positions and he quickly checked the item. At no time did he find that anyone had deliberately smashed anything.

On January 23–24, with about nine people watching, glasses, shot glasses, and an old cowbell crashed to the floor, according to author Susy Smith. "The activity got so fast and furious that no human, unless he had been on roller skates, could have rigged up enough devices to trigger things so fast." The witnesses, she wrote, watched "incredulously as objects dashed about inside the building while outdoors thunder crashed and lightning flashed and the rain poured down."[2] The shipping clerk was in the area, but could not have caused the mayhem on that day, nor likely none of the other incidents, added Smith, who spent nearly a month at the warehouse and took statements from witnesses for about 300 incidents. "How a young man like Julio could invent a device so sophisticated that magicians and psychical researchers and policemen could not detect it was beyond me."[3]

After seven days of intense investigation, Roll had to return to North Carolina for a few days. When he came back to Florida, he brought fellow researcher Gaither Pratt, who was working at the University of Virginia, and they stayed at the warehouse from January 27 to January 30, keeping Vasquez under close surveillance. At one juncture, they told Vasquez to put a tray on a shelf. Pratt recalled what happened when the tray tumbled to the floor: "The point on the shelf where it was standing (in Aisle 2) was not visible from my observation point. I could, however, see Julio. He was separated from the disturbance by the tier of double shelves. I could see both his hands...no one was in Aisle 2 where the tray fell and broke, and Julio was the nearest person. I was not able to conceive of any way in which the falling of the tray could have been caused to happen in a normal manner."[4]

A few moments later, two ashtrays fell and broke.

Pratt and Roll set up other experiments in which objects mysteriously broke. In one, Roll placed a glass on a shelf with several small items in front of it, blocking its path to the floor. The glass *did* smash to the floor, reportedly without disturbing the other objects. Then Roll took a previously damaged beer mug and placed it on a shelf. Young Vasquez joked to Roll that the ghost might not prefer damaged goods. Roll went along with it and handed a new mug to Julio. Half an hour later, Roll said, the new mug inexplicably crashed to the floor.

Roll and Pratt noted that incidents seem to happen more frequently when Vasquez was irritated or tense, but the police and researchers cleared him of any tomfoolery, and he was not charged with causing damage. Strangely, Vasquez didn't seem concerned with all the damage and said that he sometimes felt happy when the items broke.

The two parapsychologists wrote down everything they saw or put their observations into a tape recorder. In all, they registered 32 incidents, none of which, they say, Vasquez could have caused through physical means. The following list shows, according to Roll, the number of incidents when Vasquez was different distances from the falling object:

- 1 to 5 feet: 10 incidents
- 6 to 10 feet: 10 incidents
- 11 to 15 feet: eight incidents
- 16 to 20 feet: two incidents
- 21 to 25 feet: one incident
- 30 to 35 feet: one incident

(Note: the warehouse was 30 by 40 feet.)

Roll concluded that the closer Vasquez was to objects, the more they moved, and he felt that Vasquez was causing things to move with his mind, perhaps subconsciously.

A total of 222 paranormal incidents were recorded from mid-December 1966 to February 1, 1967, by a number of witnesses, including about 70 by Roll. He said 44 incidents took place in the presence of himself or co-researcher Pratt. Probing further, Roll interviewed Vasquez about his emotional health, discovering that his family life had been troubled, and he yearned for his mother and grandfather, who were back in his native Cuba. Moreover, he apparently had feelings of unworthiness, and low self-esteem. In December 1966, just before all hell broke loose in the warehouse, Vasquez's stepmother had asked him to move out of her house. He began having nightmares, which revealed, according to psychologists, a need to be punished, and even suicidal tendencies. According to Roll, Vasquez also experienced feelings of hostility, particularly toward parental figures, but he could not express them openly.

When an object would move, Roll would ask Vasquez how he felt. Vasquez replied that they often made him feel good, that they released some of the emotional tension and frustration he had been feeling about his family and situation.

While he was wrapping up his investigation, Roll came to the conclusion that the force causing the warehouse damage posed a *curvilinear field*—RSPK energy was not bowling over the objects like a train, but carrying them along in a falling trajectory until it was closed off from the source (Vasquez) or became too weak to keep the object in motion. Roll consulted a mathematician, an engineer, and others, who charted the moving objects rotations and the distances they moved. Roll concluded that the poltergeist force did not follow the standard inverse law that holds for forms of electromagnetism, which are characterized by a linear field. Instead, the poltergeist energy faded faster, resembling processes such as radioactive decay. The energy seemed most potent when Vasquez's back was turned to the objects, and often the objects moved in a counterclockwise direction, Roll said.

If the whole thing was fraud, it was certainly elaborate and fooled a lot of people. Throughout the course of six weeks, *no one*, including the researchers, the police, the magician, and fellow workers, reported that Vasquez was caught faking the incidents. However, after Pratt went back to Virginia, Roll and Smith went over possible scenarios whereby someone could manipulate objects by trickery. For one experiment, they placed ashtrays on the edge of shelves, held in place briefly with dry ice (frozen carbon dioxide). When the dry ice dissolved, the ashtray would tip off and fall to the floor. But the dry ice left traces—which were never found in the warehouse.

Unfortunately for Vasquez, the owners could not take the chance of more damage and he was eventually let go from the Tropication warehouse. No damage was reported after he left. By this time, Vasquez was persuaded by researchers Suzy Smith and Roll to go back with them to the psychical research foundation in North Carolina. Under controlled conditions, researchers say they saw a bottle fall off a table while Vasquez was nearby, and in another instance in a laboratory, a vase allegedly moved while he was standing with researchers. He was also tested with a dice-throwing machine and apparently showed better-than-chance averages.

It should be noted that Vasquez also became sick: Within three months of the beginning of the disturbances, he came down with measles, chicken pox and mumps.

When Vasquez returned to Miami from North Carolina, he was arrested for shoplifting a ring from a jewelry store and spent six months in prison. There, he was tested by a psychologist, who found him to exhibit "early family tenderness," love, and training in high moral standards, but, as Roll related to me, "also feelings of unworthiness, guilt, and rejection."

Two years later, Vasquez was working as a gas station attendant. When two armed robbers demanded that he turn over money from the register, Vasquez refused and was shot twice during the scuffle. He recovered from his serious wounds. After that incident, Roll reported, Vasquez's physical—and psychical—lives settled down.

CHAPTER 7

Sarah *and* the Pinwheel

"She does some interesting phenomena."
Dr. Michael Persinger

What I saw on a hot summer's day in 2010 hardly resembled a link to the *other world*, or evidence that the power of mind over matter exists: a tiny pinwheel, crafted from an eraser, a sewing needle, and a piece of folded paper. But then—oh my God—it started to move. For more than 20 minutes, I watched the paper pinwheel spin around and around, seemingly without the help of human hands.

This startling phenomenon was demonstrated for me on July 22, 2010, by a woman in her 40s, calling herself Sarah S., during a Skype audio/video conversation between our computers. Sarah sat close to the pinwheel as it turned lazily but consistently, mostly clockwise, ever onward for as long as we wanted. She believed she was moving it with her mind and/or perhaps her unusual electrical powers. Either this was long-sought-after evidence for psychokinesis, the power of the mind to *consciously* affect matter without physical contact, or she was the female edition of magician David Copperfield.

As I watched, transfixed, on my computer, Sarah seemed relaxed and sometimes talked to the wheel as though it were her child or a pet. "Don't worry, keep going," she said to it. "Michael has seen you do it for a while now."

In four decades as a journalist, I've recorded some amazing stuff—Tiger Woods hitting a golf ball a country mile, a man surviving a plunge over Niagara Falls in a barrel, and police officers transported into a slow-motion zone during gun battles. But I'd never seen anything quite like this. The skeptic in me told me to reserve judgment for now, because, for all I knew, she could be moving the pinwheel with an off-screen fan. (Okay, so let me retract that word *transfixed*.)

But apparently I was not the only one who had been transfixed by Sarah. A student at one of the world's foremost laboratories for studying anomalies of the human brain, the neuroscience lab at Laurentian University in Sudbury, Canada, told his boss, respected neuropsychologist Dr. Michael Persinger (BA, MA, PhD) that he saw Sarah's pinwheel move unaided three months before I did. (Persinger said the student should not go public with his observation or he might feel the scorn of the skeptical scientific community and be blackballed from getting a job.)

According to Sarah, the pinwheel is the safety outlet for controlling her RSPK and turning it into PK. Sarah says she is no poltergeist or monster, yet she is afraid of her unpredictable RSPK powers. When she gets emotional, she says, things sometimes take on their own life: lights and machines wink and burp, plates and chairs move—and sometimes people get hurt.

In 1995, she said her first husband grabbed her and threatened her in their home. "I was afraid for my life, but suddenly our house came alive," she recalled. "The lights came on and off; radios and TVs came on and off. There were weird lights that kind of looked like people."[1] Sarah's macho husband became terrified, released her, and scampered out of the house. A missing persons report was filed and police found him two weeks later, but he was never the same, and Sarah fears that her mysterious powers may have eventually led to his premature death.

Is she a witch? One of her colleagues thinks so. A gifted trickster? An extraordinarily gifted case study for psi? Persinger and his colleague, parapsychologist William Roll, continued testing Sarah on the chance that she may have a form of PK. The normally skeptical Dr. Persinger says her brain shows patterns and sensitivities he has never seen in his 40 years of research, and they are "clearly not in the obvious scientific literature."

Roll, who coined the term *RSPK* in 1958 and tested many people for PK, went further: "I think her psychokinesis is genuine. I think she is a very sincere individual and has extraordinary ability in PK."

Sarah suspects she has both RSPK and PK, and perhaps other abilities such as mind reading and the ability to see ghosts, but she is not 100 percent certain of any of this, and continually questions herself and her abilities. She believes they may be related to two near-death experiences she had following traumatic accidents. She is so eager to find out, and to find a cure for her condition, the former military woman is heavily researching the topic and keeping a log of her experiences, although she is earning her PhD in a scientific field unrelated to psi.

"Sarah" is a fictitious name. She does not want her current husband to know everything she does, partly because her condition upsets him. And she doesn't want to become "some kind of a public freak show. I've read about others like me who have had their lives turned upside down when people found out about them. I don't want anyone to ever see me doing this stuff." The interviews for this book were the first Sarah allowed. She wants to cooperate with me anonymously to aid understanding of psi and to help others understand their abilities and try to cure them or perhaps even develop them. "This isn't something I want to be famous for," she says. "This is not about me; it's about the science."

For much of her life, Sarah has been the center of strange activity, particularly when she gets upset or emotional. For example, the year 2010 was a normal year for her...not so normal for most anyone else. During a geomagnetic storm, she became ill, and there were loud tapping sounds on her bedroom walls. On other occasions, pens and coins slid across a table on their own, and a computer acted up when a colleague upset her. "One guy I don't get along with calls me a witch," she says.

At home, the television remote reportedly acts up so much around her, her husband won't let her hold it. Horror movies can set her off. When she watched the 1973 movie *The Exorcist* with her boyfriend years ago, "all the electricity in the house went on the blink," she said. There was a similar occurrence in 2009 when she watched the flick *Zombieland*.

Her husband, whom she describes as rational, skeptical, and scientific in his thinking, often triggers her powers. "My weird stuff is upsetting for him and that sets me off, and he tries to ignore it and won't talk about it." Her husband suspects she has unusual gifts, she said, but most often he ignores them. "He can't imagine the universe that I live in as being a possibility. It breaks my heart to know that I can never be myself with him, and so I try not to let my universe leak into his and mess it all up."

In May 2010, her husband got angry at another driver who took his parking spot, and road rage developed. Her fear response as a passenger reportedly took on some unusual manifestations: Their car radio went to static, the car's signal lights started blinking on and off "faster and faster" under their own power, and the steering wheel became difficult to operate. "I get afraid when hubby is angry," she said. "It doesn't matter if he is yelling at another driver or getting upset at sports on TV... it sets off my RSPK. Glasses vibrate and light bulbs pop. I'm afraid of my RSPK hurting my husband." Following an argument with him, she said, the walls in their bedroom started banging, but only when she was asleep. "It really upset him, but when I'd wake up the banging would stop." Then, in the summer of 2010, she set off her own minor earthquake, several days before one actually occurred. "My husband and I were having an argument and glasses on shelves and a table started rattling," she said.

During the Christmas season of 2009–2010, Sarah says their relationship became strained. "I don't want to get into the details, because it really isn't fair to just present one side of an argument," she said. "My husband is a nice man who is dealing with issues in his life, but things went unresolved between us and we had a house full of holiday guests to entertain. I built up some very negative thoughts about someone that I truly love, and had no way to let off any steam. Instead of getting an ulcer or drinking too much alcohol like some people might, I let off steam in a different way. We went through a lot of light bulbs over the holidays; when I get stressed, they go poof! Of course, my husband went about replacing the bulbs as fast as they were burning out—maybe his way of denying we were having problems. As long as all the lights were on, everything was fine. Problem was, I didn't feel very fine. It got to the point where I hid new bulbs around the house and changed them without him knowing, so he wouldn't get upset."

The light bulbs finally stopped poofing, but then there were loud noises like someone was banging on the wall. "I remember thinking that talking to my husband was like banging my head against the wall," she said. "Maybe my unconscious took that too literally. The banging would get loudest when I was sleeping. Hubby kept waking me up to ask if I had heard anything, and he commented that the volume dropped sharply as soon as he woke me up. At one point I told him that it was just the house settling, I went back to sleep and the noises started up again louder than ever."

Also around that time, Sarah says her anxiety resulted in a washer and a dryer moving about two feet along the laundry room floor. She and her husband had trouble pushing the dryer back into place. "He wouldn't touch me for days after that," she said. "I felt really bad that on some subconscious level I might have pushed him to the edge [with RSPK]."

Another day, the back hatch of their car came down hard on her husband's head for no reason, she said. "Then a door slammed shut in his face with no one near to have pushed it, and then there was the taser kiss...on New Year's Eve, he stayed up to kiss me at midnight. We were trying to get over our differences, but I was still upset. My husband has this thing about not saying he's sorry. Never has, never will. He just expects me to know he's sorry. He doesn't think saying such things is important. But they are important. Anyway, when he kissed me he got one heck of a wicked zap. I could see the sparks. It didn't really bother me, but he said it was like kissing a taser. I laughed and blamed it on wearing wool socks. And it is quite possible that those socks are to blame, but that kiss really did seem to say a lot about how I was feeling towards him at that moment in time."

Sarah doesn't like how she feels physically when the RSPK comes on. "Sometimes I feel overheated and other times it's so cold, it's like walking into a refrigerator. I have walked to the thermostat and suddenly have the furnace come on; then it shuts off when I walk away."

She still frets that she may have contributed to her first husband's premature death. In 1995, Sarah says, her reaction to his physical threats set off poltergeist-type activity, which made him flee the house. After police found him two weeks later, she remained afraid of him, even though he asked for forgiveness for the way he had treated her. "He was a relatively young, physically fit man when our marriage ended, and yet he didn't live for very long after our divorce," she said. "He actually died shortly after I had been told that he was attempting to track me down again. I had gone off the radar as best I could to avoid all contact with him, so hearing that he was looking for me again was pretty upsetting. I know that there is no way to know what really caused his death, but a part of me worries that maybe my fear of him played a role in what happened. I'm pretty certain that RSPK saved my life the night our marriage ended, but what if it kicked in when my old fears of him were brought to the surface again?"

Mostly, Sarah does not like her condition, her alleged powers, to the point that she's seeking not only a meaning and cause for it, but also a cure. "I want to understand it in order to fix it, 'cure' it, and make it stop so I'll be normal," she said.

Roll believed her. "She's more disturbed about her circumstances than happy about them," he said.

Another one of Sarah's quirks, she said, is the ability to pick up other people's thoughts and feelings, particularly when she gets close to them on a bus. She often sees lights around prople, not so much like auras but more like the Northern Lights. "I hear a lot of noise coming from them and it makes me uncomfortable; I can pick up too much information from them—their emotions, whether they're hungry or not, and images of what they've been doing that day. I don't know where this comes from; maybe the human consciousness can be seen outside the body? Sometimes I feel like moving away from people, to the wilderness."

Sarah has considered taking drugs to make her condition more bearable, but so far has resisted, partly because she is allergic to some drugs and painkillers. For now, she copes by using meditation, knitting socks, activating her simple pinwheel, and leaning back on a newly found support system of paraspychologists and sensitive people such as herself through an Internet blog she started.

In 2008, she contacted parapsychologist Loyd Auberbach in California. "At first, I was pretty sure he would think that I was nuts," she laughed. "I couldn't blame him if he did; in fact, that might have made him appear to be even more credible as a scientist. Secondly, I didn't really know if there was anything the guy could do for me. At the time all I really wanted was a cure for seeing ghosts."

sudbury tests

Sarah's new contacts eventually led her to getting her brain tested at the neuroscience lab in Sudbury, Ontario, Canada. There, in April of 2010, she was tested by Persinger and Roll.

Persinger's main focus is on the commonalities that exist among the various sciences, and integrating fundamental concepts among them. In the 1980s, he produced what has been termed the *god helmet* by stimulating people's temporal lobes with a machine with a weak magnetic field to produce in the wearer the sense of an ethereal presence in the room, similar to a religious experience. Through the decades, Persinger has come to believe that many UFO sightings and ghosts have a scientific basis and may be produced by magnetic fields or hallucinations, but he remains open-minded, unlike some scientists. Though Persinger's experiments could prove groundbreaking, he remains doubtful about his controversial findings being accepted by his colleagues: "I think the critical thing about science is to be open-minded," he said. "It's really important to realize that the true subject matter of science is the pursuit of the unknown. Sadly, scientists have become extraordinarily group-oriented. Our most typical critics are not mystic believer types; they are scientists who have a narrow vision of what the world is like." In fact, because he also studies parapsychology, Persinger said he was shut out of research grants for years.

Roll has been loosely called a *ghostbuster* for his numerous investigations and books authored on poltergeist activity, yet he tended to look for human and physical explanations for mysteries in which people claim things are moved by the human mind.

In the week leading up to her tests, Sarah was nervous about going to a strange place to be tested by people she didn't know. "I'd never made my pinwheel move in front of anyone before," she said. "And I wasn't sure whether I was afraid they wouldn't find anything unusual about me, or that I really was different." She believes her nervousness that week caused three light bulbs to go out in her house. "I know light bulbs can burn out on their own, but this stuff happens more often when I'm nervous or emotional."

In the lab, Sarah had an EEG machine hooked up to her head to monitor her brain activity. But during the test to try to make the pinwheel move with her mind, Sarah could not do it. She said she was ill and exhausted. "Often these things happen when you aren't really trying," she said. "So if I try to move them on purpose, sometimes it doesn't work."

A disappointed Sarah was allowed to go to her hotel room. Call them, the researchers said, if she felt better. That night she did feel better and was able to make the wheel move on her own in her room, and so she called Persinger's student, who went to her room with a portable EEG machine and tested her there. This time, she was able to make the wheel move in front of the young researcher. At first, the wheel started and stopped, and then it went on a good run, she said. Persinger, who was not there, was told by the student that the pinwheel had indeed moved, seemingly through unknown forces.

The machine showed changes in Sarah's brain activity while the wheel was moving, she said. "There was increased coherence in the brain patterns, like when people meditate," she said.

"She does some interesting phenomena,"Persinger said, "but we need more proof. Unless she can move the wheel when it's under glass, for example, it's insufficient. People can do some amazing tricks and these things can easily be duplicated by animators for YouTube."

Following the tests, Roll said he believed Sarah is an agent for poltergeist or RSPK activity. "I have never seen or heard of a case quite like hers," Roll said.

Persinger wants to put her through a further series of tests before he comes to any conclusions of paranormal activity, but he was extremely impressed by Sarah's brain. "She has a unique brain with EEG patterns I have not seen previously and are clearly not in the obvious scientific literature," he said. "If she lived closer, we would invite her to the laboratory for measurements weekly." Persinger went further, claiming that in his 40 years of research, he had never seen a person so sensitive to her immediate environment, particularly the earth's magnetic field.

Sarah remains encouraged. "Dr. Persinger says we need more tests and I agree with him," she said. "The two days in Sudbury was very preliminary work. Mostly, they wanted to see what my brain was doing. I'm not even sure if I have PK, or how I do these things."

Part of the purpose of the trip to Sudbury was to help Sarah try to cope with her condition. Persinger is also a clinical neuropsychologist who helps people with head injuries, and he suggested that she try to quieten the noises and images in her head and reduce her RSPK experiences by listening to loud music through earphones—and it worked. "Loud music sort of disengages the circuitry, disrupts the phenomenon bothering her," he said. "Now the intensity of her subject RSPK can be modulated by her, according to the intensity of music to which she is listening."

Sarah said the Sudbury testing was a better experience than she was expecting. "The researchers were happy to see PK occur. I didn't feel like a monster for a change. I did get overwhelmed sometimes...my favorite part was making the PK wheel spin while hooked up to an EEG machine. The researcher operating the machine was truly and honestly happy to see the wheel move. That made the trip worthwhile."

the wild, happy kid

If Sarah S. does indeed have psi powers, where did they come from? She says she had a happy childhood, apart from school, as the daughter of two parents who worked, and having two brothers. As for school: at age 10, she was expelled and was taken to a child psychologist. "I guess you could say I was a wild kid. The school did all kinds of psychological tests on me and wanted to put me on drugs," she said. "Counseling sessions and all kinds of testing finally stopped when I was 12 when I was old enough to pretend to be normal. They never did find any learning disabilities or anything "wrong" with me. Because of that, I ended up becoming distrustful of adults and became a bit of a wild teenager. Strangely enough, being a wild kid is considered normal, but having imaginary friends that nag you to do your homework, which I did, and tell you not to get into a car full of drunken teenagers, is not normal. Figure that one out!" She believes she was gifted at a young age, but never noticed it. "I think a certain amount is how I'm wired," she shrugged. She knows of no one else in her family who has such powers.

Into her teens, Sarah started seeing colors around people, but in high school she learned to keep her gifts to herself in order to appear normal. "In my life I've spent a lot of time and energy trying to seem normal," she says.

During numerous telephone interviews with me for this book, Sarah did appear normal—a warm, sensitive person to talk to, seemingly not a witch or a freak. She seems caring, intelligent, and funny, with a nervous laugh in which the bottom falls out of her conversation for a moment, as though she is not sure if people will believe or digest what she's said.

Sarah says a near-death experience in 1993 changed her life and awakened her unusual gifts after they had started to wane or become neglected. She was driving home from an outing with her pet terrier on a bright winter's day when her new car radio went to static and its music died. The radio had done the same thing near the same spot on the highway earlier in the day.

Suddenly, her car skidded on black ice and was sheared in half by an oncoming heavy truck. Sarah does not remember the accident, but she recalls being transformed into another world, finding herself on a balcony with her grandmother, who had died several years before, looking down at her dog in a meadow. "There was this really soft beautiful light that kind of rained down...glittering like sunshine through raindrops," Sarah said." It made me feel so warm inside, and it was so real to me." It did not seem like heaven. "I'm not a religious person, and I've always had trouble with the concept of "god," she said. "However, I did feel very loved. It was like I became part of something much bigger; the raindrops and the cool and soft light all connected. It seemed like all my senses, emotions, and thoughts mixed together in that place. Everything seemed to make so much sense and now I actually miss it. You could say I sometimes get homesick for the NDE place."

In that other world, her pet terrier barked at Sarah to join her as it went towards a forest, but Sarah's grandmother said she could not leave the balcony. "She held my hand and said I would have to go back, wherever that was supposed to be." Eventually, Sarah and her grandmother went inside the building for tea and cookies.

Sarah said she also had a brief out-of-body experience, seeing herself being attended to by medics at the crash scene. When she regained consciousness three days later, she was in the hospital, recovering from broken bones and head trauma. "My eyes were swollen shut, there was a gash on my forehead, and my face was badly bruised and cut up. My whole body was bruised and broken. I was told I'd never walk again without help." She said at one point doctors had not expected her to live, but she made a remarkable recovery. After that, her anomalous experiences became more intense. She says she saw more ghosts, and the lights around people "became more meaningful somehow. We started having a lot of electrical problems in our home, and suddenly I didn't like being in crowds; I started picking up too much information from them."

Also following the accident, her attitude toward life changed. "I suddenly wanted to go back to school and finish a science degree. My marriage didn't survive the accident, so while doing my BSc, I went through a divorce. I got married a second time while writing my MSc thesis." Now she is working her PhD. "Intuitive knowledge wasn't enough for me anymore," she said. "I wanted to know why things are the way they are. Somehow, the accident turned me into a scientist. Yet the whole thing seems backwards; as a scientist, it's much harder to accept the possibility of the world being intrinsically conscious. And it is really hard to accept the sorts of anomalous cognition that seems to have been enhanced by the near-death experience. How can you explain why the universe takes someone who is very connected to the bigger picture and then transforms her into someone who would be overwhelmed at the thought of such a worldview? Before the accident, I didn't need proof of my connection to the universe; now it's a struggle for me to accept such things—although the proof is constantly biting me on the backside! It seems like becoming a scientist was just one step in the process, and now I see the universe as asking me to integrate the girl I was before with the woman I am now." Sandra chuckled, "I'm pretty much stuck between two worlds, both figuratively speaking and literally."

She says that if she had not had her experiences, she would likely be a disbelieving skeptic. "I don't like being associated with the new-agers or people not willing to test their own experiences; rather, I want to bring science to these things because a lot of people need answers. I think my experiences can hold up to investigations. Sometimes, I struggle with wanting to be a scientist while slipping into scientism out of habit because it feels safe and familiar."

Her 1993 NDE experienced changed her enough that Meyers-Briggs personality tests given to her before and after the accident showed different results, she said. "Before that I was extroverted, a party girl; now the tests show I'm more introverted."

It was not Sarah's first near-death experience; as a toddler of 2 1/2 years, she fell down stairs and cracked her head. During that purported NDE, she said she saw pretty lights, and then the grandmother from her mother's side, who died before she was born, picked her up and suddenly all her pain was gone. But little Sarah asked to see her father, and then her father appeared and held her, she said.

Roll believed that Sarah's two serious accidents may be the major cause for her PK and RSPK powers because they impacted her brain. "I think they knocked out some systems and enhanced others." Roll said he couldn't prove it, but he thought there was a shift in power from her brain's left hemisphere, which controls logical and rational thinking, and the right hemisphere, which is more intuitive and is "our psychic hemisphere."

emotional and electrical triggers

Sarah isn't sure what's behind her RSPK powers, but suspects it may be related to her unusual brain and sensitivity to electricity. She does know that her mood and emotions are triggers to the events. "Different types of emotions bring on different types of things," she said. "I think some of it has to do with fear. When I'm in fearful situations, it can bring on RSPK. I know this could be a way of expressing myself, but I know it is not appropriate, but I can't talk about it with my husband. I can't express myself properly with him, and so this type of stuff happens."

Reactions to other people can also set it off. When she was in the military, Sarah was standing at attention for a parade when a superior pinched her butt. "I was furious, but I couldn't move"—because she would have broken rank. She can't prove it, but she believes that her subsequent RSPK was responsible for the officer hurting his foot on a forklift machine nearby.

In 2010, her bad relationship with a supervisor at college resulted in the breakdown of machines and lights going on and off, she said. "Sometimes when I get under stress, this happens. I guess I might have a passive-aggressive RSPK."

However, Sarah says she has shown she can also produce PK when she is in a good mood, and when her husband and others are not there. That makes her case highly unusual, Roll said. Two other peculiar aspects of her PK and RSPK, he added, are that her events have gone on for years, whereas the average case he studies lasts only several weeks to several months, and that she is in her mid-40s, in contrast to most other RSPK agents who are younger than 20.

Like Roll and Persinger, Sarah believes she has an electrically sensitive body. "I zap people all the time, give them a little shock when I touch them." She says she can make machines go down. In 2009, a lamp in her house exploded, and she says that alternators in her cars never last long. "I have to keep grounding myself," she said. "I visualize creating lights to protect myself, to ground myself." When she goes near power lines, she feels disoriented, and yet thunderstorms can quiet her. Additionally, geomagnetic storms can give her headaches, nausea and even hives.

In 2009–2010, she had two cases of rare ball lightning in her home. In the former incident, the lightning appeared in a hallway, flashed, and went into the bathroom. In the other, the lightning appeared in the corner of a room, like a crystal forming outside of a solution and "bloomed into existence, then popped." In both instances, there was a storm outside, yet it is highly unusual to have two cases of ball lightning in the same house.

living with psi

Sarah tries to enjoy the benefits of her condition and cope with the bad parts. "Some of my experiences are wonderful. I would miss talking to [the ghost of] my Grandma. I'm so used to the colors being around everything, maybe I wouldn't recognize a world without such things. I remember when I wondered how people could get by without them. As I got older, I just stopped thinking about it."

But seeing ghosts and colored lights everywhere can get on her nerves. Sarah says she often sees ghosts (often elderly people talking to their dead relatives), and sometimes talks to them, but she is reluctant to talk to researchers and scientists about them for fear of losing some credibility in their eyes. Sarah hopes she can live with that part of it. "Most of this stuff is either neutral or sometimes even good if you can get over the creepiness of it. Only a very small percentage of the weird stuff is bad. But it can happen, and people can get hurt and it can make me feel like a monster. It would kill me to hurt someone. The thing is, often I don't control the energy and sometimes it scares me. I worry about flipping out emotionally."

Mostly, she worries about the physical effect she seems to have on people and objects around her, particularly when she gets emotional. "Rattling plates, noises in the night, car malfunctions, [and] popping light bulbs seem to happen all the time around me," she said.

the Pinwheel

Sarah is grateful for her little pinwheel for turning her unpredictable and often destructive RSPK into controlled PK. "I'm trying to focus on using up the energy in harmless ways." she said. "It isn't a cure, but it is helpful."

Following her mixed test results in Sudbury in April 2010, Sarah reported more consistent success with her pinwheel. By late July 2010, when she put on the Skype demonstration for me, she could make it move almost every time on demand. However, she still could not make it move under a glass or a jar for long, which she calls "canned PK."

She describes how she moves the wheel: "I put it close to me, sometimes near my hand, but I almost have to ignore the wheel before it moves. But then I can feel it in my body when the wheel is moving. It's kind of an electrical feeling. My hands get pin-prickly. I see lights around the wheel and sometimes I look at that."

After watching her in action in Sudbury—albeit with disappointing results—William Roll made some interesting insights: "If she thinks someone is looking at the [pinwheel] before it begins to spin, the spinning doesn't occur. If she tries to make a video of it, if the camera is started before the PK starts, it won't spin. But if someone watches [her] before the pinwheel starts, it has no effect, or it may increase the possibility of PK."

In spring 2010, though, while watching the Oscars on TV, Sarah said she was nervous about a meeting the following day and was able to make the wheel spin while making a video of it. She sent copies of the video to her friends, who are now trying to move their own wheels (she says a college professor has succeeded, but the professor would not give an interview for this book). "I've heard that seeing someone else do it makes it easier, so I was making a video for her to practice with," Sarah said. "I think it overcomes a certain resistance."

Society needs to acknowledge such forces, which tend to be outside the mainstream of thought, she said. "There are many people who use their gifts very subtly, but they don't pay attention to it or they don't acknowledge it. Most people don't talk about these things."

Meanwhile, she keeps the wheel by her telephone for an outlet, in case the conversation gets emotional. PK, she says, is her friend.

⊚ PART II ⊚

THE THEORIES

"There is no mystery greater than that posed by the poltergeist. The noisy ghosts of folklore and legend represent some of the most complex phenomena known to science."

The late parapsychologist D. Scott Rogo, written for promotional material for his book On the Track of the Poltergeist

We have seen in the previous section that there are enough credible eyewitness accounts to suggest that poltergeist activity may exist, however rare it may be. If it does exist, what is behind it? How could objects possibly be moved without being touched by human hands? The central theory of this book revolves around a person, usually young, moving objects or creating disturbances with his or her mind, perhaps subconsciously (RSPK). The facts in most cases suggest this scenario, and it has become the most popular theory among paranormal investigators. However, we will also touch on other theories, such as that the activity is caused by electricity or electromagnetism, magnetic fields, spirits, possession of a person by spirits or evil forces, or simply pranksters.

CHAPTER 8

Mind Over Matter?

"It is possible that there exist emanations that are
still unknown to us. Do you remember how electrical
currents and unseen waves were laughed at?"

Albert Einstein

Many skeptics and scientists cannot fathom the idea of moving
things with the mind (PK, or, in poltergeist cases, RSPK). Leading
the skeptics are Paul Kurtz, a professor of philosophy at the State
University of New York at Buffalo, and professional magician James "The
Amazing" Randi, who are members of the Committee for Skeptical Inquiry
(CSICOP: *www.csicop.org*). The organization's magazine, published six
times a year, is the *Skeptical Inquirer*. Randi, who offers $1 million to any-
one who can prove the existence of such paranormal events as RSPK, says
that if people could make things move off the ground with their minds it
would amount to "a repeal of the basic laws of physics."

Perhaps, though, there are forces in the universe and inside the complex human brain that we still do not understand or have not been able to
identify or document. Certainly, we are discovering things all the time that
we once thought to be out of this world. For example, demonstrations of
Thomas Edison's first phonograph were laughed at by some early scientists
as a cheap ventriloquist's trick. Other groundbreakers were also ridiculed,
such as French chemist Louis Pasteur. Even the famous British mathematician Lord Kelvin once said that X-rays would prove to be a hoax and that
air flight was impossible. And, of course, Albert Einstein's General Theory
of Relatively was scoffed at by leading scientists of his day.

"Science, then, is not a set of immutable truths, but rather a method of inquiry," wrote investigative reporter Michael Schmicker in his 2002 book *Best Evidence*. "Scientific theories and hypothesis change as new evidence appears to challenge existing views of reality, as it always does."

William Roll disagreed with Randi's theory about the laws of physics: "It's not true that physics says that objects cannot be affected without contact—we know that the moon revolves around the Earth and magnets can attract pieces of iron. RSPK does not require a repeal of the laws of physics, but an extension," he said to me.

Of course, many cases originally thought to be from poltergeist activity actually turn out to be due to natural causes or hoaxes. But there does seem to be a small number of cases that defy explanation, reported throughout history in every country, exhibiting similar characteristics: mysterious loud noises and movement of objects and furniture, usually happening in the presence of a young person, even though that person is closely watched by others and is cleared of tomfoolery. Although these *genuine* cases seem to be rare, there is no way of putting a number on them because often they are not reported or documented. "I expect it's happening every day. It certainly isn't a frequent occurrence, though," Roll told me. "Reporting of the occurrences is rare because people tend to think they are possessed or they are afraid of being accused of being crazy, so you don't get people coming forward."

According to Stephen Mera, founder of Manchester's Association of Paranormal Investigators and Training (MAPIT), in Manchester, England, only about 12 percent of poltergeist cases are investigated by parapsychologists. One reason is that they usually do not last long— generally from one week to several months, although some have gone on more than a year.

If we are to believe there are such things as poltergeists, how do we get past the basic questions of how things seem to *get life* under their own power, or how someone can move something without touching it, particularly when we hear incredible reports of chairs rising into the air and glasses flying through a kitchen? Even the most hardcore parapsychologists don't profess to have proof of mind over matter on such a large scale, or how it comes about; however, there are many theories and much speculation. One theory is that poltergeist agents have unusual brains, with an ability to tap into outside energy sources, such as perhaps tension in a home or an actual electrical power source.

Roll, who has likely spent more time than anyone studying poltergeists in recent times, believed that some people unconsciously unleash a rare and mysterious force that interferes with gravity. Some people call this the *zero-point theory*. According to Roll, during the actual movement or levitation of objects, there is a brief suspension of gravity. "It's still just speculation," he said to me. "But I think something interferes with inertia and gravity, allowing objects to [levitate]. Scientists have found an electromagnetic field that fills the universe, but it's hard to detect. But it is detected in experiments. It's called *zero-point energy* and it interacts with gravity and inertia. The theory in cases of RSPK is that the weak electromagnetic signals from the brain affect this field. It's temporary and it cancels gravity and inertia."

In this unproven theory, the person who has the mysterious energy—the agent—causes the zero-point energy to cohere and thereby loosen the hold on gravity and inertia that ordinarily keeps things grounded, according to physicist Dr. Harold Puthoff, director of the Institute for Advanced Studies in Austin, Texas, who conducts theoretical studies in gravitation, energy generation, and space propulsion. Puthoff says that inertia is the effect that causes stationary objects to remain at rest and moving objects to remain in motion: "If you stand on a train at a station and it leaves with a jerk, inertia may cause you to topple backwards, and lurch forward if the train suddenly stops." It is thought that inertia is due to pressure from the zero-point energy.[1]

There may be something abnormal about the brains of poltergeist agents that causes this temporary suspension of gravity. In 92 poltergeist cases, Roll found that four agents were diagnosed as epileptic. That's higher than the world average of 0.5 percent of people with epilepsy. Andrew Green, a London parapsychologist, agreed that some of the agents suffered from front temporal lobe epilepsy, a brain disorder in which people can suffer blackouts lasting from one minute to half an hour. During these blackouts, an unknown power of the mind may be released, which can cause objects to move, as Roll and Green believe.

The late parapsychologist D. Scott Rogo discovered a 15-year-old boy who had temporal lobe dysfunctions following disturbances in Tucson, Arizona, in 1983. When rocks were thrown at the home of his mother and father and three siblings, a vandal was suspected, but when they were mysteriously hurled at police, the officers had no answer. The disturbance occurred on and off for several months before Rogo came to the conclusion it was the teenage boy projecting the rocks with his mind.

Green also suspects that a higher-than-average number of poltergeist agents suffer from schizophrenia, which may also lead to unusual mental powers. He investigated the 1956 case of a 15-year-old girl in London named Shirley Hitching, who was said to cause loud rapping noises with her mind. She had, prior to the paranormal occurrences, been diagnosed as schizophrenic.

It is possible that some agents suffer a type of partial seizure in which their brains are subject to sudden electromagnetic discharges that interfere with gravity and stationary objects, Roll said. (In the next chapter, we will examine the possibility that electricity within the brain or body, as well as electric fields, may influence poltergeist activity.) Other agents are said to be susceptible to hysteria, phobias, and high anxiety.

telekinetic temper tantrums

These days, most parapsychologists believe that poltergeists are haunted people. Most often the phenomena happen in the agents' homes, but if they leave the home, it sometimes follows them. "Research tells us poltergeists are not caused by spirits or demons, but are creations of the mind," Rogo told me. "The research indicates poltergeists focus on families, which tend to repress and sublimate large amounts of anger and inner aggression. The anger tends to build within the unconscious mind of one of the family members, until it explodes in the form of the poltergeist. This theory has been honored by parapsychologists for a long time, but it may not be the whole answer."

Rogo, Roll, and others say they've found trends in their investigations. They have even come up with this psychological profile: Typically the agent is an adolescent of above-average intelligence with a low tolerance for frustration, repressing feelings of aggression and hostility. Yet,

Green says he knows of poltergeist cases involving people from 3 to 40 years old, who have usually suffered some sort of mental trauma. In many, if not most cases there seems to be a buildup of stress, fear, frustration, or anger in a household and/or in the poltergeist agent. Often these emotional issues are said to be unresolved. The theory for this is called *repressed psychokinetic energy*, and was first put forward in the early part of the 20th century. (Prior to that, agents were thought to be possessed by demons or attacked by ghosts.)

"Agents can be people who typically have no method of dealing with the stress on any normal level, so the subconscious takes advantage of the psychokinetic ability to blow off steam," says California parapsychologist Loyd Auerbach. "You can think of a poltergeist scenario as a type of telekinetic temper tantrum." This can even occur with adults, he added: "If a husband doesn't want his wife to work, instead of asking her to stay home with a new baby, kitchen appliances may act strangely when the subject is brought up in discussion. Water bursts may be representative of pent-up guilt."[2]

Author and screenwriter Alexandra Sokoloff theorizes that there may be a hormonal component to the link between young people and poltergeists. When she was 16, Sokoloff had an unusual experience while she and a group of friends were playing with a Ouija board. "It was scary, disturbing," she recalls. "At a particularly tense point of the séance, a glass candlestick holder suddenly shattered in front of us. I never believed there was an actual entity present, but it did make me think that the hyped-up hormonal energy of teenagers can sometimes cause random movements or breakages of objects. And it started a real obsession for me with the question of whether paranormal experiences are supernatural or psychological or perhaps a combination of both." The experience became the basis for her award-winning first horror novel, The Harrowing, in 2006. "I believe there are a million layers to reality, and it's all out there in front of us—and if we pay more attention to the signs, there's no telling what we might discover," Sokoloff said.[3]

Or, some poltergeist cases may be mass delusions or hallucinations by several people in a stressed-out household, according to Allentown, Pennsylvania psychologist Robert Gordon. He believes a type of hysteria may take over, similar to that prevalent during the Salem witch trials.

A Hungarian-American psychic investigator, Nandor Fodor, said that repression of creativity can on rare occasions lead to paranormal events. For example, in the house of retired firefighter Edgar Jones in Baltimore, Maryland, in 1960, Jones's 17-year-old grandson, Ted Pauls, was suspected of causing soda bottles to burst from within, piles of firewood to explode, pictures to fall, and windows to break by subconsciously willing them to do so. At one point, with the whole family watching, a ceramic flower pot reportedly lifted from a shelf and crashed through a window, and a sugar bowl floated up to an overhead ceiling light and dumped its contents all over a table. Fodor investigated and suspected that the shy, brooding Ted, who had dropped out of high school because he was bored, was a brilliant, frustrated writer with no outlet for his talents. And he apparently felt he was not getting enough attention from others. "He had created a psychic disassociation," Fodor speculated. "The human body is capable of releasing energy in a matter similar to atomic bombardments as this force was apparently able to enter soda bottles that had not been uncapped and to burst them from within."[4]

Hatred seems to be a trigger for some agents. In the 1980s in Bournemouth, England, a house was plagued for years by the mysterious breaking of windows and upturning of paint cans. Parapsychologist Mary Rose Barrington suspected it was caused subconsciously by a young man who lived with his cousin and his aunt, whom he apparently hated . The incidents stopped when he left the house, Barrington said. "If this attribution is well founded, it certainly broadens the scope of poltergeist investigation by adding the routine question, 'And is there anyone who hates you?'"[5]

As Rogo told me, the poltergeist agent often focuses his or her energies toward authority figures, such as parents or employers, using defenses such as repression, sublimation, and denial to deal with their frustrations. "When the [poltergeist] agent can't control his or her intense anger, the [RSPK] is unleashed, sort of like a safety valve for frustration." In this way, the agent can also maintain a conscious innocence about the events.

As an example of this, a 15-year-old boy from a Muslim family who had recently moved to the rural village of Druten in the Netherlands may have caused RSPK occurrences in 1995 because he was confused and frustrated by the clash of cultures in his life. The boy came from an orthodox Islamic school in Turkey, in which stonings were discussed as punishment for some crimes. Among the poltergeist events surrounding him in the Netherlands were numerous airborne stones, as well as flying sand, reportedly breaking windows and hitting people. Several police officers set up a dragnet around the family's house and reported that stones continually and mysteriously hit the house. Two officers said they had sand thrown in their faces by unknown forces.

Parapsychologists Johan Gerding and Rens Wezelman of the Parapsychology Institute in Utrecht, Holland, and Dick Bierman of the psychology department of the University of Utrecht, believed the boy set off RSPK unconsciously. But secretly, they may be pleased with the irritation or damage it is causing in a home or to people, said Roll, who studied written reports of 116 suspected poltergeist cases spanning four centuries and more than 100 countries.

People who have suffered extreme trauma may also be at risk for poltergeist events. Psychologist Joel L. Whitton, professor of psychiatry at the University of Toronto Medical School, believes that some cases may be linked to post-traumatic stress disorder, or PTSD. He says the agent may unconsciously re-create stressful situations from infancy, which explains why a large number of poltergeist cases involve bottles, food, and eating utensils—they all might relate to the powerful oral needs of infants.

In 1961 in the Felix Fuld Housing Project in Newark, New Jersey, Mabelle Clark shared an apartment with her 13-year-old grandson Ernest Rivers. It was said that over a two-week period, cups, bowls, and ashtrays would sail across the small apartment. Clark apparently tried to keep it secret because she had lived in the home for 20 years and didn't want to be evicted, but the neighbors complained and housing officials eventually entered.

The officials and several other people reportedly saw a string of unexplained events, including a heavy steam iron floating from a linen closet into a bedroom. A team of parapsychologists investigated and found that the incidents stopped when Ernest was removed from the building. They discovered he had been highly stressed ever since his mother was murdered by his abusive prizefighter father five years earlier. And just before the phenomena began, the boy's mother had escaped from a women's reformatory.

People who have RSPK powers often suffer from mental health issues, Roll told me. He added that many are treated by professional therapists, who often dismiss their psi abilities as impossible and may use the idea against them to label them as delusional, or worse. What is called for, Roll said, is a profession of clinical parapsychologists, trained to understand people with RSPK and other experiences.

our amazing fear energy

Perhaps poltergeist activity is not black magic but stress magic; perhaps PK and RSPK are rare weapons or byproducts of the magnificent fight-or-flight system, which is hardwired into our bodies and has helped our species survive on a harsh planet for hundreds of thousands of years.

I have written four books on fear and the fight-or-flight response, and the more I study our fear reaction, the more I realize what amazing powers we all possess, many of them possibly still untapped. When you feel afraid or angry, your body goes through a whole series of chemical changes that effectively turn you briefly into a different person and give you substantial new powers. This occurs through your sympathetic nervous system, or what I call the *emergency fear system*.

Here are some of the changes that may or may not occur when you experience fear, depending on the severity of the threat, or what you see as a threat:

- ◉ The heart goes from pumping one gallon of blood per minute to five gallons per minute.
- ◉ Pupils dilate for maximum visual perception.
- ◉ Arteries constrict for maximum pressure to pump blood to the heart and other muscles.
- ◉ Blood is rerouted away from skin and internal organs toward the brain and skeletal muscles. Muscles tense and you feel stronger.
- ◉ Breathing becomes more rapid and nostrils flare, creating an increased supply of air.

◎ Pain threshold increases.

◎ Concentration can sharpen to the point that a phenomenon known as *tachypsychia* (Greek for "speed of the mind") occurs and all the action in front of you seems to happen in slow motion, allowing you to expand your ability to deal with a threat.

At its peak, this emergency fear system produces a big-bang response known as "fight or flight" as potent hormones, such as adrenaline, dopamine, testosterone, and endorphins come to your aid. (This is occasionally seen when people perform superhuman feats of strength to rescue relatives.)

At times, this fear energy produces altered states of consciousness. For example, tachypsychia is reported by many police officers and soldiers when they are faced with death. Police Corporal Ron Thompson reported reaching a twilight zone of superior focus while he was in a gun battle with a suspect in 1984 in Woodstock, Ontario. He told me: "A gray mantle, like a blanket, was rolled down. Suddenly everything was gone the street, the traffic, the moon, my partner. All that was left was the gunman and me. His head was transformed into a white oval egg. Very sharp. I shot him between the eyes...and killed him."

Altered states are also reported in less threatening circumstances. The late Barbara Brown, who was a brain and behavior researcher, told me that during a speech she gave at the University of California at Los Angeles, her consciousness sort of divided itself: "My perceptions and conscious sensations were suddenly in a pastoral image, where I was resting on a green lawn under a tree, calm and totally relaxed. I was faintly aware that something related to me was on a platform, speaking with inspired words and thoughts. The separate *I* had no idea what the other *I* was talking about." The audience said it was a remarkable speech.

This sounds similar to what may be another fight-or-flight symptom, the out-of-body experience, in which people say they see themselves floating above their bodies to watch surgeons operate on them, for example.

As an amateur athlete and a journalist writing to deadline, I have had similar experiences with being able to expand time, or at least expand my ability to deal with time constraints. During basketball games in the 1990s,

I summoned an altered state to produce perfect shooting performances. While shooting, I saw in a sort of split-screen a version of the ball leave my hand about one-quarter of a second before it actually did, then I saw the real ball. And then I saw the split-screen ball enter the basket shortly before it actually did. Some athletes call this "being in the zone." When I queried some biochemists and psychologists about this afterward, they suggested I had had a type of mini seizure. I have been in this zone more than 30 times in my life and every time it is only when I trusted myself and did things unconsciously.

What does all this have to do with RSPK or PK? I suspect both are rare characteristics of fear energy and the fight-or-flight system. In most of the poltergeist cases in this book, the poltergeist agent seems to be suffering from stress, anger, fear, or trauma. It follows that the person's sympathetic nervous system, and perhaps the fight-or-flight response, would kick in. Physical examinations of some poltergeist agents often show high levels of adrenaline and noradrenaline in their nervous systems, which are traditional fight-or-flight hormones. If the agent is showing unconscious hostility toward someone in the home, then his or her fear energy would be directed at that person. If he or she has PK powers, then it might manifest itself in objects moving.

British parapsychologist and author John Spencer suspects there is a connection between the fight-or-flight response and RSPK. When people are in their normal mode, they cannot do superhuman things physically or mentally, he said, but when they are really fearful or angry, "when their unconscious and sometimes irrational mind takes over, it appears to be able to call on more extreme resources than otherwise. There are accounts of parents performing incredible feats of strength, physically lifting objects in order to rescue or safeguard their children, when, in normal conditions, they would not be able to show such extreme strength." Spencer believes this may also be true of mental strength. "Perhaps RSPK is generated by a part of the brain beyond conscious or rational control, where much greater potential lurks. Indeed, maybe those parents were being assisted by some form of PK or RSPK when they acted in those extreme situations."[6]

But how could fear energy project itself outside the body? That, of course, is unproven, and yet great athletes and performers have shown they

88

use their mind and their willpower to influence physical results, such as golfer Tiger Woods and former basketball great Michael Jordan, who have used controlled anger to vault themselves into the zone. In 1993, an amateur bowler, Troy Ockerman, raised his adrenaline levels through heavy metal music and anger at his opponent and got his fear energy working to the point that his concentration powers became enhanced, and he bowled three consecutive perfect games in Corunna, Michigan.

And so, perhaps PK and RSPK are anomalies that have been lost in our strange evolution as human beings, or perhaps they are yet to be discovered and developed.

the Puberty angle

A popular theory about poltergeist agents is that they are youths just entering or going through puberty, which somehow triggers an unknown energy force and perhaps transformations in brain chemistry. Or perhaps it is released by suppression of sexual energy. Certainly, in a general sense, sex can be a powerful force, and many super-achievers say they redirect their sexual energy into creative production.

The complex, multifaceted period of puberty usually begins in girls between 10 and 11 and in boys between 11 and 12. Children go through a series of profound psychological, emotional, and physical changes, and if they are exposed to a stressful home during that time, it could alter their behavior or brain chemistry, change the way they view themselves and others, and perhaps make them more aggressive.

Two Italian physicists hypothesize that changes in the brain, which occur during puberty, involve fluctuations in electron activity that, in very rare cases, can create disturbances up to a few meters around the outside of the brain. Piero Brovetto and Vera Maxia had their research published in 2008 in *New Scientist* magazine and *NeuroQuantology*, a scientific journal that crosses the boundaries of neuroscience and quantum physics. "Poltergeist disturbances often occur in the neighborhood of a pubescent child or a young woman," wrote Brovetto, who once taught physics at the University of Cagliari in Italy. "Puberty is a modification of the child body which involves various organs, chiefly the brain."

In a highly publicized poltergeist case in London in 1977, parapsychologist Guy Lyon Playfair traced the problems of a poltergeist agent, said to be 11-year-old Janet Hodgson, partly to the fact that she was entering puberty. Playfair believed this was related to her pineal gland, located at the center of the brain and responsible for controlling the release of sexual hormones. Playfair believes that during puberty the gland can secrete a type of creative energy. "When a child suddenly acquires this new type of force," he told me, "there is a need for an outlet. If the outlet is not there, the energy will be available for a poltergeist force to steal." Playfair compares this energy to what he calls *psychic soccer*: "Along come spirits who do what any group of schoolboys would do—they go and kick it around, smashing windows and generally creating havoc." And yet, Playfair admits there are many things we do not know about puberty, never mind RSPK.

CHAPTER 9

The Electrical Connection

"...we can now enter realms of real scientific possibilities...
some very strange doors begin to open."

*Albert Budden, an investigator specializing in the scientific study
of the paranormal as well as electromagnetics and health*

In the previous chapter, we saw that some parapsychologists believe that poltergeist agents may have unusual brains, which are subject to sudden electromagnetic discharges. These discharges may somehow interact with physical energies, including electromagnetic energy, to set off poltergeist activity.

Let us now examine an overall electrical theory a little further, and the possibility that, throughout the human brain and body, electricity could spark RSPK. This theory was suspected more than a century ago.

angelique cottin

In 1846 in La Perriere, France, 14-year-old peasant girl Angelique Cottin was weaving gloves on an oak frame with other girls when the frame suddenly began to shake. Many witnesses said the frame would only shake when Cottin was near it, although she was not touching it. After she was checked by a minister and a doctor, her effect on objects around her seemed to accelerate, and it was reported that a 60-pound chair rose up from the floor in her presence, a bed rocked, and she gave people electric shocks. When she was examined by doctors, they established that her heart rate rose to 120 beats a minute during the mysterious activity, and she sometimes suffered convulsions and would run away frightened. Observers noted that she had more effect on objects around her when she was standing on bare earth and less when she was on a carpet or waxed cloth. But her powers were said to be intermittent, and sometimes would be dormant for several days.

Cottin was tested at an observatory in Paris by a group of scientists, appointed by the Academy of Sciences, and they were convinced her powers were genuine and perhaps somehow related to the electrical makeup of her body. (In all human bodies there is electricity in the beat of the heart, and electrical signals also move along your nerve cells. When you walk across a carpet, your body can pick up or rub off extra electrons and this slightly changes your body's electrical potential. Then, when you touch a doorknob, the small electrical shock you get is the electrons leaving your body.)

A respected physicist, Dr. Francois Arago, published a report in the *Journal des debats* (February 1846) in which he called Angelique's power "a kind of electromagnetism." He said the force seemed to be coming more from the left side of her body, which was warmer than the right. She was also affected by unusual movements and shakings, and her apparent power was more prevalent from 7 to 9 o'clock in the evenings. When a pen or light object was put on a table, it would reportedly fly off when Angelique approached it with her left hand. On one occasion, two strong men tried to hold down a chair, but when she came near it, it was said to shatter in their hands. Arago said the girl was very sensitive to magnets; needles reportedly swung quickly when her arm was near but not touching them, and she often got a strong shock when she approached the north pole of a magnet.

nina kulagina

In another case, electricity (bodily or otherwise) also seemed to be present. It was said that Nina Kulagina (pseudonym Nelya Mikhailova), during the 1950s, '60s, and '70s in the Soviet Union, was the center of poltergeist activity in her apartment. She was tested throughout a span of 30 years by top Soviet scientists, who claimed she was often able to move things with her mind in laboratory conditions through sheer focus. A military physiologist, Dr. Genady Sergeyev, studied the electrical potentials in her brain, which, he said, had strong voltages and could expose undeveloped photos in a sealed envelope. In addition, he said that Nina's abilities seemed to diminish during stormy weather.

The chairman of theoretical physics at Moscow University, Dr. Ya. Terletsky, said that Nina displays a new and unknown form of energy. With this focused energy, scientists said, she was able to move things as her pulse rate soared to about 240 beats per minute at the peak of the PK.

virginia campbell

In Scotland in 1960, unusual noises were heard coming from an 11-year-old girl named Virginia Campbell. Strange movements of furniture were reported at home and school around her, and when a physician, Dr. William Logan, examined her, he reported noises coming from her, similar to sounds heard during a magnetic resonance imaging (MRI) scan.

where does the electricity come from?

Parapsychologists are not sure whether such a poltergeist agent generates internal energy to make objects move, or whether his or her energy interacts with outside sources. The late German paranormal researcher Hans Bender developed a theory that in some (or many) instances, agents tap into alternate sources of energy, such as electrical supplies. He said it doesn't seem possible for such agents to generate the power they need to move heavy furniture, and so they somehow, perhaps without knowing they are doing it, "organize energy sources rather than project their own energy."[1]

The controversial Uri Geller, a psychic from Israel whose claim to fame is bending spoons with his mind, said he got his unusual powers from a strong electric shock. Geller said that when he was 5 years old, he saw a blue spark coming out of his mother's sewing machine, and when he tried to touch it, he received a severe shock and was knocked off his feet. He said that after that, he was able to read his mother's mind and could make the hands speed up on a watch by focusing on it. In 1972 at the Stanford Research Institute in California, Geller impressed scientists by correctly identifying numbers hidden from him, although tests meant to prove his metal-bending abilities were inconclusive.

Another psychic, Matthew Manning of Cambridge, England, was tested in 1972 in Toronto at the age of 17. Measurements of his brainwaves while he was reportedly bending cutlery suggested that he produced unusual patterns of electrical energy, emanating from his limbic system. As a child, Manning was purportedly the agent for poltergeist activity in his home.

magnetic fields and a poltergeist machine

One theory to explain poltergeist activity is that it sometimes occurs on or near unusual magnetic fields. "Magnetic field strengths of some locations of unexplained phenomena are significantly different from magnetic field strengths in other areas," said Andrew Nichols of the American Institute of Parapsychology and City College in Gainesville, Florida.[2] In 1996, Nichols investigated movement of objects, rapping noises, and bizarre appearances of water in a home in Jacksonville, Florida. Tension between an 11-year-old girl and her grandmother was cited as one of the reasons for the disturbances, but electrical interferences may have come into play; high voltage transmission towers were located near the family home, and a Naval air station was close by with its radar transmitters and other high-tech equipment. Nichols suspected this electrical interference may have affected the girl, whose brain may have been wired in an unusual manner.

Some parapsychologists believe energies from poltergeist agents and/or outside sources create zero-point energy to temporarily suspend gravity. The idea of gravity being temporarily suspended on Earth is not a new one; world powers have reportedly been investigating the possibility for many years, beginning with the Nazis in the Second World War, with hopes of using such a force for lightning-fast aircraft and weapons. (For a further look at this subject, read the 2002 book *The Hunt for Zero Point* by Nick Cook, who was editor for 10 years of *Jane's Defense Weekly*, the bible of the defense establishment.)

Canadian electromagnetics pioneer John Hutchinson claims to have reached a type of zero-point energy during experiments in British Columbia. And with it, many people believe, he created what has been called *the poltergeist machine* because it reportedly triggers poltergeist-like phenomena. Hutchinson says he came upon his findings by accident during an experiment. He crammed into a room a variety of devices that emit electromagnetic fields, such as Tesla coils, van de Graaff generators, RF transmitters, and signal generators. After they had been operating for a while, bizarre things reportedly began to occur: Objects levitated into the air and hovered about, or moved about and then fell; fires broke out around the building; a mirror smashed 80 feet away; metal distorted and broke; water spontaneously swirled in containers; lights appeared in the air and then vanished; and metal became white-hot, but did not burn surrounding materials. And yet, just as in poltergeist cases, the phenomena were unpredictable—Hutchinson would watch the room for days and nothing would occur, and then suddenly coins would fly into the air, water would act strangely, and transformers would blow. On a video taken in the room, a 19-pound bronze cylinder is seen to rise into the air.

Of course, Hutchinson's machine is not at work in any of the cases in this book, but it shows that perhaps electricity and magnetism are important parts of some poltergeist puzzles. "This certainly does not mean that if we identify poltergeists as electromagnetic in nature, we can all pack up and go home, mystery solved," said Albert Budden, an investigator and author specializing in the scientific study of the paranormal as well as electromagnetics and health. "In fact, the situation is the reverse, as we can now enter realms of real scientific possibilities...some very strange doors begin to open."[3] Budden speculates that the bodies of some poltergeist agents may act as electrical apparatus to interact in an unknown way with electromagnetic pollution from power lines or transmitters near their homes, thus causing objects to move and household appliances to be disrupted.

These energies could also interact with earth energies such as geomagnetic and geoelectric fields at hot spot locations inadvertently built on fault lines, said Budden. Furthermore, cases of poltergeists and hauntings occur slightly more often in days of higher-than-usual geomagnetic activity, according to researchers H.P. Wilkinson and Alan Gauld.

other electrical poltergeists

From 2003 to 2004 in Leawood, Kansas, strange disturbances were occurring in a house—doorknobs jiggling, electrical malfunctions, cold spots, doors opening and shutting, and strange footsteps, according to ghost hunter Kelli Patrick. After an investigation, her group noted that a girl in the home was just entering puberty, and, in addition, there was an unsettled geomagnetic field around the home, which constantly set off electromagnetic field detectors and gave some people migraine headaches. The occurrences subsided a few months after the girl had entered puberty. "They were a really nice and sane family," Patrick told me. "They definitely didn't make anything up."

Many instances are explored further in this book in which household electricity and appliances reportedly worked in weird ways. In Columbus, Ohio, in 1984, electrical problems plagued 14-year-old Tina Resch, the subject of Part III: The numbers on her digital clock radio were said to race without power, and numerous malfunctions were reported with a baby monitor, a television, telephones, and a hair dryer in her home. A utility company checked the house, but could find no trouble with electricity or wiring. In a London case, there were reports of metal bending, teapots rocking, electrical equipment malfunctioning, and an entire frame of the gas fireplace wrenched out of a wall. Investigators did report that their magnetometer registered *deflections* as objects moved across a room. But Budden suggested that researchers at the site did not investigate the electromagnetic possibilities deeply enough because perhaps it was not a welcome explanation for the phenomena they witnessed.

In the Virginia Campbell case, it is possible that she caused the events subconsciously through a type of PK or RSPK, as several observers noted. At one point, her physician, Dr. William Logan, made a curious finding when he checked Virginia while she was in an agitated state, "both physically and emotionally." Despite the agitation of MRI-like noises coming from her, her pulse rate remained normal and quite slow. "I thought this rather unusual, but I can't explain it," Dr. Logan said. "It was as if the subconscious part of her brain was aware that the phenomenon was emanating from her and there was nothing to fear, and the irrational side was producing a standard fear response."[4]

In the following chapter, we will see that one respected scientist believes paranormal experiences are actually hallucinations, sparked by electromagnetic signals in the brain.

esther in nova scotia

In 1878, 19-year-old Esther Cox in Amherst, Nova Scotia, Canada, was said to have caused things to move while she was staying with relatives. She also developed a fever and her skin turned bright red. Witnesses reported hearing a loud bang like a clap of thunder, which seemed to come from under the bed, shaking the entire room. Later Esther said that during her sickness, she had felt that electrical currents were passing through her body.

One of the investigators of her case, Reverend Edwin Clay, a Baptist minister, came to the conclusion that Esther's body had become a type of electric battery, which was emitting subtle and invisible lighting. The family physician, Dr. Gene Carritte, declared that Esther was suffering from shock to her nervous system. The doctor heard claps of thunder from under her bed and reportedly saw a pillow move under her head, without anyone touching it. He said that Esther was not behind any trickery, but he would not write about his experience in medical journals because he thought no one would believe him.

A book about the case written by friend and magician Walter Hubbell, titled *The Great Amherst Mystery*, shows an affidavit signed by 16 witnesses who claimed they had seen unexplained events surrounding Esther.

The occurrences went on for three weeks until Esther went into a trance and told an incredible story: Earlier that year, she had been threatened with rape by a local man, who allegedly pulled out a pistol, put it to her breast, and said he would kill her if she did not go into the woods with him. When she refused, he drove off. The trauma stayed with Esther for months.

Esther's own theory about her powers was that she was being haunted by ghosts.

The Electric Family

Parasearch, a group that investigates paranormal activity in England, suspects that a family with two small children in the West Midlands was predisposed to ghost and poltergeist activity because of personal and household electricity.

In 2002, the family reported apparitions, electrical disturbances, loud banging on the ceiling of their home, and a child's protective gate swinging back and forth on its own.

Parasearch discovered that the father had been hit by lightning as a child and had received two severe electrical shocks as an adult.

Their home had high readings for electromagnetic fields and ultrasonic sources. Furthermore, one child's cot was made of metal and was near a satellite dish. Additionally, the central heating system was suspected of acting as both a receiving and transmitting antenna for radio signals. After the heating system was replaced, the family reported that the phenomena dissipated.

Parasearch speculated that the family hallucinated the phenomena because of the complex electrical connections between their brains and their environment.

CHAPTER 10

The Super Static Girl and More Electricity

"Achtung! Die Lampe!" (Watch out for the lamp!)

We probably all know coworkers who change the atmosphere of an office when they walk through the door. But this story goes a bit further.

When 19-year-old secretary Annemarie Schneider walked into the lawyer's office of Sigmund Adam in 1967 in the Bavarian town of Rosenheim, Germany, at 7:30 each morning, it was said that any of a number of things could occur: light bulbs could explode, pictures could rotate then fall to the floor, light fittings could swing as she walked beneath them, and telephones could supposedly dial on their own. A typical incident is described in Richard S. Broughton's 1991 book *Parapsychology, The Controversial Science*: Annemarie walked down the entrance hall, taking off her coat as she went. As she passed under the hanging lamp, it began swinging, but she did not notice it. As she continued toward the cloakroom, the lamp began to swing more animatedly. An employee shouted: "Achtung! Die Lampe!" When Annemarie ducked for protection, a bulb in the hall lamp exploded. Calmly, she got a broom and swept up.

To all of those in attendance, this commotion was puzzling, and even frightening, during the first day or so; a little funny the next day; and exasperating from then on. The damage alone concerned Mr. Adam—there had been considerable electrical malfunctions since Annemarie joined the company, and fluorescent lights high on the ceiling kept popping, sometimes preceded by a loud bang and sparks. An electrician was summoned, but he broughtmore questions than answers. On one occasion, he scurried up a ladder to discover that each of the fluorescent tubes had been twisted 90 degrees in their sockets, snapping their connection. He fixed them, but suddenly—bang! The same thing happened all over again. Electrical fuses blew and the cartridge fuses were ejected from the sockets.

As for the telephones, all four of them would sometimes ring at once—and no one was at the other end of the line. When lawyers and secretaries were on the lines, sometimes they were suddenly cut off. And the telephone bills ballooned, including some calls that had never been made. Across the room, the photostatic copiers would act up, or have their fluid spill out. Not to worry—engineers from the municipal power station and operators of the phone system were on their way. They were prepared to get at the root of the problem and installed monitoring equipment on the power lines to detect unusual surges. Immediately, the monitors revealed large and unexplained power surges. To isolate the problem, the office was disconnected from its main power sources. An emergency power unit was put in, and yet the disturbances continued. Whatever was happening electrically was happening in the confines of the office building.

A similar system was set up for the wonky telephone lines. All calls made from the office were recorded. Strangely, calls were registered even though no one was in the office, and some lines were dialed up to six times a minute. On October 20, 46 unexplained calls were made in 15 minutes. There were up to four calls a minute, which connected with a line giving the local time. Was someone in a hurry to get work over for the day? Annemarie?

Technicians had no answers, even after they had ripped up the road outside to get at underground wires. One technician claimed that someone inside the office must have been making some of the calls, but all of the employees denied it. Somebody please get a lawyer! Mr. Adam, who, of course, *was* an attorney, filed formal charges with the police. If the person responsible was ever caught, he or she would be prosecuted for mischief. And so the Rosenheim Police criminal investigation division took over the case.

Paranormal investigators got involved as well, including Professor Hans Bender of the Parapsychology Department at the University of Freiburg, a veteran of paranormal cases, who came on December 1 with some of his colleagues. A week later, a physicist from the Max Planck Institute for Plasma Physics, Dr. Friedbert Karger, arrived to take another run at the telephones and the power system.

After all of this snooping around, it was established that:

◉ The disturbances took place only during office hours. (How about calling this "the Nine to Five Poltergeist"?)

◉ Variations in the power supply, electrostatic charges, loose contacts, manual interference, and other physical issues were all ruled out as possible causes.

◉ Annemarie had something to do with the problems. The power-monitoring system would kick in whenever she walked through the door.

Dr. Karger said the phenomena seemed to be the result of unpredictable, short-duration forces, yet he did not know what these forces were, except that they seemed to be intelligently controlled.

Could Annemarie unconsciously, or consciously, be controlling these events with her mind? Bender thought so. After studying many poltergeist cases, he developed a theory that in some or many instances, poltergeist agents tap into alternate sources of energy, such as electrical supplies. He said it doesn't seem possible for such agents to generate the power they need to move heavy furniture, and so they somehow, perhaps without knowing they are doing it, organize energy sources rather than project their own energy. In the case of Annemarie, he speculated that she was tapping into the electric supply of her office.

By this time, Annemarie was becoming self-conscious and tense with everyone scrutinizing her. It was not uncommon for workers to find her shouting or crying. "I never had influence over anything," she said. "I was very hurt indeed."[1] According to Bender, Annemarie had emotional problems—she was insecure and had difficulty handling frustration. "She seemed to instigate [RSPK] in response to her emotional problems," Bender said.[2] He wanted to hypnotize her to try to learn more about her issues, but her parents refused to allow it. Becoming more and more nervous, Annemarie displayed hysterical contractions in her arms and legs, which sometimes temporarily paralyzed her.

When she was sent on leave, nothing happened in the office. As long as Annemarie was around, the disturbances did not dissipate with the arrival of all the technicians and investigators, who said they were witness to paintings swinging off the walls, loud, mysterious bangs, and sparks. Some of the action was caught on videotape, including a picture rotating 320 degrees allegedly on its own power.

The Freiburg researchers reported that papers moved mysteriously and drawers opened without help, or they became ejected. All the while, the police suspected Annemarie—until an oak cabinet, estimated to weigh 400 pounds, moved twice away from a wall. It took two burly cops to push it back. The researchers were able to get a video recording of a lamp swinging unaided, and they also got an audio recording of loud bangs, which sounded like electrical discharges. At no point did police or anyone else see Annemarie or others in the office playing tricks. In all, there were 40 witnesses to the incidents, including police, journalists, and clients of the lawyer.

The office was quiet over the Christmas holidays that year, although things got back to "normal" when Annemarie returned to work on January 9. The intensity soon increased, and on January 17, Annemarie was said to have received electric shocks, as did several coworkers.

Meanwhile, the media had a field day, and some journalists started referring to Annemarie as the Super Static Girl. Two German television firms made documentaries, one of which appeared in Britain. Finally, in early 1968, the damage was becoming too expensive and Annemarie was dismissed. The incidents abruptly ended. Final bill for the damage: about 15,000 deutschmarks, or $7,500.

After leaving the firm, Annemarie got a job at another office. The peculiarities followed her there, but they were not as pronounced, and eventually subsided. When she was taken to laboratory settings for tests, researchers said she had strong ESP abilities, but she did not score well on PK tests. The latter was not unusual, however, because PK and RSPK are said to dissipate in a poltergeist agent as time goes on.

Bender said the Rosenheim case was the most impressive of his more than 35 previous investigations. In fact, the widely publicized Rosenheim case changed the German public's view of poltergeists; before Annemarie, 18 percent of the people polled believed in poltergeists, and after the case it was 28 percent.

Feeling Others' Pain

After experiencing what he felt were paranormal incidents in his office in Rosenheim in 1967, lawyer Sigmund Adam sympathized with another so-called poltergeist case in Nicklheim, Germany, in 1968. Adam visited a laborer and his wife, who reportedly were victimized by loud knocks and flying objects and stones in their home. Apparently, the activity was centered around their 13-year-old daughter. Adam told them of his experiences with Annemarie Schneider, and it seemed to make them feel less alone in their troubles.

electrical brain bursts?

Before he considered paying out on such an outlandish insurance claim, James Holland, a senior loss analyst for a major insurance company, wanted to make sure that water damage at a Florida home in 1996–97 was indeed from a paranormal source. He knew whom to call: Andy Nichols, a parapsychologist with the American Institute of Parapsychology and City College in Gainesville, Florida.

Nichols and a colleague, Russell McCarty, showed up at the seven-year-old single-story house in an affluent suburb of Jacksonville. The occupants were Mary Barton, a 62-year-old financial consultant, who also owned a pet grooming business; her son, Keith, 28; her granddaughter, Krista, 11; and her mother, Lillian, 87 (all pseudonyms).

Mary Barton told Nichols that the occurrences were episodic and unpredictable, and began on November 7, 1996, with a series of unexplained rapping noises heard from several interior walls. Lillian Barton said that she got light sprinkles of liquid or water on her head while she was sleeping and occasionally during the day as she walked through the house. The sprinklings became more frequent, falling on other members of the house, until puddles of water accumulated on the floor.

One day, Mary said she was standing in the kitchen when a small paper cup filled with water, which had been 8 feet behind her on a counter, became airborne and lodged itself in the handle of a lower cabinet. No one else was in the area and Mary was surprised to find that the cup still contained most of its water. Lillian became the most popular victim of liquid attacks and sprinklings in the next few weeks; sometimes she got soaked, and no one could establish where the water was coming from.

A heating contractor checked the heating/air conditioning system and found nothing wrong, and a plumbing contractor could find no leaky pipes, despite the fact they both got wet from the mysterious liquid. A plumbing assistant, Mike Thigpin, was so alarmed from getting soaked in the living room that he left the house, believing it had to be haunted.

The Bartons started to think that something supernatural was at work when a large, gilt-framed mirror, which had been securely mounted on a wall for years, suddenly fell, narrowly missing Lillian, who was lying on a couch. "When the mirror was examined, it was found that the wire which secured it to the wall was unbroken and the heavy mounting screws which protruded from the wall were also intact," Nichols told me. At one point, Mary, Krista, and Lillian all fled the house after getting soaked by the unidentified liquid, only to have it drench a van they tried to leave in.

In total, the incidents went on longer than a month. Nichols said that they occurred only in the presence of 11-year-old Krista, but Mary Barton doubted her granddaughter could have faked the disturbances because she was closely watched by the others. Nichols and McCarty interviewed witnesses and conducted many psychological and electromagnetic tests. It turned out there were high magnetic fields in the area, perhaps from high-voltage transmission towers within a quarter-mile of the house, and from the Jacksonville Naval Air Station, five miles away, with its numerous radar transmitters and other sophisticated equipment.

As for the psychological tests of the family members, Nichols was wary of criticism he'd seen in other cases, in which psychologists knew the people they were testing were suspected poltergeist agents and therefore may have been biased in their interpretations. So, after interviewing the Bartons, he sent their answers to Dr. David Bortnick, a clinical psychologist, without telling him who the people were. Dr. Bortnick said that the answers suggested that both Krista and Lillian had what he called "high temporal lobe liability," meaning that they may have had an increased number of minor symptoms associated with temporal lobe epilepsy, but without having a seizure, and they were subject to bursts of electricity in their brains. Krista had reported having repetitive dreams, hearing unexplained buzzing or sizzling sounds, and having a strong sense of déjà vu. Lillian had reported repetitive dreams, unusual sensations of cold, the smell of burning rubber, and a sense of presence in the house. Both ladies said that these sensations were more common when family stress levels were high.

Mary Barton was also tested, and she, along with her mother and granddaughter, showed a high degree of aggression in her interpersonal relationships, Nichols said. "All show unhappiness, insecurity and a recourse to an unrealistic fantasy life." He added that Krista showed aggression towards others and an inability to handle even minor frustrations. "Krista was also typified as harboring a potential for physical violence, which is kept in check by her reliance on repression...she displayed the typical profile of the poltergeist personality," Nichols said. "Her relationship with her great-grandmother, Lillian, seemed particularly strained. It is significant that Lillian was most frequently the target of the RSPK activity." Nichols added that the Bartons, "while outwardly displaying the façade of a happy home, were a deeply troubled family."[3]

The source of the mysterious liquid or water was never identified, because the occurrences had reached their peak by the time researchers arrived at the home, and they were not able to get sufficient quantities of the liquid for testing.

After Krista entered psychotherapy in January 1997, the occurrences stopped. However, she continued to have emotional problems, and a short time later, she was arrested for shoplifting. "Like the poltergeist, the incidents of theft may represent another outlet for displacement of her inner turmoil," Nichols said. "Although no specific symbolic correlations were apparent in the Barton case, such metaphorical expressions of unconscious processes—so often seen in dreams—cannot be discounted. Cases of this kind emphasize the need for researchers to be aware that poltergeists, like hauntings, may take a variety of forms reflecting the interpersonal dynamics, psychopathologies and emotional needs of the witnesses."[4]

Meanwhile, Nichols never found out if the insurance company paid the claim for paranormal damage.

the Polish Phenom

Joasia Gajewski was 13 years old when things began happening in her apartment in Sosnowiec, a mining town in Poland. Her mother was a telephone operator and her father was a plumber. Just after the death of her beloved grandmother, Joasia was about to enter puberty. At this point her family and friends noticed she seemed highly charged with static electricity. They said she crackled with it so much that it sounded like someone snapping his fingers. She was also suffering from headaches and fever.

On April 4, 1983, while Joasia was in bed with her grandfather, plates and glassware reportedly started flying about the room, windows rattled, furniture shook, and some shattered glass struck the girl, cutting her. The frightened family fled the apartment. Later, several police officers, including Sergeant Tadeusz Slowik, said they saw glasses, screws, and other small objects fly at unusual trajectories. While city engineers were checking for abnormalities, they said they saw a mustard jar fly through the air. In all cases, Joasia was nearby, but witnesses said she did not throw anything.

Dr. Eustachiusz Gadula, a respected surgeon and vocational rehabilitation specialist, put together a team of scientists and psychologists to test Joasia under laboratory conditions. They said that the girl had unusual thermal spots or warm areas, around her fingers, toes, head, and just above her solar plexus. She also evidenced rapid changes in body temperature and very high static electrical charges on her body, which did not dissipate when she was grounded.

During tests, a number of scientists say they saw incredible phenomena: An armchair moved with Joasia sitting cross-legged in it. When she got out of the chair, it continued to move, they said, and then it went into the air and rotated. Three men reportedly tried to hold the chair down, but they could not. On another day, a blanket, which had been rolled up on a couch, allegedly moved into the air across the room and covered Dr. Gadula.

Joasia turned down offers to try to perform her unusual skills on tour, and reportedly went into the healthcare profession.

Fires

In rare instances, poltergeist agents can create fires through spontaneous combustion, leading to people having their possessions damaged, says Professor Andrei Lee, head of the Emergency Poltergeist Service in Moscow. In these cases, fires often stop after a few weeks, the activity allegedly replaced by moving objects.

In Formia, Italy, in 1983, it was said that mysterious fires started in the presence of 10-year-old Benedetto Supino, burning books and wood furniture and scorching plastic. Reportedly, he also caused electromagnetic effects on machines and motors. It was said that a parapsychologist, Dr. Demetrio Croce, worked with the boy to try to teach him how to channel his powers, but the results are not known.

CHAPTER 11

Ghosts and Exorcisms

"A ghost haunts; a poltergeist infests. A ghost likes
solitude; a poltergeist prefers company."
Parapsychologist Harry Price, in his book Poltergeist Over England

Some parapsychologists, including psychiatrist Dr. Ian Stevenson, a professor at the University of Virginia, believe there is a link between spirits of the dead and poltergeist activity, and they sometimes suggest to victimized families that a séance be held to cleanse a home. Others believe that a poltergeist agent is possessed by a spirit or a demon, and they sometimes suggest a type of exorcism to try to bring the person back to him- or herself.

For example, Reverend Colin Grant conducted an exorcism at the historic Greyfriars Churchyard in Edinburgh, Scotland, in 2000, after numerous reports of hauntings and poltergeist-like occurrences, but incidents reportedly continue to this day.

Rather than ghosts, some people find it easier to believe in RSPK as an unexplained energy force, because with the former, one must consider that there is life after death. Alternatively, Auerbach suggested to me that rare instances of apparitions in poltergeist cases are due to a "projection of stress, guilt, anger, fear, or frustration from the subconscious." There are a handful of cases in this book in which people involved in so-called poltergeist cases say they see an apparition. That does not necessarily mean that there is life after death, but possibly that the people are hallucinating. In fact, hallucinations of ghosts are relatively common in people undergoing trauma. Michael Persinger, a neuroscientist at Laurentian University in Sudbury, Ontario, has done studies that show that many people who claim to see ghosts are activating a part of their brain's fight-or-flight system in order to deal with a situation that cannot fathom, such as the death of a loved one.

William Roll did not know of any case in which a spirit was responsible for a poltergeist incident. "We should not close our minds to that possibility, but they always seem to occur around a living person," he said to me.

In England, poltergeist investigations are being hampered by researchers and parapsychologists who too quickly jump to the conclusion that spirits are responsible, according to Wayne Pickrell, investigations coordinator for the Black Country Paranormal Society. "In all my years of being interested in the paranormal, I have never seen so much rubbish flying about," he told me. "We dealt with some people having poltergeist activity. Psychics had been in and exorcised the spirit. To add insult to injury, they charged the poor family for their services. And guess what? The spirit was back the next night. Yes, I do believe in ghosts, but sometimes other more plausible explanations are found."

When paranormal investigators do not attend, it is often left to the family to come to their own conclusions. In March 2010, a family in Cork City, Ireland, abandoned their three-bedroom house after reported occurrences throughout several weeks that they blamed on evil spirits: flying ashtrays and glasses, screams in the night, glowing orbs hovering in the air, a cooker turning itself off and on, cushions flipping over on a couch, a chair shaking while someone was praying, and a young boy getting tossed out of his bed. "It was our dream house, but we have been driven out by an evil spirit," said a pregnant Laura Burke, 21, who lived in the home with her fiancé and her 5-year-old son, Kyle. "My son Kyle can't come near the place. He was thrown out of his bed and thrown across the room...I will never bring a child into this house. I really am petrified."[1] The boy reportedly saw a pair of eyes staring at him through a window at the time he was thrown. Local lawyer David McCarthy also witnessed strange goings-on, and suffered a stroke a few days later. Two priests celebrated Masses in the home, and a Shaman, Paul O'Halloran, led an exorcism, but the occurrences continued. O'Halloran believed three restless ghosts caught in a time warp were haunting the property. "The reason they are making so much noise is they want the issue to be sorted and they want to be freed. I feel the energy is an angry one and needs to be moved on," he said.[2] Clairvoyant John O'Reilly inspected the house and said he felt a strong presence of an angry spirit; perhaps a younger man who hanged himself.

Interestingly, Adrian Payton reported no incidents while living in the house for 26 years before Laura Burke, and yet he became a believer when he revisited it in 2010 and found the house to be chillingly cold. "I was chatting away to the owner when all of a sudden a drawer fell to the ground," Payton said. "I also saw a table levitating. This is genuine. They have no reason to say this is happening."[3]

an aquatic haunting

"Unlike [in] *The X-Files*, real-life paranormal investigators usually arrive weeks, months or years after an incident."

Peter A. Hough, *chairman of the Northern Anomalies Research Organization in England*

"Spooky Spills Scare Family," read the headline in the *Manchester Evening News*. It was August 1995, and paranormal investigators Stephen Mera and Peter Hough of MAPIT became interested in a story about a family in Rochdale, England, that was being ousted from their council home (a type of government-sponsored housing in the UK) by mysterious outpourings of water, supposedly destroying their furniture. "At first, I was wary of the fact that it was council property and it wouldn't have been the first time council residents had blamed phenomena, hoping to move to a better home," Mera told me. But his skepticism eventually melted like the 85-degree temperatures of that unusual summer.

At the home in question, in Hill Top Close, Jim and Vera Gardner lived with their daughter, Jeanette, 33, and their granddaughter, Alison. It was a prefabricated bungalow meant only as temporary accommodations. Jim had lived there for 13 years.

Vera told Mera and Hough that the weird occurrences had begun 10 months previously when the family noticed a damp patch on the wall of the back bedroom. Water was seeping into the bedroom, belonging to Jeannette, and the Gardners had called the housing department and then an electrician. No leaks were found in the attic, but the seeping continued. The family suspected the water was simply condensation, but then it started leaking in greater quantities, with water reportedly shooting from one corner of the bedroom to another, forcing Jim to use an umbrella to keep dry.

Then the water got into the kitchen. "An electrician dismantled the light fittings while Mr. Gardner watched, sheltering beneath his umbrella," Hough said. "He said it was coming down just like rain!"[4] Moreover, pictures and ornaments unexpectedly flew off the wall, and, on a number of occasions, the couple said they heard unexplained coughing and the smell of licorice, similar to the smell of flavored cigarette paper.

Enter the town council, landlords to the Gardners. They brought in an electrician, but nothing unusual was found—not even leaky pipes. Condensation was also ruled out. Suddenly, the Gardners said the council did a turnabout and accused them of turning a hosepipe on the ceiling, so they would be moved to another council house. Vera said that accusation was ridiculous, and that she'd lived in the home for 14 years without prior incident. The family continued to live in the house, even though the wet bedding was bringing the family to tears. When Jeannette was moved into another bedroom, the drippings followed her.

After a hairdryer allegedly flew off a dresser and hit a visitor in the head, the family turned to the local newspapers, hoping that publicity would bring professional help, which it did. On the first day the paranormal investigators showed up, something happened in front of them: "While [Jim Gardner] was explaining the past events to us, we heard Jeanette cry out in another room," Mera said. "We rushed over to see a streak of water shoot across the ceiling, as if had been intelligently controlled. I couldn't believe my eyes." For Mera, it was a watershed—"the first time I had witnessed a paranormal incident in my life"[5] According to Mera, the water forms lasted for about 15 minutes and suddenly vanished, strangely leaving no mark or even a water stain. Shortly thereafter, there was another occurrence in the kitchen, where Jim Gardner stood under what appeared to be a rain shower. "Remarkable; it sounds too remarkable to be true, but I assure you it was raining!" Mera told me.

Hough climbed up to the loft door into the attic. Directly above the water in the loft, he found it to be hot, dry, and dusty. "I pulled up some of the surrounding layers, but there was no evidence of moisture," he said. "How was it I was standing here, in broad daylight, on a warm summer's day, watching water form and drip from a dry plasterboard ceiling?"[6] Hough added that he checked for hidden hoses, buckets, and squirt guns, but found nothing.

The researchers put some of the water into one sealed container and other water from a bathroom tap into another, so that the two samples could be compared during analysis.

While the investigators were away for a week, Jim Gardner reported that several pictures flew off walls, a wooden clock floated in the air, and scissors, knives, forks, and spoons moved on their own accord. The odor of licorice and tobacco lingered, even though no source could be found. A lampshade swung back and forth, he said, and a cotton reel hit Vera. A family nephew was hit on the back of the head by a makeup case, and a radio went on and off by itself.

Mera and Hough held a vigil at the house, along with three other MAPIT researchers: Alicia Leigh, Vic Moorse, and his wife, Carole Moorse; and an unnamed psychic. They took video recordings of each room as the Gardners stayed overnight at another house. Mera and Leigh took the first shift of the night in the lounge. The first thing they noticed was that a small statuette seemed to appear out of nowhere in the middle of the floor. In the next few hours, the investigators said they heard strange noises, and Mera heard his name being called, but no source could be found. "It wasn't the first time I'd spent in a building said to be haunted, but this was different. You could feel the atmosphere was heavy with a sense of static in the air."[7]

At 2 a.m., Val, a British psychic, joined the team. She reported smelling a strong sense of hyacinth flowers in the house. Mera, Hough, Carole, and Leigh also said they smelled the hyacinths. "The smell was overpowering, but we couldn't find a rational explanation," Mera told me.

An hour later, Mera, Val, and Carole were in a back bedroom when Mera heard four long, heavy breaths from behind him. He described to me what happened next: "At first, I froze. But I couldn't bring myself to look back. When I leaned back a little, I felt a powerful blow to my back. I jumped in pain and ran into another room, and Carole and Val followed me. When [Hough] examined my back, it had a big red mark on it."

Carole said she too had heard heavy breathing, and Val reported feeling someone or something touch her arm. Hough examined the room, but found nothing out of place, and there were no suspects because the family was staying with friends. After an hour, the mark disappeared from Mera's back, but he was in pain.

When the Gardners met the researchers the next morning, Vera informed them that the statuette that had allegedly appeared on the floor had been a gift from her late husband, who had suffered from chronic asthma and was a heavy breather. At the end of his life, he had been bedridden in the back bedroom (the scene of the assault upon Mera), where he died.

Also that day, the investigators contacted a vicar from a local Roman Catholic Church, who told them that he had conducted a blessing of the Gardner home. The vicar believed that poltergeist activity was focusing on the daughter and the granddaughter. The investigators were confused. They had thought the poltergeist focused only on the family, but incidents had continued while the family was away. "We believed at this point we were dealing with a unique type of haunting," Mera told me.

When the investigators got test results back of samples of water they had taken one week earlier, from the North West Water Laboratories, there were significant differences in the sample of paranormal water from the ceiling and the bathroom tap water. Calcium, sodium, and chloride percentages were higher in the paranormal water. And the electrical content of the two samples also differed: The tap water had a conductivity of 181, compared to 1,323 for the mysterious water.

Two weeks later, the family moved out of the house for good.

The investigators then researched Vera Gardner's late husband and discovered that he had smoked Old Holburn tobacco, which is often rolled with licorice papers. Meanwhile, an Asian family moved into the

Gardner bungalow and reported no strange occurrences. However, the phenomena seemed to follow the Gardners to their new home, where they experienced similar events for about two months.

> In 2005, the Vatican in Rome was becoming so concerned about the devil and satanic practices among young people that it began offering a course on exorcism through its university, Pontifical Academy. Pope John Paul II believed the devil is alive in the world and is causing much mayhem via possession. Among the widely accepted signs of possession by the devil are speaking in unknown tongues and demonstrating physical force beyond one's natural capacity—similar to poltergeist activity. Since 1995, the Roman Catholic Church has consistently reported a rise in the number of *official* exorcisms performed around the world, which is now up to about 15 to 20 per year. But that does not include *unsanctioned* exorcists, or those belonging to other faiths.

devil girl

In 1925, 11-year-old Eleonore Zugun visited her 105-year-old grandmother, reportedly a witch, in the village of Buhai, in Romania. On the way to her grandmother's home, Eleonore was said to have found some money by the roadside and spent it on candy, which she ate. Her grandmother warned Eleonore that because she had used money that the devil had *left behind*, she would never be free of his evil powers. On the next day, it was said, stones flew against the side of the old woman's house, smashing windows, and small objects flew towards the girl. Neighbors became alarmed because they thought Eleonore might be possessed by *you know who*, and so she was sent back home to her own village of Talpa.

There, several people, including a priest, were present when objects reportedly began to fly in her room. Throughout the next three weeks, hounded by superstitious villagers fearing the devil, Eleonore sought refuge in the monastery of Gorovei, but the destructive disturbances apparently continued there and were reported by newspapers. By April, she was committed to a lunatic asylum. The newspaper accounts soon reached Fritz Grunewald, a well-known engineer and parapsychologist in Charlottenburg, Germany, who went to the asylum and took Eleonore to another monastery, where they could observe her. There, Grunewald said he saw Eleonore mysteriously struck by a salt container and a stick used for mixing, even though no one was in a position to throw them.

For a brief period after her second stint at a monastery, Eleonore fell on bad times, as her family and neighbors looked upon her as a devil child. She became dirty and frightened and wore ragged clothes. Soon, she was taken under the wing of a woman interested in psychical research and psychoanalysis: Countess Zoe Wassilko-Serecki, a beautiful Viennese woman with Romanian blood. She said she had seen some events at the monastery in September 1925, and took Eleonore with her to her apartment in Vienna. Eleonore apparently was happy there, and photographs taken of her at the time show a smiling, well-dressed girl, quite unlike photos of her just months before.

In Vienna, Eleonore was closely examined by physicians and a nerve specialist, who found her to be bright and intelligent, although emotionally immature, and with unusually sensitive skin. The strange goings-on continued in Vienna: Objects flew, sometimes appearing to come out of the air, such as a small iron box filled with dominoes. All the while, Eleonore believed that a devil, which she called Dracu, was behind the occurrences. Dracu seemed intent on hurting the girl; objects were thrown at her and she was slapped and pushed to the ground.

Beginning in March 1926, Eleonore started experiencing real pain as she suffered pricks to her hands and fingers, as if from needles, and scratches to her face, neck, arms, and chest. She was sharply bitten on her hands and arm. It is possible the girl inflicted these injuries on herself, but Countess Wassilko-Serecki believes she did not.

The countess then took the now-famous Eleonore, who was being dubbed "The Poltergeist Girl," on an extended tour of several European countries in which many psychic researchers reportedly saw the phenomena surrounding her.

On March 25, 1926, Professor Hans Hahn of the mathematics department at the University of Vienna came to the apartment. Hahn said that, as he held Eleonore's hand, strange marks appeared on her hands and forearms as though she was being bitten.

115

Also in the apartment was prominent British psychical researcher Harry Price, who said he saw a cushion move off a chair, on its own power, and scratch marks appear on Eleonore. He termed the events *telekinetic phenomena*. Price brought Eleonore and the countess to London to his National Laboratory of Psychical Research, where from September 30 to October 14, 1926, Price said he witnessed numerous object movements. Some of them could possibly have been cheating on the part of Eleonore, he said, but on the whole they seemed genuinely paranormal, including the flight of a 10-inch steel stiletto, used to open letters, across the room. "I instantly turned around...no one could have projected the stiletto. And certainly not Eleonore."[8]

The case was not without its critics, including Dr. Hans Rosenbusch, a Munich physician, who said the countess at times was helping Eleonore trick the investigators—a claim the countess denied.

In all, there were a reported 3,000 phenomena, of which 844 were seen by reliable witnesses. After reviewing all the evidence and interviews, Peter Mulacz of the Austrian Society for Parapsychology called it an extraordinary case of PK. Perhaps bolstering the validity of his claim was the fact that much of the testing of Eleonore was done by investigators and physicians outside in bright sunlight or under the glare of 500-watt lamps, thereby reducing the possibility of trickery.

The strange occurrences seemed to end with Eleonore's first menstruation in the early summer of 1927—no surprise to many parapsychologists, who, as I have said, believe that poltergeist energy is related to sexual energy as a youth reaches puberty.

The countess set up Eleonore in training to become a hairdresser, and in 1928, she returned home to Romania to work in that profession. Apparently, she went on to live a normal life. She married, but she did not have any children.

the demon of olive hill

Even the paranormal world has its "good news, bad news" scenarios.

The good news in the Olive Hill, Kentucky poltergeist investigation was that *two* paranormal researchers saw full-fledged levitation of objects in a home. The bad news was that they were not allowed to stay very long because the religious family thought the researchers had brought demons with them.

The story, which jumps from house to house in rural Kentucky, began in 1968 in Olive Hill at the home of elderly couple John and Ora Callihan. Living with them were their son, Tommy, his wife, Helen, and their five children: Beverly, 14; Roger, 12; two younger brothers; and a sister, Marcelene. Also in the home was a teenage girl, unofficially adopted by the family and helping to take care of the small frame house. (After what happened, there was a lot of cleaning to do.)

One day in late November, the family reported strange rumblings in the house. Glass shattered in a picture of Jesus and furniture moved. It was the beginning of mayhem. From then on, about 200 incidents were reported, leading to considerable damage, including the smashing of most of the Callihans' ceramic lamps and figurines. A good helper, their grandson, Roger, helped them to clean up the mess.

Believing that the occurrences had something to do with the house, Tommy and Helen packed up with their children on November 23 and moved to another home nearby on Zimmerman Hill, while the grandparents, John and Ora, stayed behind. But something apparently moved along with them, because furniture started getting legs. In early December, after Helen said she saw an apparition in her bedroom, she started to believe a ghost was responsible.

The local newspaper, the *Ashland Daily Independent*, published an article on the family that intrigued a psychology student at the University of North Carolina named John P. Stump, a budding parapsychologist. Stump went to the home for some field research and was told by the Callihan family and friends that 90 incidents had occurred, such as the smashing of knick knacks and crockery and the movement of larger items such as a coffee table, a refrigerator, and a kitchen table. Many of the events had been witnessed by family and friends, Stump was told, but the activity was sporadic, and sometimes days went by when nothing happened.

Witnesses included two of the Callihans' friends, Phyllis Cranks and her husband, Odis.

Mrs. Cranks said that on December 8, while Roger was walking towards her in a bedroom, a bedside table rose up in the air behind him, moved about 10 feet right up over his head, and crashed to the floor. Young Marcelene also said she saw plastic flowers in a bowl move slowly on a table and fall to the floor. In 48 hours at the grandparents' house, Stump said he witnessed dozens of strange incidents, including a chair flipping over, and a clock, flowers, two bottles, and a glass jar of canned berries moving by themselves while young Roger was nearby, but in no position to move them. Stump quickly checked for strings, but found none.

An amazed Stump then contacted William Roll, who first went to John and Ora's home, then over to the new home of Tommy and Helen on Zimmerman Hill. Roll noted that the latter house was well-kept and that Helen seemed a good mother. The children appeared well behaved, he said, and were not as frightened as the adults. Helen was particularly traumatized, and Roll believed that was because she had been told by her fellow Jehovah's Witnesses that a demon was causing the events.

Roll instead believed that RSPK forces were at work, but Helen didn't buy that. On December 16, while she was discussing the religious theory in the Zimmerman Hill home with Roll, Stump and her husband, they heard a loud crash upstairs. A bowl of fruit had fallen off a dresser. It seemed an innocent event, but it turned out to be the beginning of a whole series of disturbances, from furniture moving through tables being flipped over to the kitchen stove reportedly moving six inches under its own power.

Roll recalled to me that he was walking behind Roger into the kitchen when the kitchen table "jumped into the air, rotated about 45 degrees and came to rest on the backs of the chairs that stood around it, with all four legs off the floor."

On another occasion, Roll said he saw a coffee table, weighing about 70 pounds, flip over while Roger had his back to it. Altogether, Roll estimated 10 incidents occurred while he and/or Stump were watching. In all 10, he said, they had been keeping watch over Roger.

Roll wanted to document the case more closely with photographs and psychological tests of all the family members, but Helen Callihan was becoming more uncooperative. The family brought in a minister from the Jehovah's Witnesses, but the incidents continued. And then Helen delivered a bombshell: She told Roll and Stump that they had unintentionally brought demons with them from John and Ora's home nearby.

Helen hoped the demons would follow them back to Duke University, yet the disturbances apparently continued in the home, and an exorcism failed to stop Helen's demon. Finally, the family moved away from the house for some time, and when they returned, there were no more incidents.

Roll came to the conclusion that Roger Callihan was the agent for the poltergeist activity and that he exhibited the subconscious ability of mind over matter. He speculated that the boy was frustrated by having to spend time with his grandparents, and that was part of the explanation for the breakages in their home.

Despite all the theories and speculations, many parapsychologists, never mind mainstream scientists, often throw up their hands in dismay when asked to pinpoint the cause of the unusual activity. As parapsychologist Maurice Grosse continued to investigate the subject of poltergeists into his 80s, he said he was convinced that society was far from understanding the poltergeist. "There are many theories, and I've heard them all," he said to me. "Nobody has come up with a convincing theory. All this talk about electrical disturbances behind poltergeists...we just don't understand yet. I think it's a type of mind force, perhaps with something else attached to it. It's an intriguing phenomena."

CHAPTER 12

Things That Go Sneak in the Night

"I knew what to do. She was scared stiff of ghosts."

*A London man's plan for scaring his family out of
a house by pretending to be a poltergeist*

Some poltergeists are outright frauds.

Many suspected cases of poltergeists have proven to be no more than the fantasies of distraught minds or the actions of jokers, according to the late parapsychologist Maurice Grosse, who investigated many cases throughout the years, some of them peppered with cheating. In fact, many of the serious paranormal researchers in this book, including Grosse, William Roll, and Tony Cornell, have admitted they have been duped by people from time to time.

Cornell, considered one of England's leading paranormal experts and the author of a book on poltergeists, once caught a cheater with a video camera. A fisherman who lived in Kent, England, said that a poltergeist had been cutting him with an invisible razor blade, and he showed hundreds of cuts on his body to prove it. Cornell installed a camera in the man's home and it showed that he always went into the bathroom before the attacks occurred. The video also showed a razor blade and a thumbtack fall out of his jacket.

A few months later, the man claimed the poltergeist was setting fires in his house, but by this time, Cornell suspected the man was starting the fires himself to get attention because his second wife's children did not like him. Shortly thereafter, the man was convicted of burning down a barn and was jailed for two and a half years.

In another case in London, Cornell became suspicious of an elderly man whose Victorian house was said to produce loud, poltergeist-type noises that had driven away his son, daughter-in-law, and grandchild. After investigating, Cornell discovered the man had rigged an ingenious device in which he created the peculiar noises. At night when his relatives were in bed, the man would pull on a wire at the side of a downstairs fireplace, setting off a noisy contraption hidden under floorboards, which consisted of two tin mugs, an iron bar, and a biscuit tin with two wooden balls in it. When the wire was pulled, it started the noises, which became amplified in two upstairs bedrooms.

It turned out his motivation was not to get attention with authorities or the media, but to be rid of his kin. "The man and his wife did not like his daughter-in-law," Cornell told me. "When his wife died, his son and daughter-in-law moved in with him, which made him uncomfortable. When the daughter-in-law tried to get the man committed to an old people's home, he knew what to do. He knew she was scared of ghosts…"

Skeptic Paul Kurtz once told me that some people are predisposed to believe in a paranormal explanation and may be easily fooled by a smart trickster: "If a situation is charged with emotion and some drama, it's likely to arouse an affirmative response," he said.

Although many people, including psychic observers, were perhaps more superstitious and gullible in the past, the late Hans Driesch warned of fakes in the early part of the 20th century. "What human being, however meticulously conscientious, is not liable to be deceived?" wrote Driesch, an embryologist, professor of philosophy, and president of the Society of Psychical Research in England from 1926 to 1927. "Even the greatest men of science have sometimes made mistakes and fallen victims to deception… now in psychical research, in which the subject of the investigation can himself actively contribute to the deception, in which there is not, as in the normal natural sciences, a determined state of affairs itself incapable of active deception, everything is infinitely more difficult."[1]

In modern times, hoaxes can be played on the Internet, such as a story that became known as the "Strange Case of Katrina Landrou," in which a 14-year-old Long Island girl was supposedly the focus of mystifying and terrifying poltergeist activity. The story, posted on the Internet with a photo showing a girl being accompanied by a floating loaf of bread over her shoulder, was quite a clever cliché of many poltergeist cases and included rapping on windows, ping-pong balls dropping down a chimney, and Tom Jones songs coming from inside a toilet—apparently all caused by Katrina in her entry into puberty. "All I gotta say is, don't get her mad," her brother was quoted as saying. At the end of the Internet article was the punch line: April Fool. It was on the Website of Stephen Wagner ("Your Guide to Paranormal Phenomena"), who isn't afraid to poke fun at himself and his genre from time to time. (For other such spoofs, check out Wagner's page at *http://paranormal.about.com/cs/paranormalezines/a/aa042803.htm.*)

Apart from an April Fool's joke, why would someone pretend to be a poltergeist? There seem to be lots of reasons, including those from people who are looking for a way to move out of their house, to get someone to relocate them, or to lower property value.

- In Bristol, England, in 1761, it was said that Richard Giles's two daughters were terrorized by a poltergeist. No satisfactory explanation was discovered, but one theory was that it was a hoax set up to lower the value of the property.

- In 1948, according to a state's attorney, 13-year-old Wanet McNeil set fires at her uncle's farm in Macomb, Illinois, while posing as a poltergeist, because she was unhappy, didn't like the farm, and wanted to see her mother, who was living elsewhere. But many members of the local fire department did not believe her confession, claiming to have seen numerous mysterious fires and other unexplained occurrences, which they say Wanet could not have faked.

- In recent times, landlords of British council houses have claimed that some tenants have faked poltergeist incidents in order to win relocation to a better home.

Even the higher-ups are sometimes guilty of hoaxes. In Delain, France, in the foothills of the Alps in 1999, the village mayor was suspected by police after allegedly feigning poltergeist activity such as throwing candles and toppling statues. The mayor, who had apparently been lurking in the shadows, tossing the objects, and then appearing moments later with an expressions of horror, was not charged but ordered to see a psychiatrist. He apologized for his mischief.

And then there are the good, old-fashioned grudges. In 2005, a Polish woman, who apparently harbored a grudge against her husband's boss, was sentenced to four months in jail for pretending to be a ghost or poltergeist in the boss's castle estate in Innsbruck, Austria. The 42-year-old woman, whose name was not released in court proceedings, allegedly terrorized the boss by slamming doors late at night. She was captured on videotape creating the disturbances.

We can't forget the suspected poltergeist cases that turn out to be related to psychological or degenerative illnesses. In Bradley Stoke, England, in 2009, writer/researcher Charles Fort and paranormal investigators went to a house after a 78-year-old retired legal clerk claimed his late wife had appeared in the form of a poltergeist to move items around his home. It turned out the man had progressive Alzheimer's.

a skeptical analysis

The skeptics, of course, often have a field day when frauds are caught. *See, we told you!* they exclaim. But should the nabbing of a cheat mean that all poltergeist cases are rubbish? Should we close our minds to paranormal possibilities?

In 2004, I mentioned the case of the alleged St. Catharines poltergeist (given in Chapters 2 and 3), which included testimony from many police officers, to the ultimate skeptic of the paranormal and of poltergeists, James Randi. I had hoped Randi would digest the synopsis and get back to me with his thoughts on whether it was possible the 11-year-old boy was indeed a poltergeist agent. "I dunno," Randi said. "I wasn't there, and neither were you. I've heard similar reports of what [alleged spoon-bending psychic Uri] Geller has done—until the stories fell apart under investigation."

I replied to Randi, "Is it possible there is such a thing, however rare, as psychokinesis?"

"Yes," he said. "But there is also the possibility (however unlikely) that Richard Nixon is alive and living in Argentina with Martin Borman..." According to Randi, it's no coincidence that poltergeist cases almost always revolve around young people. "It's a way of these kids getting attention," he said. "They either move the objects themselves or pretend they have seen them moving."

true and false

If we are to really get to the bottom of the poltergeist issue, we cannot let the frauds turn us off, and we cannot throw out the cases that seem to be legitimate because of those that are not, said Maurice Grosse.

We have established that there are many cases of fraud in poltergeist investigations, but there may also be instances of fraud and genuine paranormal activity *within the same case*. In a number of cases in this book, youths who were said to have paranormal powers were either caught cheating at some point or confessed to using trickery, but that does not necessarily mean other occurrences that happened in their presence were phony. Sound confusing? Not really, if you examine human nature.

Let's say a young boy unconsciously causes objects to move with his mind. Police, family members, and parapsychologists all testify to the legitimacy of the events because they have all been closely watching the boy and rule out trickery. But genuine poltergeist events seem to be fleeting and difficult to produce. And so, his abilities may start to wane. A young poltergeist agent may have become enamored with all the attention he had been getting, and doesn't want to give up the center stage. Most children like attention and being stroked by adults, especially if journalists come to their home and make a big deal of it in the newspapers and on television. If they cannot immediately reproduce the genuine events, such children may resort to cheating to keep the attention on themselves. They may nudge a chair when they think no one is watching or bang on a wall around a corner. Some parapsychologists call this *imitative fraud*.

In the big picture, let us call this the *When the Circus Comes to Town Syndrome* because, in many of these well-documented cases, that seems to be what happens: The local media sniff out the story and descend

124

upon a home with their notepads and cameras, and sometimes the national media get involved. Pretty soon, police, neighbors, parapsychologists, and the nosy woman across the street are trampling through the home. It really does become a circus.

In 1974 in Powhatan, Virginia, Dr. Gaither Pratt and his investigators found evidence that two children had moved some objects purposefully to look like poltergeist activity. When caught, the kids said they did it to please the scientists, but they added they were *not* responsible for earlier movements of chairs and a magazine which had apparently flown through the air. Indeed, Pratt said the children could not have been involved when he saw a number of unexplainable events, including a chair mysteriously tilt backward and slam against a wall.

In the highly celebrated Enfield case of 1977–78 in London (detailed in Chapters 15 and16), many witnesses, including police, reported seeing furniture and toys move on their own power while in the presence of 11-year-old Janet Hodgson. As the case dragged on and the girl became a mini-celebrity, the voice of an old man started coming out of her mouth. Janet's sister reportedly told a newspaper that she and Janet had played tricks to fool observers in order to keep the case from dying out in the media. Journalist Ray Alan said it was obvious that the girls loved the attention they received when objects started moving, and that they decided to keep the mystery going by inventing the voice. Another investigator said that a videocamera had caught Janet attempting to bend spoons and an iron bar by force and *practicing* levitation by bouncing up and down on her bed. When faced with this evidence, Janet admitting to faking some of the events, but not all of them, because she said she wanted to see if the investigators would catch her.

"Where children are involved, accusations of trickery flow thick and fast," said Grosse, who was in charge of the case. He further told me that numerous legitimate paranormal events took place prior to the trickery "but the real experience cannot be confused with their pranks."

A similar situation occurred in Columbus, Ohio, with Tina Resch, who witnesses believe caused many objects to move with her mind, including a telephone, but was then caught cheating by a videocamera, pulling down a lamp. Tina said she did it to give journalists something to write about after they refused to leave her parents' house after a vigil of more than nine hours (Tina's story is detailed in the next two chapters.)

It is also possible that in some of these cases, the disturbances are *both* paranormal *and* traditional, William Roll said. In other words, a youth may take his or her hostility out on family members by moving things with the mind *and* the body. "It may help us understand the psychological process which results in genuine phenomena if we know that this can also result in ordinary destructive behavior," Roll said to me. "And vice-versa: It is important to know that destructive impulses in a person can not only find an outlet in ordinary acts of aggression, but also in [PK] activities."

However, once cheating is found, everything that happened prior to it can be called into question. "If a person is once caught cheating, then the further display of his or her powers should be highly suspect," wrote Paul Kurtz.[2] He suspected that Tina was a con artist who fooled everyone right from the beginning in order to get attention, and perhaps because she was jealous of others in the house. Kurtz believes that Tina cheated several times, although he was never in the Resch house, and that Roll and others were duped because they had a predisposition to believe in a poltergeist. And yet Kurtz left a small window open for the possibility of the paranormal: "Perhaps [Tina] does have these marvelous powers and perhaps it is the skeptics' will to disbelieve that causes them to refuse to accept the testimony of others."[3]

Apart from the lamp incident, Tina denied cheating in other instances, and indeed, Roll said that she went on to move objects with her mind later under test conditions at his lab in North Carolina.

Like Randi, Kurtz tends not to believe in poltergeists. When I asked him if poltergeists might actually exist, he said it was "very doubtful."

Confessions have been elicited from youths in other famous cases, but not everyone bought them. In 1960–61 on a farm near Mena, Arkansas, many members of the Ed and Birdie Shinn family and their neighbors reported seeing kitchen utensils, books, and chairs float in the air on numerous occasions in the presence of 15-year-old Charles Elbert Shaeffer, the Shinns' grandson, a gawky, overweight boy with thick glasses. After about 11 months of mysterious events, Charles confessed to police to overturning chairs and lamps and tapping on his bed frame with steel pliers because his grandfather had been picking on him. But Charles Albright, a columnist for the *Arkansas Gazette*, who covered the story, rejected the confession: "[Charles] can't make biscuits float through the air any more than we can!" he said. "Our theory is that he took the rap so that everybody could get some peace." Indeed, during all the rumors and publicity surrounding the case, the Shinn farm had been overrun with curiosity-seekers, police, and investigators, who all left once the confession was published in the papers.[4]

Although the media is sometimes quick to embrace a poltergeist story for its unusual qualities and potential human-interest angles, journalists can also turn against a case at the slightest hint of a hoax. That was true even in more superstitious times in the early 20th century, according to Hans Driesch. He added that the press was often too quick to come to conclusions. "There are journals that empty whole buckets of sarcasm as soon as psychical research, which they usually confuse with the specific spiritualistic hypothesis, is so much as mentioned, without having made any attempt even to glance at the serious literature of the subject."[5]

oakland: hoax or hurried confession?

It is rare for a poltergeist to be reported in an office, as opposed to a home. But it happened in Oakland, California, in 1964, in the office of court reporter George Wheeler, whose job was to record testimony in the courts in Alameda County.

It began in the newsroom of the *Oakland Tribune*, where city editor Roy Grimm received a tip on the police radios that strange things were going on in an office on Franklin Street, and officers had been called. Journalists can be a rather skeptical, even cynical group, and Grimm found himself chuckling as he assigned the "p-p-p-poltergeist!" story to reporter Jim Hazelwood. But according to the police radio, objects were moving around in the office with no rational explanation.

Hazelwood arrived to find people converging on the third floor of the office building, which housed three suites belonging to Wheeler. It was a nondescript setup, with filing cabinets, telephones, electric typewriters, a water cooler, and wall cabinets to store papers.

In other ways, it was *not* such a cliché workplace. Almost immediately, Hazelwood heard a crash coming from an empty room, and he went inside to find that a metal cabinet had fallen onto the floor. Intrigued, Hazelwood interviewed the people who regularly worked in the office and who had recently become accustomed to weird noises and reportedly flying objects. They were George Wheeler and his wife, Zolo, also a court reporter; two other court reporters, Robert Caya and Calvert Bowles; and two transcribers, John Orfanides and Helen Rosenberg.

Zolo showed Hazelwood her husband's office, which was a mess of smashed crockery—an ashtray, a flower vase, and a glass water pitcher. No one knew who had done this damage, although Officer Charles Nye of the Oakland Police Department told the reporter that the crockery had seemed just fine, sitting on a shelf, when he had arrived earlier in the day.

As Nye was talking to Hazelwood, a banging noise emitted from another room. Apparently a telephone had "removed itself" from a table and had crashed to the floor. The police officer and the reporter rushed inside to find the room empty. Believing this was turning out to be a legitimate story, although he was not exactly certain what the story *was*, Hazelwood summoned Jim Edelen, a veteran photographer from the *Tribune*, to snap pictures of the damage.

Edelen took shots of the broken items with transcriber John Orfanides posing with them. Seconds later, another crash occurred behind the men—a large jar of Coffee-Mate had reportedly flown out of an adjoining room and crashed onto the floor, spewing its white powder all over the place.

This kind of stuff had been transpiring for about two weeks, according to Helen Rosenberg, who said she had witnessed much of the damage, or at least its aftermath. Telephones had been malfunctioning, she said, with rows of lights along the lines lighting up, even though no one was on the line. The local telephone company investigated, but found nothing askew. They changed the telephones, but the new ones acted up as well.

On June 15, Hazelwood reported that all eight telephones in the office kept sliding off the desks and falling to the floor, many times over. A metal piece of a typewriter was said to have flown across the room and hit a wall. A porcelain cup on Wheeler's desk reportedly jumped nearly 10 feet into the air and smashed against the ceiling. And the electric typewriters! Coil springs under the keys strangely twisted together, making the machines useless. When the type writers were replaced, the new machines became damaged in the same fashion. On June 16, typewriter repairman Bob Goosey said he saw a cabinet turn sideways and fall over, with no one near it.

Meanwhile, media coverage of the events attracted widespread interest. Dr. Arthur Hastings of Stanford University, who had done some parapsychology work at Duke University in North Carolina, came on the scene. He investigated, and began to suspect that the occurrences were paranormal in nature and not pranks or magic. In no instances were people seen to cause the damage.

On the morning of June 17, Orfanides and Cal Bowles had just opened the office when the water cooler fell over, covering the floor with water and broken glass, and then an 8-foot-high wooden cabinet filled with office supplies tumbled down in the middle of the room, dumping its papers, they said. A small machine also flipped over. The 20-year-old Orfanides became a suspect in the damage and police took him down to headquarters for questioning. He was released, but he did not immediately go back to the office to work. When he was not at the office, no incidents occurred.

Then, on June 29, a bombshell hit: After being questioned for a second time by police, Orfanides allegedly confessed to tossing objects around the office and bending the typewriter springs. But Hazelwood did not believe the confession because he said he had seen things that Orfanides could not have done. Curious, Hazelwood visited Orfanides at his apartment. The reporter claimed that Orfanides had confessed because he felt pressured by the police and wanted the case to simply go away. He denied to Hazelwood that he had thrown any objects. In fact, Orfanides said he was talked into confessing when the police said that he would not be prosecuted. Orfanides told Hazelwood that the occurrences in the office building were as much a mystery to him as to everybody else.

If so, how did these things occur? Dr. Hastings came to his own conclusion. During his investigation, he discovered that Orfanides had been teased by other men in the building because of his effeminate behavior, even though he was newly married. Hastings said that the young man's stress levels had risen and became manifested in the unconscious poltergeist activity.

natural causes

Not all poltergeist cases are real *or* fraudulent. There is often a natural explanation for unusual bumps and noises, for example, faulty pipes, raccoons in the belfry, or seismic disturbances.

In 2002, what was initially called an outbreak of poltergeist activity in the village of Boquate Ha Sofonia in the African country of Lesotho when a large stone smashed into a cooking area in a village, turned out to have a heavenly source. One resident also had pieces of rock bounce off her roof. Another of the village residents, Malino Mantsoe, blamed a thokolosi (poltergeist) and sprinkled holy water around her house and on the stone. But the stone turned out to be a rock weighing a ton that had been circling the sun for 4,600 million years and had exploded into thousands of pieces when it hit the earth's atmosphere—a meteorite.

In 2003 in Marathon County, Wisconsin, strange knockings, gushing water taps, peculiar habits of a helium balloon, and a radio that, for no apparent reason, suddenly played big-band music, were reported in a home. Members of the Wausau Paranormal Research Society said they could not rule out the possibility of paranormal phenomena, but they believed that some of the occurrences were caused by:

- A pump connected to the plumbing, causing fluctuations in the magnet field.
- Temperature changes that caused drafts.
- Faulty faucet valves.
- A weak radio signal that allowed the big-band station to slip in and out.

In another theory, physicist David J. Turner says that lightning may play a role in explaining reports of paranormal activity, including poltergeists. If conditions are stormy, he said, some reported ghostly appearances or poltergeist effects might be manifestations of ball lightning.

Then there are the animals. In 1999 in Sandwell, England, a family had their home exorcised to get rid of a poltergeist. John and Jackie Bambrick said they were forced out of their home on Lansbury Road by loud bangs and scratching noises which seem to move the house. It turned out to be nothing more than a wild cat, which had become stuck up their chimney.

the skeptics' view of why people believe

As I've stated, millions of people believe in ghosts and the paranormal, but why? Michael Shermer, founder of *Skeptic Magazine*, listed a number of reasons in his 1997 book *Why People Believe in Weird Things*:

- ◉ *Credo consolans* ("it feels good"): It is comforting to believe that there is a god and an afterlife.
- ◉ **Immediate gratification:** People call psychics for comfort regarding their personal lives, their career, or their future. But they tend to remember only the positive or comforting answers they get.
- ◉ **Simple explanations:** People want simple answers for a complex world. Superstition and belief in fate can provide simple explanations for complex science.
- ◉ **Morality and meaning:** Without a belief in a higher power, why be moral? What is the meaning of life? Science often seems cold, but pseudoscience, superstition, magic, and religion offer simple and consoling meaning.[6]

As far as poltergeists or ghosts are concerned, a large segment of the public and the media are far more fascinated by demons and ghosts than the possibility of a prank or fraud, Kurtz said. Some parapsychologists agree. Cornell warns that if people can find no logical explanation for a case, they often automatically believe that the paranormal is at work. "It is as if beliefs developed in less enlightened times lie dormant in the unconscious, then they become revived," he told me. "This has more chance of happening when the beliefs are authorized by a clergyman or spiritualist medium."

A predisposition to believe may be hard-wired into us. In fact, paranormal experiences may be partly (or wholly) hallucinations or altered states of consciousness, some scientists believe. Neuroscientist Michael Persinger believes that mystical experiences, such as poltergeists, ghosts, out-of-body experiences, alien abductions, and psychic and religious experiences are somehow linked to excessive bursts of electrical activity in the temporal lobes, the area of the brain responsible for regulation of emotions, the fight-or-flight response, and motivated behaviors.

People with sensitive temporal lobes, or *temporal lobe lability*, get frequent bursts of electrical activity and may be more susceptible to paranormal hallucinations than others, he told me. They may also be creative, and have experiences resembling those of epileptics. Persinger believes these people are particularly susceptible to hallucinations when they are near an electromagnetic field. He says he has been able to prove his theories in the laboratory by putting helmets on people and exposing them to electromagnetic signals. Four of five people, he said, report a mystical type of experience; a "feeling that there is a sentient being or entity near them." Some weep and some feel God has touched them, but others say they feel in the presence of demons or evil spirits. "And that's in the laboratory!" Persinger told me. "You could just imagine what would happen if that was late at night in a pew or place of worship." Meditation can also cause these effects, he added. In fact, people prone to paranormal experiences are sensitive to weak magnetic fields and to man-made electrical fields, which are becoming more prominent in the communication age.

A lack of exposure to science may be another reason so many people believe in the paranormal. Karen Lohman, a former teacher, said she joined the Cleveland, Ohio–based South Shore Skeptics, a group of scientists and science buffs, because of the lack of scientific literacy in America. "We don't have an understanding of even the most basic principles about why the sun comes up in the east and sets in the west," she said. "We want magic to exist, whether it's clairvoyance or crystals, because it's an awfully cold and cruel universe and we want to control the uncontrollable."[7]

The late astronomer and author Carl Sagan said that science has "beauty and power and majesty that can provide spiritual as well as

132

practical fulfillment, but superstition and pseudoscience keep getting in the way, providing easy answers, casually pressing our awe buttons, and cheapening the experience."[8] Sagan added that pseudoscience speaks to powerful emotional needs that science often leaves unfulfilled, and caters to fantasies about personal powers we lack and long for.

Then again, maybe some poltergeists, ghosts, and UFOs *are* real? Indeed, Sagan tried to stay somewhat neutral on the subject of the paranormal and called for both skeptics and believers to remain open-minded to the possibility of other ideas. "It seems to me what is called for is an exquisite balance between two conflicting needs: the most skeptical of all hypothesis that are served up to us and at the same time a great openness to new ideas," Sagan said. "If you are only skeptical, then no new ideas make it through to you...you become a crotchety old person convinced that nonsense is ruling the world. There is, of course, much data to support you. On the other hand, if you are open to the point of gullibility and have not an ounce of skeptical sense in you, then you cannot distinguish useful ideas from worthless ones."[9]

Bernard Carr, professor of mathematics and astronomy at Queen Mary University in London and a member of the Society for Psychical Research says that there remain enough questions about the paranormal that science should not close the book on it: "Although we don't fully understand these phenomena, scientists should investigate them," he said.[10]

⊙ PART III ⊙

THE STRANGE CASE
OF TINA RESCH

This section is reserved for the Tina Resch case in Columbus, Ohio, in 1984—one of the most publicized poltergeist cases in modern times. It remains controversial.

CHAPTER 13

The of House Styrofoam Cups

"The extent to which it is possible to observe poltergeist
events under good conditions will determine whether
or not science can take them seriously."
*Parapsychologist William Roll**

W hen a family packs up and moves to a motel near their home
for three days, leaving all the lights blazing, you know something is amiss. And so it was for John and Joan Resch and
their daughter, Tina, in Columbus, Ohio, in March of 1984, in what
became perhaps the most famous poltergeist case in the United States.

In the beginning, 5242 Blue Ash Road seemed another middle-class
brick and stucco home on a quiet street with lots of couches, plants,
family photos, and Pete, a Siberian husky. It was well-kept despite the
fact that, through the years, the family had taken in about 250 foster children and had been honored for community service. In 1984,
John and Joan had six children living in their house—their natural son,
Craig, 24; their adopted daughter Tina, 14; and four foster kids, from 6
years old down to a few months.

The focus of this story, a girl named Christina Elaine "Tina," was
born on October 26, 1969, and abandoned shortly thereafter by her
mother. Joan Resch adopted her at a hospital when she was less than
a year old. Tina was a busy, at times restless child, who had some trouble with projects in elementary school and was described as hyperac-
tive. Joan suspected she had a learning disability and even attention

deficit disorder. However, Tina did show talent in the Girl Scouts, once winning an achievement award. By Grade 3, her parents started giving her the drug Ritalin to relax her. Other students and even teachers teased her. Tina was insecure and slept with many teddy bears and other stuffed animals in her bed to comfort her. After she was beaten by bullies and left tied up in the schoolyard, Joan pulled her out of school for home tutoring. At home, Tina helped with the foster children, but this tended to make her feel bottled up in the crowded Resch household.

By 14, according to her family photos, Tina looked as though she might be a people-pleaser, seemingly forcing herself to smile in some shots. Like many girls, she enjoyed perfume, music, and sometimes Bible study, and she developed crushes on older guys. Tina was tall for her age, at 5 feet, 8 inches, a brunette who was not quite beautiful, and yet attractive. There was most often a sparkle, an energy, a brightness in her eyes, and she seemed to be someone you would like to spend time with. A neurologist who had visited with Tina, John Corrigan, described her as "kinetic and frenetic, never sitting still." But if Tina was at times restless, she also had a shy side.

By 1984, Tina's energy was becoming negative—she was starting to talk back to her parents, and even becoming angry, refusing at times to do her share of the housework. John and Joan were strict and not afraid to spank their kids. Without this firmness, they believed they could not have managed all those foster children for the Franklin County Children's Services. But Tina said the corporal punishment became too much at times; on one occasion, she said, she was beaten by John, and she threatened him with a knife if he hit her again. John was 57, described by those who knew him as a strong, well-built man, but not big on conversation. He spoke through his actions, particularly working with his hands, and he was said to be a perfectionist when building and fixing things. He had recently retired as a superintendent for a sheet metal firm, and had not been well after suffering a heart attack. His full-time job had become helping Joan with Tina, Craig and the four foster children. As his wife, Joan seemed to complement him well with her friendly, ever-smiling demeanor and easy ways. She was in her mid-50s and quite neat in her dress and appearance.

The first incident was reported by Tina herself. She said that on Thursday, March 1, 1984, the day John allegedly beat her, she went to bed early. When she looked at her digital clock radio in the bedroom, the numbers began racing on their own without her touching the clock. Then the radio came on by itself, and, after she turned it off, it came on again, and the only way to stop it was to unplug it. The following morning, the heart monitor of one of the foster children, 6-month-old Anne, kept going off. After Joan unplugged it, the alarm kept going off without any power or batteries, Joan said.

On March 3, the television was reportedly malfunctioning as Tina and the children watched cartoons. The family did not believe in a paranormal explanation for this, and so Joan blamed Tina, who denied faking anything, and said that when the instances occurred she often felt a headache and a stomach ache.

Then things started happening that Joan could not explain: a garbage disposal in the kitchen came on with no one around, a battery-operated wall clock in the family room had its minute hand start racing, lights were going off and on all over the house, and water began pouring out of sinks in an upstairs bathroom. Tina could not have been responsible for this mess because she had been with her, Joan said.

The Columbus and Southern utility company checked the wiring and power in the house, but nothing unusual was found. While workers were in the house, a stereo system came on loudly and an unplugged television set came on, Joan said. And then her husband, John, reported unusual incidents involving household appliances.

Joan then called a friend, electrician Bruce Claggett, 54, who had problems hearing her over the telephone. "There was an unearthly howling over the phone, like someone or something was preventing us from communicating," Claggett later recalled to me. At the Resch home, Claggett could find no electrical problems, hot spots, or loose joints. Before he left, he saw lights going on and off, and he did find the source: The light switches on the walls were moving up and down on their own accord. Also, while Claggett was in the kitchen with Tina and Joan, the garbage disposal came on under its own volition, he said. Baffled but not beaten, Claggett and Joan then taped down all the light switches to the walls. Suddenly, two ceiling lights in the kitchen activated, despite the tape over their switches, so Claggett re-taped them. But they soon came on again, with no one near the switches. "No way could Tina or anybody else have flipped those switches on…it made the hair stand up on the back of my head," Claggett told me. The only others in the house were the four small foster children, and they were not in a position to affect the lights, the electrician said.

This bizarre scenario repeated itself many times in the next several hours, with the Scotch tape popping off the light switches and the bulbs coming on while Claggett, Tina, John, and Joan were witnesses. Tina's reaction seemed to be one of excitement, but after her apparent glee subsided, she complained again of pains in her head and stomach. And she worried she would get the blame for the switches. Her father, John, was still not sure about Tina, and later he blamed her for water faucets suddenly coming on in a bathroom and a picture on the living room wall swinging to and fro. However, Tina's stepbrother, 24-year-old Craig, said he saw the swinging picture and that Tina had not touched it. Prior to that, Craig had also suspected Tina of fraud and was looking to catch her.

A short time later, John could not blame Tina for swinging a painting because wasn't close enough to touch it. John stopped it from swinging, but it started up again. He checked for string, but found nothing, and when he put the painting under the couch, it reportedly slid out on its own accord. Tina laughed.

Finally, John called the police. Two officers arrived and checked the house. When Tina led a cautious officer upstairs, a metal pan suddenly flew from a bathroom behind her. The officer drew his gun and pointed it into the room, but he did not shoot. The cops did not stay for long, and later, back at the station, they suggested in their brief report that the Resches were mentally ill.

On March 4, a friend of the Resch family, Joyce Beaumont, described as a level-headed payroll clerk at Rockwell International, came to the home suspecting Tina of trickery. But almost immediately, Beaumont absolved Tina of any blame when she saw two sticks of butter slide up a cabinet door, and then Tina was hit in the back of the head by a candlestick while sitting in the family room. It had reportedly flown from the kitchen. Beaumont said she also saw a clock fall on Tina's head, and later the teenager was reportedly pinned to the floor by a table. By this time, Tina was screaming and crying in pain. As Beaumont tried to free her, she said, a telephone hit her in the back of the head. No one else was in the room. "The phone was coming out from behind and hitting me while Tina was underneath the table," Beaumont said.[1]

Tina said that she and relatives were struck by flying objects, and that she had to duck once when she saw in a mirror the reflection of a paring knife coming at her. Her stepbrother Craig backed up her statement, saying that he watched Tina come from the kitchen, and the knife went past her and hit the fireplace. Tina told the *Miami Herald*, "It's a little scary when [objects are] flying. I don't feel anything. I wish it would stop. I still don't believe things like this happen." Later that day, two of Tina's stepbrothers said they saw kitchen chairs and a couch move by themselves. Joan and John, wondering if the cause was of a spiritual nature, called the minister of their Lutheran church, Pastor Heinz, who blessed each room with a lit candle and told the evil spirit to leave. But when he tried to sit on a couch, it lurched towards him. No children were close enough to have touched it, he said.

Enter the media. On March 5, Mike Harden, a reporter for the *Columbus Dispatch*, said he saw a doll's cradle flip into the air and other similar occurrences while Tina was not close enough to have affected them. "I was seeing something I couldn't understand," he told me. Also that day, *Dispatch* photographer Fred Shannon went to the Resch home. A media veteran of 30 years, Shannon thought he had seen everything. His first shot was of the only wine glass left un-smashed in the house. He took a picture of Tina holding it away from her body, as if it were in danger. A few minutes later, while he and Tina were in another room, the glass mysteriously smashed in the dining room, he said. Shannon also said that six metal coasters had crashed against the dining room wall.

Action then turned to the family room. With Tina sitting on a chair, a Princess telephone flew across her lap, according to her stepbrother Craig. (It was not the first incident involving a phone. On March 4, Joyce Beaumont said a phone had flown across Tina's lap as the latter was crying. There was no way Tina could have thrown the phone, said

141

Beaumont, who came to the conclusion there was an unknown force at work in the house.)

Craig said he also saw an afghan fly up from the carpet and land on Tina's head. Shannon took a photo of the afghan draped over her, and then a room divider fell over. Shannon checked the room for strings, but found nothing. At this point, Shannon was ready to shoot anything that moved, and he got his wish. As Tina sat on the side of a reclining chair, a loveseat situated about four feet away against a wall moved out from the wall about 18 inches. He got two pictures, one of them showing Tina looking a little surprised and appearing to brace herself for the loveseat moving towards her, and a second showing her appearing to lose her balance and fall backwards into the recliner. "I saw this with my own eyes," Shannon told me.

Shannon then heard a loud noise, and a large candlestick that had been lying on the floor next to the loveseat moved into the hallway. Then the Princess phone really took center stage: As Tina sat on the reclining chair with the phone on a small table to her left, the phone started making airborne trips across her lap or striking her in the side, again and again. It was attached to a cord, and sometimes the flying cord would stretch out six feet across the room. Tina was sitting with her arms crossed, not touching anything, Beaumont said.

Sitting on a couch nearby, Shannon saw this happen about seven times, but the flights were so fast and so unpredictable, it was difficult to catch them on film. "Each time the receiver flew like a projectile, rapidly and with great force," he told me. Several people in the room, including Shannon and Harden, said they did not think Tina could have picked up the phone and tossed it so many times without them seeing her do it. Finally, while he was focusing on the phone, Shannon got what he wanted: a picture of the phone flying about six feet across Tina's lap. Tina looked surprised and was holding her hands backward as though she had touched something hot. Harden saw the phone fly. "I was seated across the room facing Tina...I saw [the phone] in motion without it being aided in any way on her part. It moved on a level trajectory from Tina's left to right," he told me.

Before Shannon got the film developed, two of Joan's friends from the Franklin County Children's Services, Kathy Goeff and Lee Arnold (who was Tina's caseworker) showed up to see if they could help the family. They said they saw the phone jump and smack into the loveseat. Arnold said she was watching Tina and believed it was not possible for the girl to have tossed the phone, especially at such a high speed.

The following day, Shannon's photo of Tina and the flying phone appeared on the front page of the *Dispatch* and was picked up by other media around the world. After that, the family received about 150 media requests to be interviewed. With all the publicity, the occurrences and the stress piled up, and family life was deteriorating in the Resch home. The four foster children were sent to other homes, which upset Joan and particularly John, who had become close to them. And, after returning briefly to school, Tina said she was getting harassed by other students, and teased.

And so, John, Joan, and Tina packed up and went to a motel for three days and two nights. They didn't have much choice, as there were few glasses, cups, and dishes left unbroken, and they were eating out of paper plates and Styrofoam cups. No incidents were reported at the motel, but things got back to "normal" when they returned home. As soon as Tina walked through the door, several items moved, including a soft drink bottle, a candle, and a glass. At times, Tina said she thought the house was haunted, or perhaps she was possessed by the devil.

She also thought that the occurrences sometimes escalated when she got angry with others.

On March 7, the Hughes family came to offer their emotional support. Barbara Hughes, also a foster mother, and her husband, Ted, a schoolteacher, brought their two adopted children with them. They were all born-again Christians, bearing a crucifix on a chain for Tina. What they said they saw smacked of the devil's work—four metal coasters flying under their own accord, a soap dish spinning in circles, and a glass shattering. Barbara said she was struck by kitchen chairs and one of their adopted children was hit by a phone.

Once again, the people in the house claimed that Tina could not physically have caused the damage. "Tina and I were standing in the doorway," Barbara said. "[The coasters] took off—one, two, three, four. The first one I saw in the air and then the others took off. One at a time they just lifted off the pile and went around the room like someone was playing Frisbee."[2]

Insurance Claim for What??

Can one make an insurance claim for poltergeist damage?

The Resches inquired about just that from their insurance company, Midwestern Indemnity of Cincinnati, for coverage of broken paintings, glasses, and lamps. Agents said they considered the family trustworthy, but they did not know who to blame for the damage, except to put it under the category of malicious mischief and vandalism.

One agent told the family they could probably win the claim because they had an all-risk policy, but the company had some reluctance to put it through because it might open itself up to unusual or fraudulent claims in the future.

In the end, the Resches decided not to press for the insurance money.

CHAPTER 14

The Circus Comes to Columbus

"The Resch case boils down to simply a matter of faith."
Joe Dirck, columnist for the Columbus Citizen-Journal

O n Thursday, March 8, the circus came to Columbus in the form of a media conference in the Resch home. Until then, the family had granted few interviews and had been given pseudonyms to protect their identities. However, because they and the *Columbus Dispatch* had been besieged by interview requests, the Resches consented to a news conference.

Before the reporters arrived, an incident occurred while family friend Barbara Hughes was making lunch. As she served Tina at a table, two kitchen chairs moved and hit Barbara in the stomach, and she doubled over in pain. Tina had been sitting across from her at the time. Then a baby chair slid into Hughes' knee. Peggy Covert, Joan Resch's married daughter, who was a nurse, witnessed this. Covert said that Tina had been in no position to move the baby chair.

The Resches seemed tense as reporters gathered in the house, and Tina was worried the journalists would judge her and blame her for everything that had transpired in the preceding week.

By one o'clock in the afternoon, about 40 journalists had assembled in the Resch's 20-by-20-foot living room, and television lights were making things hot. "I didn't want to do this," Tina said in her opening remarks. "If I say anything, people are going to think I'm crazy."[1] But the reporters, some of whom had cast her in their stories as a cross between the main characters in the movies *Carrie* and *Poltergeist*, were easy on her, and they asked her to relax. She was asked if she was afraid when objects moved. "No," Tina said. "But it's scary when they're flying. I wish they would stop. I still don't believe things like this can happen."[2]

Her father, John, agreed. "I see it and I still don't believe it. How a glass can fly at a 90-degree angle through a doorway and around a corner, or the television run with no electricity? I just try to clean up, to turn my head away when it happens." Joan Resch explained that she had packed away her valuables "so they wouldn't get broken or hurt someone."[3]

The conference was supposed to last for one hour, but the journalists wanted to stay, hoping to catch something paranormal. Four hours passed and the house still resembled a carnival with reporters and cameramen waltzing through the rooms and peaking around corners, mostly following Tina. Videocameras were set up at various locations, but no phenomena were seen. By 9 o'clock, the family's nerves were getting frayed, and so Joan took Tina aside and suggested she *do something* to get rid of the reporters. The mild-mannered Joan didn't have the courage to tell them to leave, but she reportedly told her daughter that something had to happen before they would.

The only paranormal incident during the conference was reported by United Press International writer Jodi Gossage, who said she saw a chair overturn inexplicably when Tina entered the opposite side of the living room.

But at about 9:30, a large table lamp fell to the floor. Drew Hadwal of the Columbus station WTVN-TV believed he had caught the action on camera and he hurried to his station to check. What he discovered was that Tina had apparently intentionally knocked the lamp down with her hand. The video tape revealed that Tina had been unaware she was on camera when she knocked the lamp to the floor, and then looked surprised, as though it had crashed on its own. The footage was shown on television, and suddenly, sympathy for the family plummeted. When faced with the facts, Tina admitted that she had pulled the lamp, but she said she did it to give the reporters something so they would finally leave. "To me, what happened was understandable," parapsychologist William Roll later told me. "Nothing paranormal was happening that afternoon and she wanted to get rid of the reporters." Her mother agreed, believing that Tina grabbed the lamp just to get rid of everyone.

Some media turned against the family and became cynical. Jay Maeder, a columnist for the *Miami Herald*, wrote, tongue-in-cheek, "Miss Tina read her boyfriend's mind and broke up with him on the spot."

And yet some journalists remained open-minded, including Hadwal, who could not explain other bizarre happenings. "I was seated at the kitchen table with Tina and all of a sudden the chairs spread out," he said. "I don't see how she could have sent them out in three directions like that."[4]

Meanwhile, unusual events continued to be reported. The day after the press conference, Hughes said a heavy kitchen table kept moving on its own near Tina. The same day, Hughes and Joan said a chair flipped Tina off it, dumping her onto the floor with such force that her glasses fell off. By this time, though, Tina's credibility had fallen—but not in the eyes of her family and others who had seen what they called amazing occurrences.

Roll still believed the case was worth investigating. He had been following the story in the newspapers, and he arrived, along with his assistant Kelly Powers, on Sunday, March 11, three days after the media conference. Although Roll wondered if Tina had been playing tricks all along (especially after finding a book on magic in her room), he tried to keep an open mind. The first thing Roll noticed about Tina was her clumsiness; her habit of bumping into walls and furniture, like many growing teenagers. If she was a sleight-of-hand magician, she didn't show it. Tina even experienced spells of dizziness, and her clumsiness had led to many falls and broken bones in previous years.

In Roll's first two days in Columbus, no incidents were reported. That was not unusual in poltergeist cases, he said, because the action often subsides when an investigator shows up, and then picks up again after he or she has been in the presence of the poltergeist agent for a while. But Roll was able to interview many witnesses, including Tina. She seemed to bond with the fatherly Roll and told him she wished there were fewer children in the Resch house. She also said that she had first believed that the paranormal incidents were related to the death of one of her only friends and confidantes, Tina Scott, in 1983, which had made her sad and angry, particularly because she had not been allowed to go to her funeral. Not long after her death, Tina Resch said she saw an apparition of Scott in her room.

Roll pursued the theory that Tina might have psychokinetic powers, partly due to sexual issues. In many other poltergeist cases he had investigated, the adolescent or youth suspected of being the poltergeist agent was going through puberty at the time of paranormal occurrences. Roll discovered that Tina had already entered puberty, but there was the possibility of other sexual tension; she told him she had been raped by an adopted brother (who is not named in this book).

On March 13, the circus stepped up a notch with the spectacular entrance of James "The Amazing" Randi, a professional magician, known for debunking claims of the paranormal. As much as Tina had been at center stage, Randi now attracted bold headlines. When interviewed by the *Columbus Dispatch* about the case over the phone before he came to the Resch home, Randi told me he had been quoted as saying, "I've always said that I don't believe in things that go bump in the night. And I don't believe in Santa Claus and the tooth fairy."

Wearing a cape and a beard, Randi came to Columbus as part of a scientific team sent by Paul Kurtz, founder of the Committee for Scientific Inquiry. The team also included Professors Steven Shore and Nicholas Sanduleak of the Case Western Reserve University in Cleveland. Despite Randi's telephone interview, Kurtz said his team was going in open-minded. "We thought that the public deserved an explanation," he told me. "And yet, it seemed to us this was a hoax fooling the entire country."

And now Randi was standing in front of the Resch home, giving an interview for reporters and TV cameras. "I've never seen a bona fide paranormal event, but that doesn't mean I won't," he said. "When you've sat by the chimney on Christmas Eve for 35 years and have never seen Santa Claus, you don't say he doesn't exist. I'm always ready for a soot-covered fat man in a red suit to bounce down the chimney."[5]

Buoyed by the videotape that had shown Tina pulling down the lamp, Randi held up from under his cape a check for $10,000, which he would present to the Resches if they could show him one paranormal event. However, Randi was not allowed in their house. He claimed that the media and John and Joan Resch had invited him to come to their home, and that it was Roll who stopped him from entering. Roll had already taken up residence at the Resch home, and, according to Randi, was hyperbolizing the events for the media. However, Joan took responsibility for keeping Randi out on the sidewalk. "It's been rough on us; we've had a circus," she said. "Now we have a magic show. No, not here." She was offended by Randi's cheap jokes and offer of money, which she refused.[6]

Some of the witnesses to events in the Resch home refused to speak to CSI (Committee for Skeptical Inquiry) investigators, including Barbara Hughes, who suspected they did not have open minds and might twist the things she told them.

Meanwhile, the incidents continued. Also on March 13, Joan reported that an unseen force pushed her against a refrigerator while Tina was with her. Throughout the next few days, Roll said he witnessed six different objects move while Tina was nearby—a tube of lipstick, a book, a teacup, candy, his Sony tape recorder, and pliers. "She clearly did not touch them," Roll told me. "I was persuaded this was for real...I had handled three of the objects immediately before they moved, precluding the further possibility that they were attached to trick devices. Now I knew it wasn't all chicanery. Things were actually flying by themselves."

Roll was coming to the conclusion that Tina was wired differently than other people and that she was somehow suspending gravity at a short distance with her tension and unusual energy.

testing tina

As noted in earlier chapters, Roll called the suspension of gravity *zero-point energy*. Hoping to prove his theory, Roll convinced Tina to come to his home in Durham, North Carolina, from March 17 to April 12, so that she could be tested at the nearby institutes where Roll had worked—the Institute of Parapsychology, and the Spring Creek Institute.

According to Roll, a number of paranormal incidents took place with Tina at the institutes and at his home, but nothing spectacular or conclusive. "I had a lot of Danish porcelain in my home and I asked her not to have anything crash to the floor," Roll mused to me. "My wife was very nervous." On March 31, while borrowing a three-wheel motorbike in Durham, Tina crashed and broke her leg. There were no further incidents until she returned home to Columbus.

In August 1984, with the strange incidents dying down, Roll became chairman for a panel on the case, which also included Randi, photographer Shannon, reporter Harden, electrician Claggett, and Dr. Rebecca Zinn, a psychotherapist who counseled Tina in North Carolina.

In October 1984, Tina returned to the Spring Creek Institute, where Dr. Stephen Baumann was setting up tests for psychokinesis. By this time, Tina's alleged powers were apparently subsiding, and yet one day, Roll, Baumann, and psychotherapist Jeannie Stewart set up a table with a 12-inch socket wrench on it, which they hoped Tina could move with her mind. According to Roll, Tina was not allowed near the table, but while Stewart and Baumann were standing between Tina and the table, there was a loud noise behind them and they saw that the wrench had moved off the table and about 18 feet along the floor, finally hitting a door.

Also in North Carolina, Dr. Zinn said she saw a number of paranormal incidents involving Tina. In one case, Zinn said she took Tina by the hand as they walked down a hallway leading to her office when a telephone suddenly came from behind them and struck the girl in the back. "There was no way anyone could have touched it," Zinn said. She was so shaken about being around Tina, she called it a lesson in fear.

Also in North Carolina, there were reportedly four movements of objects in Roll's house and 10 at Spring Creek after Tina was hypnotized to try to recapture her mindset and emotions back in Columbus.

Meanwhile, Randi and Kurtz wrote reports about the case in the *Skeptical Inquirer*, the bible of the CSI. Randi said that if the phenomena surrounding Tina were genuine, it would be a repeal of the basic laws of physics. Roll countered by saying that physics does not say that objects cannot be affected without tangible contact: "The moon revolves around the Earth and magnets attract pieces of iron—recurrent spontaneous psychokinesis requires an extension of the laws of physics, not their repeal."

In his 1985 book, *A Skeptic's Handbook of Parapsychology*, Kurtz wrote: "Our investigators came up with the following explanation: Tina Resch is a disturbed 14-year-old who has dropped out of school and is being tutored at home. She had seen [the movie] *Poltergeist* and had learned how to hurl objects into the air unobserved…if a person is once caught cheating, then the further display of his or her powers should be highly suspect. Tina Resch and Uri Geller are like [psychics] Eusapia Palladino and D.D. Home of earlier generations." (Kurtz believes that those three people also cheated.)

Randi and Kurtz thought other incidents were orchestrated by Tina and bought by the media looking for a good story. "Carefully observe the people nearby," they wrote. "As soon as they are not looking, quickly shoot an object into the air. If you tell them it is a poltergeist, and they can't easily see how it could have taken off, then they may accept the claim as genuine. If there is a predisposition to believe and the situation is charged with drama and emotion, it is more likely to arouse an affirmative response."[7] However, Randi admitted the scientists had not interviewed many witnesses, partly because, like Barbara Hughes, they would not cooperate.

Meanwhile, the *Columbus Dispatch* didn't buy the skeptics' claims. Reporter Harden, who had described himself as the ultimate skeptic of the paranormal before he first set foot in the Resch house, stood fast on his story. "I was reporting what I saw and could not explain," he said in 1985. "I saw a phone move and didn't see anyone move it. But only a fool would think that human vision is absolutely infallible. The opinion should be left up to the experts. They're going to be debating this for a long time."[8]

Shannon also stood behind what he saw and photographed, adding that the case changed his life. "On my mother's grave, it wasn't a hoax. I was scared to death. Lots of things were flying," he said to me. "Things didn't just levitate; they became projectiles."

After interviewing all of the witnesses, Roll believed there was no doubt that Tina had used trickery in the lamp incident. "When it was filmed by WTVN-TV, it showed her willingness to deceive when she thought it was to her advantage. She wanted to get the reporters off her back," he told me. But Roll denied that many of the other incidents were trickery: "The clumsy lamp trick was quite different from all the other occurrences, 34 of them in which Tina was reported to be in different rooms from the incidents. And then there were the 125 occurrences while she was being observed." Roll added that in order to pull off these feats, Tina would have needed advanced skills of sleight of hand, as well as devices enabling her to reach or activate the objects that moved, and there was no evidence of such things.

Regarding the telephone incident that led to the photograph, Randi reviewed a series of photos taken by Shannon and proposed that Tina had thrown the phone each time from left to right while sitting on the reclining chair. But Roll countered that Tina was right-handed, and that, in order to conceal her trick in front of several witnesses, she would need to be as fast and as inconspicuous as she could. That would mean, if she was being deceitful, she would have set herself up at the other side of the table to take advantage of her right hand.

Overall, Randi basically dismissed Roll as not being a credible researcher, and called him nearsighted and a poor observer. Roll countered that he was not nearsighted, but actually farsighted! Roll said that Tina was not a publicity-seeker and never felt pleased about everything that was going on.

Some people felt that John Resch, Tina's adoptive father, was a good witness. They say he had more motive to catch Tina cheating than anyone because he was a man who was proud of the material things in the house, much of which had been destroyed or damaged by the unseen force. And he was deeply hurt that the four younger foster children had to leave the home. And yet, after suspecting Tina of trickery early on, he said he never caught her cheating.

tragedy

This story ends badly.

The Resches sold their house on Blue Ash Road in early 1986 and their relationship with Tina was not good. They wanted to put her back into foster care, but there was a backlog of cases and she would have had to stay in a detention center. Instead, she married a young man she had met at a convenience store.

That marriage lasted just 17 months, amid accusations by Tina that her husband had beaten her. In 1987, John Resch suffered a heart attack and died. Soon after that, Tina began dating a man she had met at church. The relationship did not last long, but it produced a baby girl, named Amber, on September 29, 1988.

Still living in Columbus, Tina then married another man, Larry Boyer—partly for the baby's sake, she said—and she changed her name to Tina Boyer. But there were problems in that relationship, as well, and they drifted apart. Roll had been keeping in touch with Tina and he suggested that she and Amber move close to him in Carrollton, Georgia, where he was living since moving from North Carolina, and where he was a professor of psychology and psychical research at the State University of West Georgia. Tina trusted Roll and took up his offer.

Tina told Roll that her daughter, Amber, was much the way she had been as a child: bubbly, high-strung, and smart for her age. But Roll said there was tension between mother and daughter, and that Tina had problems raising Amber, so he enrolled her in a parenting class at Carrollton Tech. "Tina was starting to turn her life around," Roll told me.

Tina then met another divorcé, David Herrin, a 29-year-old truck driver, who had a 3-year-old daughter. They lived together for about six weeks. Then, on April 13, 1992, Amber died at age 3 from what police said was bleeding in the brain and swelling of the brain. Tina and her boyfriend Herrin were charged with murder and cruelty to children. Prosecutors in the Carroll County murder case filed a list of what they say were 33 alleged transgressions against the child, which were used to show a pattern of abuse by Tina. Prosecutors said the little girl was repeatedly struck, severely scolded, locked in a closet, and burned with a cigarette.

Through her attorney, Tina denied beating Amber, and she said that the child had been in Herrin's care when the fatal injuries occurred. She said if she was guilty of anything, it was of not taking her injured child to the hospital in time to save her life. But Herrin blamed Tina.

Tina pleaded guilty to felony murder and cruelty to children in order to avoid the electric chair, and, at age 25, was sentenced to life plus 20 years in prison. Herrin was not prosecuted for murder, but was found guilty of cruelty to children and received a 20-year sentence. Tina is serving her sentence at Pulaski State Prison in Hawkinsville, Georgia. She was denied parole in 2002 and 2008, and has reported bouts of depression in prison. Tina, Prisoner No. 810071, was up for parole again in 2015.

Kurtz theorizes that the way people had pampered Tina and believed her poltergeist story helped lead to her downfall in Georgia. "There's no question in our minds the girl was cheating," Kurtz said. "She was so good at it that she deceived people constantly. She was seeking attention and everybody fell for it. I think all this was a factor in a destructive course later on."[9]

James Randi agreed: "We must ask ourselves whether a proper investigation of the claims that brought this woman to world attention, which might have deprived her of the celebrity status that she attained through support by scientists [Roll and others] and media who encouraged her, might have brought her to a healthier state of mind and adult lifestyle. Such an unhappy child, discovering that she could so easily manipulate the media, becomes an adult who is not in a position to make appropriate choices in life."[10] Randi said the parapsychologists and the media used Tina, as well for their own purposes.

Before his death in 2012, Roll occasionally visited Resch in prison, and he believed she got a harsh sentence. Roll said there was not a direct link between the poltergeist activity of 1984 and Amber's death, but Tina's injured psyche prevented her from making good choices for herself and her child.

In 2004, Tina said that she still dreamed about her house in Columbus. "They're never good dreams...and I always find myself thinking—when I wake up—that I wish I could go and bulldoze that house to the ground. Like somehow, that would make me feel better."[11]

Roll wished people like Tina could be studied more closely scientifically. "I think the abilities she had were a natural endowment of the human mind," he said to me. "She's already made quite a contribution to science...but to understand ourselves fully, and to better understand our brains and their capabilities, we need to know more about people like Tina. She is a sort of natural treasure."

In 2004, Roll wrote a detailed book about the case with writer Valerie Storey, called *Unleashed: Of Poltergeists and Murder, The Curious Story of Tina Resch.* One of Tina's former neighbors in Columbus, Jim Kress, bought the book and was saddened by it. "I lived next door to John and Joan Resch when I was a teenager," he said. "I remember when they adopted Tina. She was a cute little one. Too bad things turned out the way they did."[12]

CHAPTER 15

The Ghostbuster and the Mythbuster

"The most important sense [needed] to investigate
the psychic sense is common sense."
William Roll

I n this chapter, we will discover more about two of the prominent characters in this book, who were involved on opposite sides of many poltergeist controversies throughout the years: parapsychologist William Roll and magician/skeptic James "The Amazing" Randi.

william roll

William George Roll was born in 1926 in Germany where his father was a lawyer, but his father and mother divorced when he was 3 and William went with his mother to live in her native Denmark. He grew up in Birkerod, near Copenhagen, where he had a traumatic childhood. In 1940, the Nazis occupied Denmark, and his mother died suddenly two years later. Roll became a ward of a guardian who didn't like him, and he did poorly in school.

A determined Roll joined the Danish resistance movement from September 1944 until the country's liberation on May 5, 1945, and he was a courier between the leader of the resistance and the smaller group leaders. "They were the best times of my life," Roll told me. "It was exciting and I was working for a good cause—freedom. My confidence was restored."

155

During his teens, Roll said he had out-of-body experiences. "I wondered if I was having some sort of hallucination, or a serious case of absent-mindedness, or whether my soul had detached itself from the body." A curious Roll began reading up on the subject and discovered "there was a field that explored experiences like this medically."[2]

In 1947, he moved to California to be close to his father and to attend the University of California, Berkeley. He then married a girl he had met in New York: Muriel.

For five decades, Roll, who was uncomfortable with the term *ghost-buster* ("I think we're called parapsychologists," he used to say, without ego), was been the face of poltergeist research, having reviewed hundreds of cases from around the world, as well as having investigated dozens of his own. The general field of PSI, and whether it even exists, is hotly contested these days among scientists, parapsychologists, and psychics, but it is hard for anyone to get angry at Roll. He went about his business, gathering painstaking details in highly charged family cases, and he did not seem to take it personally if his theories are called rubbish by skeptics.

Roll was a respected PhD academic with an undergraduate degree from the University of California, Berkeley; a master's from Oxford University, England, and a doctorate from Lund University, Sweden. For two decades, he worked under the leadership of another parapsychologist, J.B. Rhine, the founder of modern parapsychology, at the Institute for Parapsychology at Duke University in Durham, North Carolina.

After joining Rhine at Duke in 1957, Roll got his first poltergeist case the following year, at the home of James and Lucille Herrmann on Long Island, New York. (Recall thieir story from Chapter 4: Tops were mysteriously popping off bottles of soda and holy water and porcelain figures were flying into walls.) The Herrmanns thought that a spirit had come to their home, but after investigating with psychologist/parapsychologist Dr. J. Gaither Pratt, assistant director at the Duke institute, Roll suspected that the couple's 12-year-old son, Jimmy, was unconsciously causing the occurrences through his mind. It was a rare and complex phenomena, Roll and Pratt said, and they termed it *recurrent spontaneous psychokinesis* (RSPK). Until then, the general public—and even researchers—had believed that poltergeists were actually a type of ghost.

After working with Rhine in North Carolina, Roll became a professor of psychology and psychical research at the State University of West Georgia in Carrollton, Georgia.

From 1958 until his death, Roll investigated numerous aspects of the paranormal, including:

- ESP and its relationship to memory
- The way magnetic fields affect people's perceptions of psychic occurrences.
- The possibility of ghosts and life after death.

But he is most known for his work on poltergeists. Starting in the 1960s, Roll studied 116 written reports of poltergeist cases spanning four centuries in more 100 countries. Roll identified patterns that he labeled RSPK. Generally, he discovered, the most common poltergeist agent was a child or teenager whose unwitting RSPK was a way of expressing hostility without the fear of punishment, he said. The subjects or poltergeist agents were usually entering puberty and were girls rather than boys. The individual was not aware of being the cause of such disturbances, but was, at the same time, secretly or openly pleased that they occurred.

The mild-mannered, soft-spoken Roll believed that psychic events and poltergeist cases occur more often around magnetic fields, which often exist near geological faults. It is a complex subject and he did not claim to have all the answers, only unproven theories. In retrospect, Roll considered Columbus and a case in Miami his most convincing cases because they both had so many reliable witnesses.

Throughout the years, Roll was contacted by many people having problems with poltergeists or ghosts, and in many cases he alleviated their fears somewhat with his calm demeanor and the facts as he saw them. He was a trusting figure, but sometimes stressed-out families did not allow him into their homes or they kicked him out because they believed he brought evil spirits with him. Although he had a sympathetic ear for people, Roll said he's not easily hoodwinked and tried to go into cases with a skeptical, yet open mind. He caught some people trying to fake paranormal occurrences. As he told me, "The most important sense to investigate the psychic sense is common sense." He needed it once when he was in a room with a medium who was conducting a séance. Roll was skeptical about the validity of the séance, and so he used what he called "the toothpaste test for ghosts." He hid some toothpaste in his shoe, and when an apparition came close to him, as everybody held hands in the dark room, he took out his stocking feet and marked the ghost's foot. Later, when the lights came on, Roll found a white smudge of toothpaste on the foot of the woman who owned the apartment. She had been used by the medium to dress up as the spook.

Roll appeared on several segments of the television show *Unsolved Mysteries*, and was also on the Discovery Channel and other television programs. He wrote four books and more than 200 scientific articles. He spoke at conventions and was a regular contributor to the *Journal of Parapsychology*. In 1996, Roll received the outstanding career award from the Parapsychological Association, and in 2002 he received the Tim Dinsdale Memorial Award from the Society for Scientific Exploration.

Roll never saw a ghost, but he said he had seen things move in several poltergeist cases without any familiar physical causes. He retired in 1990, but occasionally investigated the paranormal while living with his second wife in Carrollton. He has three children who are in more conventional jobs than he was. Roll died on January 9, 2012, at a nursing home in Normal, Illinois. He was 85.

the amazingly cynical randi

"We may disagree with Randi on certain points,
but we ignore him at our peril."

The late astronomer and author Carl Sagan

If I can prove in this book that poltergeists exist, then James "The Amazing" Randi owes me a million bucks.

Randi seems to be the enemy of poltergeist, a disbeliever in the strongest sense. He goes by the nickname "The Amazing," but really, his theory about life is that Nothing Is Amazing, except for science and things that can be proven without a doubt. In Randi's world, if you didn't see it happen, it likely didn't happen. And even if you saw it happen, someone could have duped you. His many fans say there are far too many charlatans in the world; too many things we gulp down without question without examining their texture.

For decades, Randi has proudly worn the crown of the world's Number-one skeptic, and he looks the part with his bald head, white beard, and suspicious eyes glaring at you over the top of his glasses. In 2004 when I asked him if it was possible that a particular poltergeist case could be true, he cracked, "I dunno. I wasn't there, and neither were you."

Randi's skepticism seemed to develop in his native Toronto when he was a 15-year-old amateur magician. While visiting a Spiritualist church, he was irritated at seeing what he called "common tricks" being passed off as divine intervention. But when he tried to convey this to the churchgoers, they called the police and Randi was questioned for four hours.

Randi developed a career as a professional magician and staged spectacular acts such as Houdini-style escapes from chains. In 1976, he was one of the founding members of the Committee for the Scientific Investigation of Claims of the Paranormal (CSICOP), which publishes a journal, the *Skeptical Inquirer*, reaching about 50,000 subscribers.

Randi tries to expose everything: faith healers, water dowsing, superstition, the existence of the Bermuda Triangle and UFOs, and astrology. Two of Randi's main targets throughout the years have been spoonbending psychic Uri Geller and televangelist Peter Popoff. "If Geller [bends spoons] by divine power, he does it the hard way," Randi mused to me.

"Acceptance of nonsense as a harmless aberration can be dangerous to all of us," he says. "We live in a society that is enlarging the boundaries of knowledge at an unprecedented rate, and we cannot keep up with much more than a small portion of what is made available to us. To mix that knowledge with childish notions of magic and fantasy is to cripple our perception of the world around us. We must reach for the truth, not for the ghosts of dead absurdities."[2]

Randi is particularly worried about the growing popularity of exotic cures and therapies catering to sick people, who may be sidetracked from effective treatments.

He feels sympathy for people who put their money into things beyond their control—faith healing, astrology, psychics. "It's a very dangerous thing to believe in nonsense," he says. "You're giving away your money to the charlatans; you're giving away your emotional security, and sometimes your life."[3]

In 1996, Randi established his own foundation—The James Randi Educational Foundation, a nonprofit organization funded through member contributions, grants, sales of books and videos, seminars, and conferences. Its aim is "to promote critical thinking by reaching out to the public and media with reliable information about paranormal and supernatural ideas so widespread in our society today." The foundation holds lectures and seminars, and supports and conducts research into paranormal claims, using experiments. It has a comprehensive library of books, videos, and archival resources, which are open to the public.

The foundation's goals are:

- ◎ Creating a new generation of critical thinkers through lively classroom demonstrations.

- ◎ Offering scholarships and awards to students and educators.

- ◎ Demonstrating to the public and the media, through educational seminars, the consequences of accepting paranormal and supernatural claims without questioning.

- ◎ Supporting and conducting research into paranormal claims through well-designed experiments utilizing "the scientific method" and by publishing the findings in the JREF official newsletter (*Swift*) and other periodicals. Also providing reliable information on paranormal and pseudoscientific claims.

- ◎ Assisting those who are being attacked as a result of their investigations into and criticism of people who make paranormal claims, by maintaining a legal defense fund available to assist these individuals.

One of the things that makes Randi effective is his delivery—his cutting sarcasm and deft skills and stage presence as a magician. He often duplicates tricks that are passed off as supernatural events. "As a magician, I know two things: how to deceive people and how people deceive themselves."[4] With his Project Alpha, he put magicians in a university parapsychology lab to determine whether fakes could be debunked.

Randi is also an accomplished lecturer and television personality, who has appeared on *Larry King Live* and at the White House in 1974.

To raise public awareness on the issues of the paranormal, Randi's foundation offers a $1 million prize to any person or persons who can demonstrate any psychic, supernatural, or paranormal ability of any kind under mutually agreed-upon scientific conditions. The money is held in a special account that cannot be accessed for any purpose other than the awarding of the prize. Throughout the years, Randi and his colleagues have tested hundreds of applicants, but no one has claimed the One Million Dollar Paranormal Challenge. He says that, faced with solid evidence, he would be glad to hand over the prize. "That would be such an advance for our knowledge of the universe that it would be well worth a million dollars," he says. "The possibility is very, very small, but it's there."[5]

Critics of the challenge say that Randi is unfair to applicants. "[Randi] has obsessive concentration on minor or unimportant matters in order to divert attention from the major issues," said Australian lawyer and parapsychology writer Victor Zammit. He added that Randi shows "contemptuous dismissal of evidence inconsistent with his conviction that all evidence for the paranormal is bunk, and all who contend otherwise are deluded fools."[6] Other Randi critics say that many people with paranormal abilities are scared to get into the ring with him because of the chance for bad publicity if they cannot perform their usual—and perhaps unpredictable and fleeting—gifts under pressure and the bright lights of a camera. Randi is well aware of his critics, and even afraid of some of them. "I get threats all the time," he told me.

But throughout the years, he has gained some big backers, including the late scientist/author Isaac Asimov, who said, "Perhaps nobody in the world understands both the virtues and the failings of the paranormal as well as Randi does. His qualifications as a rational human being are unparalleled."[7]

Of course, Randi does not believe in poltergeists or psychokinesis. He says there are many frauds—particularly teenagers seeking attention—or natural explanations.

Randi was born in Toronto in 1928, became a naturalized United States citizen in 1987, and now lives in Plantation, Florida, with his partner of over 25 years, artist José Alvarez. He officially stepped down from his position at the James Randi Educational Foundation, but continues to make occasional appearances. A documentary about his life, called *An Honest Liar*, was released in 2014.

Randi has written many books, including *The Truth about Uri Geller* (1982) and *Houdini: His Life and Art* (1978).

For more information, contact:

The James Randi Educational Foundation
2941 Fairview Park Drive, Suite 105
Falls Church, VA 22042
Website: http://web.randi.org
Email: jref@randi.org

☺ PART IV ☺

POLTERGEISTS IN THE UNITED KINGDOM

Poltergeists have frequently been reported on the other side of the Atlantic as well, as we will see in this section, where we examine the facts, evidence, and theories of many more cases outside of North America. Chapters 16 and 17 are reserved for the most celebrated poltergeist case in modern times in the United Kingdom: the Hodgson family case in Enfield, north of London, England, in 1977.

CHAPTER 16

Watch Out *for* *the* Lego Bricks

"Poltergeist activity is so inherently improbable that most rational people simply cannot believe it. And when they see it and have to believe it, they find it very hard to convince anybody else that it really happens."

Guy Lyon Playfair, author of This House Is Haunted

From the other side of the road, Number 284 Green Street resembled so many other semi-detached council houses in the north London borough of Enfield. The neighborhood, which had sprung up in the 1920s, consisted of lots of alleyways, small gardens in front of the homes, and a school across the way. There seemed nothing foreboding about the area, yet inside the three-bedroom home at 284, all was not well with Peggy Hodgson and her four children. It was 1977, and the story of what was happening would live on for decades in British lore.

Mrs. Hodgson was a recently divorced single parent in her mid-40s, struggling to get by on welfare and support payments from her ex-husband in the working-class neighborhood. She was a short, plump woman with small eyes, which at times could be piercing. But, overall, she was chummy toward visitors, down-to-earth, and trustworthy, according to those who knew her. The family was reportedly a close-knit group, starting with Peggy's daughter Janet, 11, who looked like her mum, but was more outgoing, with bundles of energy, and was a trifle big for her age. Janet talked fast and had a somewhat mischievous look about her. Another child, Margaret, was tall and pleasant and looked older than

13. She did not have Janet's bubbly qualities. Their 7-year-old brother, Billy, seemed harmless behind a large pair of spectacles, a full head of hair, and a speech defect. Another brother, 10-year-old Johnny, was away at a hospice for sick children during most of the events that were to occur in the Hodgson house. He was suffering from brain cancer.

But Johnny was involved when the incidents began, on August 30, 1977. On that evening, he and Janet informed their mother that frightening things were happening in their room: Their bed was shaking and furniture was moving about on its own accord, and there were shuffling noises and loud raps on the walls. The mother was not too upset and believed it was just children and their antics.

The next night, Peggy heard a shuffling noise coming from Janet's bedroom. When she went to check on them, the children were apparently asleep. From their room, Mrs. Hodgson said she heard four loud knocks coming from a wall that adjoined the neighboring house. Curious, Peggy turned on the lights. What happened next was hard to explain: A heavy chest of drawers moved out from the wall, she said. It moved only about a foot and a half (18 inches), but when a heavy set of drawers moves on its own accord, 18 inches is a mile. Surprised, Peggy pushed the dresser back against the wall, but it reportedly moved right back to its position away from the wall. When Peggy tried to push it back again, it would not budge, and she started shaking like a leaf and hustled her children out of the house to the next-door neighbors', Vic and Peggy Nottingham.

Vic and a relative went into the Hodgson home and they said that they, too, heard knocking coming from the walls. They searched the home and could find no explanation.

Police were summoned and Constable Carolyn Keeps scoured the Hodgson house. While investigating, the officer became a witness to a chair moving three or four feet towards the kitchen door, apparently without the help of human hands. Keeps did not know what to think, but she was so convinced she had seen something unnatural, she was not afraid to put it down in her official report that night.

Years later, Keeps signed her report to authenticate her findings:

"On Thursday, September 1, 1977, at approximately 1 a.m., I was on duty in my capacity as a policewoman, when I received a radio message to 284 Green Street, Enfield.

I went to this address where I found a number of people standing in the living room. I was told by the occupier of this house that strange things had been happening during the last few nights and that they believed that the house was haunted. Myself and another PC [constable] entered the living room of the house and the occupier switched off the lights. Almost immediately, I heard the sound of knocking on the wall that backs onto the next-door neighbor's house. There were four distinct taps on the wall, and then silence. About two minutes later, I heard more tapping, but this time, it was coming from a different wall, and again it was a distinctive peal of four taps."[1]

The officer and the neighbors then checked the walls, attic, and pipes, but found nothing unusual. The other officer and the neighbors then went into the kitchen to check the refrigerator, leaving the family and Keeps in the living room.

"The lights in the living room were switched off again, and within a few minutes, the eldest son [Johnny] pointed to a chair which was standing next to the sofa. I looked at the chair and noticed that it was wobbling slightly from side to side. I then saw the chair slide across the floor towards the kitchen wall. It moved approximately three to four feet and then came to rest. At no time did it appear to leave the floor. I checked the chair but could find nothing to explain how it had moved. The lights were switched back on. Nothing else happened that night, although we have later reports of disturbances at this address."[2]

From that night on, the Hodgson family would have the attention of the police department. On the third night of the strange occurrences, Sergeant Brian Hyams and an unnamed officer heard loud thumping, even though apparently no one was in the home, and Peggy Hodgson remained in a hallway where she was in plain view of the officers. In a downstairs room, Hyams and the other officer reported that toys began flying about the house. "Lego bricks just started to levitate, or move about I should say, jump about like jumping beans," Hyams said. "There was a bird in a cage that started squawking. And suddenly, one or two

Lego bricks started to fly towards us." Hyams became afraid and he ran out of the house. "I'm no hero," he said. "I went straight out of the door and I think there was a rush between us who got out the swiftest."[3]

Some time later, he returned to the house along with reporter Douglas Bence and photographer Graham Morris of *The Daily Mirror*. Morris set up his expensive Nikon camera to try to record the events as the journalists talked with the officers, and was reportedly smacked in the face by a flying toy brick. When it was developed, the picture strangely showed nothing but a hole where the flying toy should have been, Morris said. And when picked up, the small plastic bricks felt hot, according to Morris and Bence.

As the days went by, weird occurrences continued in the Hodgson home, even after clergy and mediums were brought in. On September 4, 72-year-old Bob Richardson, Mrs. Nottingham's father, said he was in the kitchen of the Hodgson home when "two marbles passed me at terrific speed and hit the bathroom floor. When I picked them up, they were hot."[4]

Another newspaper, the *Daily Mail*, joined in the coverage. Meanwhile, the *Daily Mirror* sent senior reporter George Fallowes to investigate. He became so impressed that he suggested that the family contact the Society for Psychical Research (SPR), founded in 1882 by a group of Victorian enthusiasts who wanted to apply rigorous scientific method to the study of the supernatural. And so Maurice Grosse, an investigator with the SPR, arrived on the scene on September 5, one week after the events had begun. Grosse was a middle-aged business-man and inventor, who had just made a lot of money by designing a dispenser box for newspapers. Just two years earlier, Grosse had lost his own daughter, aged 22 and also named Janet, in an automobile ac-cident. With his glasses, shirt and tie, heavy moustache, and trustwor-thy appearance, Grosse looked every inch the investigator, perhaps like Sherlock Holmes.

On September 7, Fallowes heard knocking on a wall at the side of Janet's bed and he later reported that he did not consider it possible for Janet to be responsible. And there were reportedly more flying Lego bricks, one of which struck Bence.

In the wee hours of September 8, Grosse and three journalists from the *Daily Mirror*, Bence and photographers Graham Morris and David Thorpe, assembled on the upstairs landing, leading into three bedrooms. At about 1:15 a.m., they heard a crash in Janet's bedroom and rushed in to find her bedside chair had moved about four feet across the room and was lying on its side. Thorpe saw the chair topple. Janet, who was alone in the room, appeared to be fast asleep. A short time later, she awoke and started crying, before falling asleep once more. An hour later, Thorpe said he saw with his own eyes the chair move and fall to the floor on its side. The four men looked at Janet, who still appeared to be fast asleep. Fallowes said it was almost as though she was in a trance. Grosse lifted her eyelid to find the eyeball up in its socket.

All of this was beginning to impress Grosse as being a poltergeist event. He returned that night to hear that the Hodgsons had seen marbles flying through the air, and a sideboard drawer had opened by itself. Then, at about 10 o'clock, Grosse said he saw a marble fly past him out of nowhere. It seemed to move over the heads of the children, although the investigator believed that none of them had thrown it. A short time later, chimes hanging on a wall started swinging to and fro, even though no one was activating the front doorbell.

Later, Grosse was called to a bathroom, where he saw a door open and close on its own—not once, but three or four times. Grosse felt a cold draft, though no windows were open. Nearby in the kitchen, Grosse said he saw a T-shirt move off the top of a pile of clothes, down to the table, and finally to the floor. He said that no one could have touched the T-shirt without him seeing them do it. And there was more action soon after: three airborne marbles apparently just missed Janet. Grosse noticed something unusual about the marbles—rather than bounce a little or roll when they fell to the floor, they simply came to an immediate halt. There were also unexplained electrical disturbances and mechanical failures in the house.

Through all of this, the family seemed nervous and at times downright scared, but they were comforted by Grosse's presence. In all of his poltergeist cases, Grosse made himself available to counsel families "because there is a social-services side to our job," he told me. "Most poltergeist

169

cases are caused by high stress—marriage problems, drinking problems, and illness." Also, Mrs. Hodgson was able to keep relatively relaxed and focused by starting a logbook of the occurrences.

After a cardboard box *jumped* off a table as Janet walked past, Grosse came to the conclusion that the 11-year-old girl was the epicenter for all or most of the activity, and that she was not faking the incidents but rather was somehow causing them through highly unusual emotional or mental forces.

According to her mother, Janet had been acting strangely in the previous few weeks, perhaps partly because she was entering puberty. Otherwise, she seemed like many other girls her age, waiting to grow into her large teeth while wearing braces and a hair style like singer Olivia Newton-John, watching John Travolta movies and listening to the rock group Bay City Rollers.

To be safe, Grosse asked the investigators and journalists to carefully watch Janet. What they did notice was that, from time to time, there was tension among the family members, particularly between Peggy and her children. They put that down to the fact that she was a recently divorced single mother. Peggy sometimes became irritated with Janet, especially when objects started flying around the house. The girl thought her mother often blamed her for the occurrences. "Mum winds up shouting at me a bit," Janet said. "Cause it's happening around me. That's what I say—'It comes to me.' I've got a lot of energy, people say."[5]

On September 9, Mr. Richardson said he found a chair in Janet's bedroom precariously balanced on top of an open door. When he touched it gently, it fell off the door. He accused Janet of putting the chair up there, but she denied it. A few minutes later, Richardson said he saw a lid of a goldfish tank "jump off" and land four feet away while Janet was in another room.

On September 10, the case made the front page of the *Daily Mirror* with the headline, "The House of Strange Happenings." In the story, Fallowes wrote that, because of the emotional atmosphere at the house and in the neighborhood, "ranging from hysteria through terror to excitement and tension, it has been difficult to record satisfactory data. Nevertheless, I am satisfied the overall impression of our investigation is reasonably accurate. To the best of our ability, we have eliminated the possibility of total trickery."

More media became involved and the story was picked up by the London television show *Night Line*, which interviewed on the air Grosse, Peggy Hodgson, and a neighbor. Other media followed, including the BBC Radio 4 news show *The World This Weekend*. That show's reporter, Rosalind Morris, said that in the early hours of September 11, 1977, she saw Janet's chair fly across the room and her bed shake up and down on its own power.

On September 12, parapsychologist Guy Lyon Playfair joined the investigation after researching poltergeists in Brazil and writing two books about them. The first thing he noticed was that the house resembled a photographer's studio with cameras and tripods everywhere. Graham Morris showed him a bruise on his forehead where a piece of Lego had reportedly smacked him. Playfair established that in the previous 12 days and nights, at least 10 witnesses outside the family had seen phenomena, including police, Grosse, and journalists. "I wanted to convince myself beyond reasonable doubt," Playfair said.

For the next few evenings, Playfair, Graham, and others kept a vigil outside Janet's room, where marbles that fell off her bed seemed oddly to stick to the floor immediately, rather than rolling; the bed shook; drawers opened; and chairs fell over. When Playfair and Grosse tried to repeat the strange antics of the marble, they could not get it to stop dead. It always rolled when dropped.

On September 20, Playfair said that a book did some bizarre things in the air, flying off a mantelpiece through a door, and then slamming into a closed door of a front bedroom, although no one actually saw its entire flight. That same night, family members were near hysteria after a loud crash in Janet's bedroom. A heavy chest of drawers—too big for a child to maneuver—had tipped forward, falling onto an armchair with its drawers spilling out. "Oh my God, what strength it has!" Margaret shouted. "Whatever it is, it's bloody powerful!"[6]

"It's getting more powerful every day," Janet said. "I saw that. I was looking there. I saw it move, I saw it tilt over. I heard creaks on the floor."[7] When queried, Janet said she did not know what force was at work, only that she was not trying to hoodwink anyone.

The following night, Grosse was alone in the kitchen when a teapot next to the stove started to rock back and forth for about seven seconds, "doing a little dance right in front of my eyes." When he examined the pot, it was empty and quite cold. "There was just no way it could do that normally," he told me. Janet was nowhere near the kitchen at the time.

Also that night, Grosse and Playfair were looking for ways to document the goings-on, so they brought in the production manager and chief demonstrator of Pye Business Communications. PBC officials set up cameras in various locations, including Janet's bedroom, but soon discovered their equipment was malfunctioning for no apparent reason: The buttons on the video recorders would all come on at the same time, and the tape would not rewind. Some of their equipment inexplicably jammed, which cameraman Ron Denney said had never happened before.

It was the second time in a week that cameras had failed to operate in the Hodgson house. On September 13, photographer Graham Morris said that three of his expensive electronic flashguns developed faults simultaneously after being recharged in the Hodgson home. Reportedly, as soon as they were set up, they started to drain themselves of power. They had never given him trouble in the past and were considered foolproof, he said. As soon as he took them out of the house, they worked normally.

When Denney did get the video equipment working, there was no unusual activity for several days, which made Grosse and Playfair suspect two things: either Janet did not want to be caught cheating, or her poltergeist entity was mischievous and did not want to be discovered.

moving next door

The strange incidents were not confined to the Hodgson home. From time to time, the Hodgsons were too tense or frightened to stay in their house, so they went to neighbors'. Peggy Hodgson did just that after an incident on September 25, when she awoke at about 6:45 a.m. to what she said sounded like footsteps. A small chair by the bed jumped, Peggy said, then as she got out of bed, it jumped again. Five minutes later, a large chest of drawers inexplicably moved and fell onto its side, Peggy said. She believed that Janet, and no one else, had physically caused it to happened.

Peggy then decided to take Janet and two of her other children, Margaret and Billy, to visit her brother John Burcombe and his wife, Silvie, at neighboring 272 Green Street. That afternoon, John reported paranormal phenomena in his house. He said that while he was in an upstairs bedroom, an old television set, likely too heavy for a child to move, moved to an angle of 45 degrees, and two skirts placed upon a bed suddenly became crumpled. The only person in the room with Burcombe was his daughter Denise.

At one time, John Burcombe had been skeptical when his sister Peggy Hodgson had told him of the goings-on in her home. He believed things had moved because of vibrations, but he said he became a believer after he saw a number of incidents in his own home as well as his sister's home, including a drawer opening by itself, a lamp slowly sliding across a table and falling to the floor, and a strange light about 12 inches long suddenly appearing very intensely in the air, then fading away. Months later he would say he was petrified by the experience of seeing things move which he could not explain. His 16-year-old daughter, Brenda, also said she saw objects move in her bedroom.

Also on September 25 at the Burcombe home, John's wife, Sylvia, was making tea and chatting with several people, including her daughter, Denise, and her sister-in-law Dianne Hyde. As she was pouring water from the kettle, Sylvia said that a plastic rod, which had been part of a toy set, suddenly appeared in front of her face. She screamed and dropped the boiling kettle onto the floor. The piece of plastic, which was about six inches long, then jumped in front of her again, she said, and finally dropped onto the kitchen countertop. It had not been thrown by anyone, she insisted.

Janet's bedroom

Back in the Hodgson home throughout the next few months, crazy things were reported around Janet, such as bending and snapping of spoons and other small metal objects. And then things went one step further: Janet said that a curtain beside her twisted several times into a tight spiral and attempted to wrap itself around her neck. Her mother said she tended to believe her. Automatic cameras set up by investigators did catch some strange movements of curtains and bed sheets in Janet's bedroom in mid-December, 1977: Two cameras were set up in the bedroom, controlled by a button outside the room. Whenever investigators heard something, or suspected something was going in inside the room, they activated the cameras, which were set to flash at half-second intervals. Grosse said that the still cameras clicked on a sequence of events showing that bed covers moved up a wall with Janet and her sister Margaret apparently asleep. The windows were closed and there were no drafts in the room, Grosse said. In the final photo, the curtains had twisted and the bed clothes had also mysteriously twisted.

The cameras also snapped pictures of a pillow moving in a zigzag fashion. And then, incredibly, Janet claimed to have been levitated in her room. She said she was picked up and tossed about by an unseen entity, which was witnessed only by neighbors passing by and looking up through a window into the girl's bedroom, but their testimony was inconclusive and they could have seen the girl simply jumping. Janet claimed she had been moved many times by the unseen force, often being chucked off her bed. On one occasion, the same automatic cameras caught her airborne off her bed as her mother and Margaret watched in the bedroom. The set of pictures show her soaring like Peter Pan, with her body upright and both her legs tucked under her. She is high off the bed and about to land hard onto the floor. She either jumped off the bed or was tossed (critics say she could have jumped because she was a good athlete, although the bed was reportedly hard, with stiff springs—hardly a trampoline).

"A lot of children fantasize about flying, but it wasn't like that," Janet said in a 2007 interview for Channel 4 in England that Grosse provided to me. "When you're levitated with force and you don't know where you're going to land it's very frightening. I still don't know how it happened." Her mother told Grosse and Playfair that Janet did not jump off the bed. "Janet was lying in bed and I was talking to her... Janet was suddenly flying through the air," Mrs. Hodgson said. [8] The mother added that on several previous occasions, she had seen Janet come off the bed in a similar fashion.

Meanwhile, Grosse was becoming skeptical of some of Janet's claims, but he tended to believe that she had been levitated at least once. While reviewing the case years later, Grosse said that Janet's levitation was possible because in 1982, four years after the occurrences ended at the Hodgson home, Professor John Hasted, head of the physics department at Birbeck College in the University of London, put Janet through some tests to see if she had some paranormal ability. He had her sit on an electronic weighing machine. Over a 30-second period, her weight briefly dropped by nearly one kilogram (2.2 pounds), Hasted said. The professor could not explain this, unless Janet had some ability that allowed her either to levitate or to mentally affect the machine's recording mechanism.

Grosse and other investigators believed that some of the activity involving Janet occurred while she was in a trance. Some of the episodes turned violent as Janet became hysterical. "At one point, I thought she was actually going to kill herself," Grosse said. "She rushed up against a wall and smashed her head, cursing. How dreadful it was." At those times, doctors gave her 10-milligram injections of Valium to calm her.

The possibility that the occurrences had a spiritual cause was not overlooked—mediums Annie and George Shaw prayed for Janet and held a type of séance for her. Their visit was uneventful, although Annie believed that Janet was possessed by several spirits.

Although some people still suspected Janet as being a trickster, on October 15, Playfair said he witnessed the phenomena firsthand. He said he was getting off a chair in the Hodgson kitchen when a table suddenly turned upside-down with a thud. Janet was with him, he said, but she could not have caused the table to flip because he was watching her at the time and she was not within its reach. He seemed gleeful and exclaimed to Janet: "I saw you standing there the minute that thing went over. Well, you didn't do that one!"[8] Later, Playfair said that he and Grosse discovered the table was too wide and heavy for one person to flip over.

The following week, things got dangerous. An iron grille, which had been under a fireplace in the children's bedroom, somehow came flying across the room and landed on little Billy's pillow, narrowly missing him. Two days later, someone or something ripped a heavy iron frame weighing about 50 pounds out of the fireplace and severely bent it. "This was a major demolition job, for the thing was cemented into the brickwork," Playfair said to me.

outside influences

Meanwhile, Janet was having problems adjusting to her new school, which may have had some impact on the occurrences. The nightly events were affecting her schoolwork and she often fell asleep, exhausted, in class. Additionally, Janet claimed that some phenomena occurred at school, and that her chair jumped from time to time. Grosse said he and Playfair interviewed Janet's teachers, and they believed something paranormal was at work.

Other incidents were reported outside the Hodgson home. According to Playfair, there were many occurrences at local stores, on buses, and on the street. At an optician's store, a box of lenses allegedly began shaking as Janet went near it, and a door opened and closed on its own. At the supermarket, vegetables often rolled onto the floor, Playfair said. Grosse and Playfair did not document many of these cases because they said they did not want to draw too much outside attention to the Hodgsons, who had been given anonymous names in the *Daily Mirror* and on BBC TV. Their true identities as the poltergeist family were known only to their close family and neighbors.

However, some people did discover their real identities, and that caused problems. There were some threats from annoyed neighbors and a group of Jehovah's Witnesses, who warned the Hodgsons to be wary of devils and demons. At one point, according to Grosse, a letter was sent to the family, from some residents of nearby Beachcroft Way: "Get off this estate. We don't want to live with witches and devils like you. You made your flat [home] catch fire and when you let your cat and dogs out, you had better watch where they are. We smashed your car light in the other night. Next time we will smash you in."

Also in the fall of 1977, Janet and Margaret were sent for a rest to a council care home (a government-sponsored care home, operated by nuns). There, Margaret said, a wardrobe shook in their presence, a cupboard fell over, and bedclothes mysteriously moved on their beds. Janet told Grosse the events were starting to feel commonplace for her, yet she seemed confused about whether she was psychically causing them, or whether an entity was doing it in her presence or working through her. She did report, however, often getting a funny feeling in her tummy about the time the incidents were taking place.

Curiously, her mother said she was also feeling poltergeist symptoms. Just prior to some of the events, Peggy reported feeling an unusual type of pain in the front of her head. Right after the events, it would subside. During her youth, Peggy had had numerous bouts of epilepsy, although she had not suffered an attack in many years. (Some paranormal researchers report a high incidence of epilepsy among poltergeist agents.) However, few people ever suspected that Peggy was the poltergeist agent in this case. A social worker, who had known Peggy a long time, described her as being a down-to-earth woman, a respected member of the community and "not prone to hysteria." She added that the Hodgsons were a close family, and well-liked by family and friends.

On October 29, the emotionally and physically tired family left for a vacation at Clacton-on-Sea. Few incidents were reported around the family while they were away...

CHAPTER 17

The Voice

"If you show me a girl who can imitate that voice for
three hours I'll give you five hundred pounds."
Maurice Grosse

Either some children are as good as Cirque de Soleil performers, or
poltergeists really do exist—or both.

back home in enfield

The Hodgson family returned to their home in from their week's
holiday and were joined by Grosse and Playfair on November 5, 1977.

One night, as everyone was going to bed, knocking and rapping
that appeared to be coming from the second floor began in the house.
Grosse confirmed that the children were not responsible, because he
was watching them. It was hard to pinpoint where the banging was coming from—perhaps the skirting boards or in the walls—but it seemed to
have a rhythm or pattern to it: "Rat tat-a tat-tat...tat tat."

Grosse thought, if something was intelligently making these noises,
he would try to make contact with it. He did so while in the presence
of Playfair, Mrs. Hodgson, Janet, Margaret, and Billy, along with neighbors John Burcombe and Peggy Nottingham. Grosse asked the knocker
what five and five added up to. The reply was fast: 10 quick knocks.
Later, everyone in the room would attest to the fact that they heard the
answer, and no one admitted making the knocks. In fact, it seemed as
though everyone was watching everyone else.

178

Then Grosse developed a system for the knocker to answer: one knock for no and two for yes. But for the next while, he could get no replies to follow-up questions. "Are you playing games with me?" Grosse asked. The answer hit Grosse in the head: According to the other witnesses, a cardboard box containing small cushions jumped off the floor next to the fireplace, flew over a bed a total of about eight feet, and hit Grosse in the forehead.

"Oh crumbs!" Grosse laughed.[1]

The people in the room believed no one could have tossed the box; certainly not Janet, who was in her bed at the time.

the voice emerges

The strange movement of objects was soon to be replaced by another mystery. In December, the Enfield case took on its own voice—literally. Janet, who had turned 12 on November 10, started talking in the voice of a gruff, old man.

In early December, two psychologists from the Society for Psychical Research—Dr. John Beloff, head of the Edinburgh University psychology department; and Anita Gregory, of North London Polytechnic—came to the house. They heard strange barking noises and loud, piercing whistling, which seemed to come from Janet's direction, but they could not be directly traced to her. Janet denied making them.

Grosse believed that if Janet did indeed have a poltergeist entity or spirit, which was trying to communicate, it might be productive to try and get it to talk, as Professor John Hasted had suggested. Grosse started the bizarre proceedings in the upstairs bedroom, which Janet shared with her sister Margaret and her mother, Peggy. (Some of the conversations between Grosse and Janet/poltergeist are available on YouTube, titled "Enfield Poltergeist Real Voice Recordings (Bill).")

Much of Grosse's conversation with *the voice* happened while his back was turned to Janet or from behind a closed door, which made Grosse suspicious that Janet was faking the voice and did not want to be found out. By December, *the voice* was calling itself Bill, an old man who had died in the house. Bill said that Janet's bed sometimes shook or moved because he was sleeping in it, apparently as an entity. One night it reportedly told Janet to get out of the house.

Grosse began to believe that Janet was not playing tricks. "If you show me a girl who can imitate that voice for three hours I'll give you five hundred pounds," he told me.

On December 13, a new investigator entered the picture—Grosse's son Richard, who had started work with a law firm in London and had been skeptical of his father's assertions about a poltergeist. As Playfair noted, it became the first time that a poltergeist has ever been submitted to cross-examination by a lawyer. Bill told Richard that he had died on a chair after he went blind and had a hemorrhage. Richard later wrote of the incident that he believed *the voice* could not have been produced by an 11-year-old girl.

Maurice Grosse then brought in speech therapists, who came to the conclusion that the girl was not speaking with her normal voice, but rather through a second set of *false* vocal cords that everyone has, but few people ever use or even know exist. Actors are sometimes trained to use this second voice, though it can be painful for both sets of vocal cords. But Janet's normal voice did not seem to be affected or weakened, despite the fact that she often talked for hours in the gruff voice.

Janet's *second* voice was recorded and run through a larynograph, a machine that registers patterns produced by frequency waves as they move through the larynx, designed by Professor A.J. Fourcin of University College in London. The tests were carried out by Professor Hasted, who said that false vocal cords are a type of auxiliary cord that protect the trachea from damage. The speech carried out through these rare vocal cords is called *plica ventricularis*. When someone uses them, he or she gets a sore throat within two minutes, because there is not enough liquid to lubricate these auxiliary cords and they become inflamed.

Hasted showed Playfair and Grosse the wave forms of Janet's normal voice and her other voice, and they were completely different.

During questioning from Grosse, Playfair, and Richard Robertson of Birbeck College on December 15, 1977, Bill went into great detail about girls' menstruation. He seemed to know this was the first day that

Janet had a period. Playfair believed that one of the possible sources of poltergeist energy may be from a youth's pineal gland, which is located in the center of the brain and controls the release of sexual hormones. "When a child suddenly acquires this new force, there is a need for an outlet," he told me. Playfair added that if there is no outlet, the energy could result in poltergeist activity.

Discounting the mysterious voices, the Hodgson home was looking like any other in London at Christmastime, with bright lights and colored streamers and gifts under the tree, including a box of chocolates for Bill. *The voice* was still a part of the nightly ritual, but it was becoming more relaxed and allowing Grosse, Playfair, and others to be in the room when it spoke—sometimes for up to three hours. They observed that Janet's mouth seemed to be moving, but not in the way of normal speech patterns.

Meanwhile, physical incidents continued, several in which Janet wound up with materials around her throat, including a curtain that tightened like a noose in front of several witnesses. On other occasions, the investigators had caught, with their automatic cameras, bed sheets doing strange things in Janet's bedroom, like billowing about on their own, despite the fact it was winter and the windows were shut tight.

On New Year's Eve, Peggy Hodgson reported a cupboard jumping to and fro for about 10 minutes, and a small Christmas tree lifting up off a table and moving across the living room. Then *the voice* spoke through Janet's 13-year-old sister Margaret. It didn't say much, but it was clearly similar to the old man's voice that had been coming out of Janet, albeit somewhat more fluent and communicative. Could the poltergeist, if there was one, also involve Margaret? Could it be a discrete entity that attached itself to more than one person, or did Margaret have the same unique abilities and stresses of her younger sister? Or was the whole thing a fraud? The investigators now revisited Margaret's history in this case: She had been in the room, or nearby, during many of the occurrences of objects moving or Janet talking with *the voice*. On one occasion, Margaret reported that her own bed had shaken up and down a number of times.

the newspapers cry fraud

Early in 1978, the *Daily Mirror* returned with a team of journalists to do a feature article. They brought along a ventriloquist, Ray Alan, to check out Janet's mysterious voice, and he became skeptical, telling the newspaper, "These little girls obviously loved all the attention they got when objects were mysteriously moved round the house, and they decided to keep the whole thing going by inventing the voice."

Anita Gregory of the Society for Psychical Research, who had spent a short time at the Hodgson home, said the mysterious men's voices were simply the result of Janet and Margaret putting bed sheets to their mouths. In addition, Gregory said that a videocamera had caught Janet attempting to bend spoons and an iron bar by force and *practicing* levitation by bouncing up and down on her bed. When faced with this evidence, Janet admitted to faking some instances, but not all of them, Grosse said, because she wanted to see if the investigators would catch her. "They usually did," he told me.

If indeed Janet had faked some or all of the occurrences, it may have been related to what I refer to throughout this book as the "When the Circus Comes to Town Syndrome," in which it may be possible that a case has some genuine paranormal activity, but it turns to trickery on the part of one or more of the people involved, usually a youth. The theory is that a child may bask in the attention afforded to him or her by investigators or the media and may start throwing things around (or in this case putting on a pretend voice) to keep the case going.

By now, the Enfield case had become known across Britain and was catching on abroad as even the *National Enquirer*, America's sensational tabloid, arrived on the scene. Another newspaper, the *Daily Express*, had run its own story accompanied with a photograph of actress Linda Blair from the popular movie *The Exorcist*. Some people noted the resemblance between Blair and Janet Hodgson. And *The News of the World* had a large story about the case with the headline, "Ghost Hunters Clash Over Mystery of Spook or Spoof Kids."

But Grosse and Playfair believed that most of the incidents had not been trickery, noting that, early in the case, police did not believe that Janet, Margaret, or anyone else had been cheating.

Peggy Nottingham said that one mainstream media publication had offered her 1,000 pounds (around $1,600) to say that what happened in the Hodgson home had been faked. She said she refused the offer.

However, Playfair said that Janet and Margaret likely *did* play a few tricks during the case, but none of them involved the major events of moving objects or *the voice*. "All children play tricks in their own house—what do you expect children to do? But you can't fake the real thing," Playfair said to me in 2005. "I am sick of answering questions about their cheating. This case was legitimate."

After *the voice* controversy died down, the case got back to "normal," as the physical movements and knockings continued. On May 30, 1978, the Hodgson children had a spat with children of a nearby home across the garden wall. Showers of stones, milk bottles, and bricks were thrown by children or by unseen forces. Gardens of at least five homes were damaged, and yet none of the neighbors reported seeing anyone throw anything. The incidents reportedly continued even after Peggy Hodgson had brought Janet and her other children inside their home. The children denied throwing anything. Bob Richardson, the brother of Peggy Nottingham, said a clod of earth had moved through the air in a mysterious fashion, and he saw no one throw it.

Meeting of the Unusual

It was the most unusual meeting—two people who had both been so-called poltergeist entities. On December 17, 1977, Matthew Manning visited Janet Hodgson in Janet's home at the request of investigators. By this time, Manning was a famous psychic, who helped people deal with their paranormal abilities and experiences. But when he had been a boy, Matthew had allegedly caused things to move in his home and at his school.

With Janet, Manning shared his feelings and got *the voice* to talk, although it did not make much sense and answered "dunno" to many of his questions. He said that during his poltergeist case as a boy, he got headaches similar to those that Janet was having. He tried to convince Janet to develop what he termed "psychic abilities," as he said he had done himself since becoming an adult. During his eight-hour stay in the house, there were several loud crashes, but no paranormal events were witnessed.[2]

aftermath

Janet spent three months in the hospital, from June to September 1978. Doctors found her to be normal physically with no indication of epilepsy, which her mother had suffered from as a young woman. Upon her return, Janet looked well and more mature. Few incidents were reported after that, but the case continued to receive much publicity. In 1984, Playfair published a book on the case titled *This House Is Haunted*, and the case was one of several used for a 1998 British film called *Urban Ghost Story*. According to Playfair, another film company was interested, but was turned off by a Christian fundamentalist group, which convinced the filmmakers that the Enfield case was the work of the devil. He also believes that the 1982 movie *Poltergeist*, directed by Steven Speilberg, was partly based on the Hodgson case in Enfield, although he cannot prove it.

Not everyone was prepared to accept that a poltergeist had been at work: Dono Gmelig-Meyling, a Dutch psychic, had a theory that Maurice Grosse's stake in the case was related to the death of his own daughter, also named Janet, two years before he started the Enfield investigation. The psychic believed that Grosse's daughter's spirit drew him to the case in order for him to be distracted from his grief.

In 2007, Janet admitted that she and her sister Margaret had faked a few of the occurrences to keep the attention and the action going when nothing was happening—such as balancing the chair on top of the door—but that 99 percent of them were real and caused by a force she could not explain. "I know from my own experience that it was real," Janet said. "I felt used by a force that nobody understands...the poltergeist lived off me, off my energy. Call me mad or a prankster if you like. Those events *did* happen. The poltergeist was with me—and I feel in a sense that he always will be."[3]

Grosse remained steadfast that the case had strong paranormal elements. "I'm 100 percent—no, 150 percent—satisfied that this case was genuine poltergeist activity," he told me in 2005, one year before he died.

It was the sheer volume of events that most impressed Grosse: In a span of not more than a few months, his investigators counted more than 1,500 unexplained incidents, he said. Grosse noted that there were many "reliable, independent witnesses, who have given great weight to our evidence." He said that at least 30 people had seen phenomena, including police, journalists, tradesmen, council workers, and the Hodgsons, Nottinghams, and Burcombes—"three perfectly ordinary families who would satisfy any jury that they were telling the truth." Playfair believes the Hodgson case was very complex, perhaps involving a spirit of a dead person *as well* as Janet's unconscious paranormal ability.

As for Janet Hodgson, she apparently went on to live an ordinary life, Grosse said. She married and had four children, one of whom died young. She lives in central England with her husband, who works in child care. Her brother, Johnny, died of a brain tumor at age 14, not long after the disturbances at Enfield ended. "I don't think the family was ever told by doctors how serious Johnny's illness was," Playfair said to me. "That family has had more disasters than any family I can think of." Janet's sister, Margaret, also married. Their mother, Peggy, died in 2002.

Chapter 18

A Little Irish Gal and Wee Hughie

"It is...beyond all possibility that five responsible persons should be so deceived at various occasions over a period of two weeks."

Dr. A.R G. Owen, fellow at Trinity College

Virginia Campbell was a pretty 11-year-old Irish girl with blond hair and beautiful blue eyes. By all accounts, she wore her beauty quietly and was a shy lass. Virginia was raised by her parents (unnamed in any of the documentation) on a farm in the hamlet of Moville in County Donegal, Ireland. She was said to lead a lonely life in the country, and two of her very favorite companions were her dog, Toby, and another little girl, Anna. In 1960, Virginia's father sold their farm, and she moved to Scotland with her mother to live with Virginia's married older brother, Thomas Campbell, a miner, in a council house at 19 Park Crescent in the small village of Sauchie in the central part of the rugged country.

Also living in the house were Thomas's wife and their two children. Virginia apparently did not like her setup for sleeping—she had to share a room with her 9-year-old niece, Margaret. It was not ideal for Margaret, either, who had to give up her privacy as well.

In mid-October 1960, Virginia began attending Craigbank Primary School in Sauchie, where she made friends and seemed normal. According to her teacher, Miss Margaret Stewart, Virginia was placid, with above-average intelligence and a very honest disposition. The first sign of something amiss came on the evening of November 22, when people in the Campbell house heard a mysterious *thunking* noise, similar

186

to the sound of a bouncing ball, in Virginia's bedroom, on the stairs, and in the living room. It was probably just the little girl, fond of games, the family thought. But it seemed no game at tea time the next day, when Thomas and his wife said they saw something that had never occurred in their house, nor perhaps any other in all of Clackmannanshire County: A heavy sideboard moved boldly out from a wall approximately five inches, then returned to its original position, without anyone's assistance. Virginia had been sitting in the living room, near the sideboard, but she did not touch it, the Campbells reported.

Later that night, while Virginia was lying awake in her double bed, along with her niece Margaret, loud knocks were heard coming from their bedroom. The puzzled and frightened family didn't know what to do, but a neighbor called in Reverend T.W. Lund of the Church of Scotland. The minister investigated and believed that the noises were coming from the headboard. He moved Virginia down in the bed, where she was sleeping alone, so that she was not near the headboard, but the loud knocks continued.

That same evening, Reverend Lund said he saw the impossible: A large linen chest, located near the bed, rocked sideways, raised itself off the floor, and traveled in a jerking motion parallel to the bed for a distance of about 18 inches. And then the full chest (27 inches by 17 by 14, weighing 50 pounds) reportedly moved itself back from whence it had come. The stunned minister and an unidentified neighbor lifted the chest, their fingers shaking a little, out onto the landing. When they suggested that Margaret join Virginia in the double bed, an even louder knocking reportedly came from the headboard. The minister and the neighbor said no one—certainly not the two girls—had caused the noise.

The following evening, Rev. Lund came back to the home and was told by family members that there had been a new type of occurrence—a strange movement of Virginia's pillow, which had reportedly rotated beneath her head at about 60 degrees. The family's physician, Dr. W.H. Nisbet, also came to the home, along with an additional minister and another doctor, both of whom asked to remain unnamed. Rev. Lund and Dr. Nisbet said they saw a curious rippling movement on Virginia's pillow, but they could not explain it and did not believe that Virginia had caused it. That same evening, Rev. Lund said he heard more rapping noises and more rockings of the linen chest.

Another witness to some of the events was Malcolm Robinson, an investigator for Strange Phenomena Investigations and its magazine, *Enigma*. He reported: "I was in Virginia's bedroom with a number of other individuals. I was standing close to the bed in which Virginia was lying; she had the covers up to her chin...seconds later, I observed the pillow next to Virginia, which had been plumped up, suddenly take what appeared to be the shape of a person's head. A clear indentation of the pillow was seen by myself and others in the room. Now during this time, strange knockings, bangings, and scratching, and what sounded like sawing noises were coming from all over the room."[1]

Another witness to the pillow incident, a close friend of the family who wished to remain anonymous, described what he saw: "I was standing close to the bed and Virginia had the bedclothes pulled up to her chin. Suddenly I observed the covers making a rippling motion from the bottom of the bed right up to her chin. I am convinced that Virginia did not do this by herself." The man said he then saw the pillow next to the girl take the impression of a person's head. "Others and myself saw a clear indentation in the pillow." He also reported strange knockings, scratching, and what sounded like sawing noises. "Virginia was very upset during all this and we could not settle her."[2]

Rev. Lund and several other ministers believed that something paranormal, if not spiritual, was happening. "People scoff about stories of ghosts and spooks, but they have not studied the subject," said Rev. Thomas Jeffrey of the Church of Scotland. "In the case of this little girl, we have examples of well-known phenomena."[3]

Apparently no exorcism was attempted, and little discussion was given to the possibility that the girl had been possessed by a spirit or demon. Although the case received national publicity, the Church of Scotland did not take an official stance or even offer much comment. However, on one evening, a prayer service was held in the Campbell home. While several members of the clergy recited The Lord's Prayer, the banging and loud noises reportedly became even louder than before, and this while Virginia was being closely watched. No one else in the home was suspected.

incidents at school

The strange incidents were having a terrifying effect on family life at 19 Park Crescent, and on November 23 and 24, Virginia was kept home from school. When she returned, her teacher, Miss Stewart, became a witness to something she later called "unnerving." Miss Stewart was fond of Virginia. She thought her student was good academically, shy and withdrawn, but pleasant, and certainly didn't seem abnormal. However, during a session of silent reading and essay writing, Miss Stewart said she observed Virginia trying to hold down her desk lid, which several times raised itself to an angle of 45 to 50 degrees. The teacher said she could plainly see Virginia's hands flat on the lid of the desk, and her legs were underneath the desk.

A short time later, when another student got up to bring a notebook to the teacher, Miss Stewart said that the unnamed student's unoccupied desk, behind Virginia, slowly rose off the floor, perhaps an inch or two, and then settled down again, coming to rest a slight distance from where it had begun. Still suspicious, Miss Stewart immediately went to the desk to check it for strings or wires, but there were none.

That night, Dr. Nisbet stayed with Virginia. While the girl was lying motionless on the bed without bedclothes over her, the physician said he heard unexplained knocks in the room. Also, the linen chest started moving again—about a foot. He moved the chest away from the bed and suddenly its lid opened and shut several times in succession. The surprised physician said he also saw horizontal rotations of up to 90 degrees of the pillow under Virginia's head and curious ripplings passing across the bedclothes. On November 26, Dr. Nisbet's medical partner, Dr. William Logan, went to the bedroom. He said he saw a puckering of the bedcover and pillow rotations similar to those reported by Dr. Nisbet. On the following day, Dr. Logan was back with Virginia. This time he brought along his pet dog. She liked it, saying it reminded her of her beloved dog Toby back in Ireland. Later, Virginia seemed to go into a trance and called out for Toby. At about 11:30 p.m., Rev. Lund arrived, and then the girl cried out loudly, striking the air with her fists. When they left the room, she fell into a quiet sleep.

Dr. Nisbet told the *Alloa Advertiser* in December 1960: "Virginia is not responsible for what has happened. The child is innocent. The child herself did not conjure up what has taken place—an outside agent is responsible. The girl was hysterical all the time the phenomena were appearing. We decided to try sedation; Virginia was given mild tranquilizers to quiet her. If the phenomena were being conjured by her own imagination, they would no longer appear if her brain were dulled. Even though her brain was not working normally, the phenomena still appeared."

It was back to Craigbank Primary School on November 28 for Virginia—and more events. While Virginia stood, hands clasped behind her back, next to Miss Stewart's large oak table, the teacher said she saw a blackboard pointer lying on a table suddenly start to vibrate and move across the table until it fell to the floor. While the pointer was moving, Miss Stewart put her hand on the heavy table and discovered the table was vibrating. Then the whole table reportedly started to swing away from the teacher in a counter-clockwise motion. Virginia started to cry and said she was not causing the disturbance, and the teacher believed her.

the poltergeist gets a name

Also on November 28, Virginia was driven by a relative to the village of Dollar, several miles away. Dr. Nisbet visited her there at a home and again said he heard knockings, louder than they had been in Sauchie. The following day, there were more occurrences at Dollar— Dr. Logan and his wife heard several bursts of knocks, which seemed to be coming from near Virginia. Mrs. Logan, who had previously been skeptical, believed that Virginia was not causing the noises, at least not in a normal physical sense.

That night Virginia reportedly went into a 10-minute trance, talking loudly in a strange voice and calling out for her dog Toby and her friend back in Ireland, Anna. She tossed around on the bed and answered questions while apparently still in the trance. Her replies to questions seemed to indicate a lack of normal inhibition, as if repressed thoughts were emerging.

No incidents were reported on the following day, when Virginia returned to the Campbell residence in Sauchie. But by now, the so-called poltergeist had become such a fixture, it had won a nickname to some people in the house: Wee Hughie. It was a sign that Virginia and her niece, Margaret, and others were trying to put a smile on the proceedings, and that the occurrences were not violent or even threatening in nature. Wee Hughie was more or a prankster than a mugger, the family believed.

At about this time, the *Alloa Journal* reported that peculiar things began to happen to Virginia, such as heavy pieces of furniture moving when she entered a room, and doors opening when she approached them. Then the national media got involved in the story and the Campbells became prisoners in their own home, shying away from publicity. Frustrated journalists were reduced to interviewing the Campbells' friends and neighbors.

On the evening of December 1, Dr. Nisbet and Dr. Logan came to 19 Park Crescent with a tape recorder and a movie camera, and captured number of loud knockings and sawing noises on the tape recorder. After that, the bizarre occurrences seemed to dissipate. There were a few minor unexplained happenings, such as when Virginia and her niece Margaret reported that they were pinched several times. One of the final incidents was on January 23, 1961, at school. Miss Stewart said that Virginia put a bowl of flower bulbs, which Virginia had attended to over the Christmas holidays, on her table, and they moved unaided across the top of the table.

At about this time, Miss Stewart noted that it seemed the disturbances in Virginia's life seemed to peak in 28-day cycles; the bowl incident occurred 56 days after one of the major incidents at the school. The disturbances, the teacher said, started off fairly violently, then leveled off and disappeared, and then came back again.

Dr. Owen interviewed many witnesses and went further in the cycle theory, positing that it could have had something to do with Virginia's menstrual cycle. The 28-day cycle, Owen said, "is a very suggestive figure, if the phenomena are related to physiological happenings associated with a quasi-menstrual cycle occurring as a result of exceptionally rapid pubescence."[4]

In the end, teachers and students seemed glad the events were waning because journalists had been hounding them for interviews. At one point, headmaster Peter Hill had the school gates locked to keep reporters at bay. In his investigation and interviews of witnesses, Dr. Owen reported other phenomena alleged to have occurred but not always corroborated: levitation of an apple from a fruit bowl, and the moving of a shaving brush, a small vase, and a china dog. In bed, the two girls were said to have had their legs pinched or poked, and their pajamas pulled off or rolled up their bodies.

Eventually, the disturbances ended altogether, and Wee Hughie seemed to die a natural death. Virginia was finally reunited with her dog, Toby, and her Irish eyes were smiling again.

In his 1964 book *Can We Explain the Poltergeist?*, Dr. Owen concluded that there were too many reliable witnesses to dismiss this case as fraud or accident. "The five main witnesses believed themselves to have heard certain sounds and seen certain movements of objects," he wrote. "It is just possible in principle to suppose that one person could be the victim of illusion or hallucination. It is, however, beyond all possibility that five responsible persons should be so deceived at various occasions over a period of two weeks. Thus we must conclude that they heard actual noises and saw actual motions of real objects."

At no time was Virginia, or anyone else in the Campbell home, caught cheating.

the theories

If these occurrences in Scotland were indeed paranormal, what could possibly have caused them? According to Dr. Owen, during the time of the disturbances, Virginia was going through rapid physical development and maturation, although puberty in the full sense had not arrived. Dr. Owen added that Virginia was probably upset during the poltergeist activity, but there was no evidence that she was mentally ill.

Dr. Logan and others suspected that having to leave her dog and best friend in Ireland were partly responsible for stress in Virginia's life.

Virginia could have caused the events subconsciously through a type of PK or RSPK, several observers noted. At one point, Dr. Logan made a curious finding when he checked Virginia while she was in an agitated state, physically and emotionally. Despite the agitation, her pulse rate remained normal and quite slow, which caused investigators to suspect the subconscious part of her brain was aware of the phenomena, but another part of her brain was producing a fight-or-flight response.

At the same time as the incidents in the Thomas Campbell house, there were minor earth tremors in the vicinity of Sauchie, but they were probably not strong enough to cause the incidents. Still, some people felt that strong magnetic fields created by these seismic disturbances could have had some effect.

Not many details are known of Virginia's life after Wee Hughie, although we know she got married and apparently went to live in Sheffield, England. She remained mum about the case and refused to discuss what happened in 1960–61 in Scotland.

CHAPTER 19

From the UK to the U.S. and Beyond

"I was amazed at the destruction of such a solidly built
piece of furniture. It would have taken two strong men
to lift it upside down and a large axe to dismember what
happened to it, all in the course of about 30 seconds."

Thomas Barrow, on what he believed was destruction caused by a poltergeist

a lively case in runcorn

There are a number of ways to expose a teenager you suspect of faking a poltergeist case: You can put a video camera on him 24 hours a day, truss him up with packing tape, or sit on him. Friends of John Glynn Jones chose the latter test to eliminate the possibility that he was using tricks to scare them in 1952 in the town of Runcorn, England. Four of them sat on top of him on a bed, and yet they said drawers in a dressing table continued to rattle under their own power.

This lively case began in mid-August, 1952, in Runcorn, located on the Manchester ship canal on the Mersey River in northwest England, a town known for its shipbuilding, production of chemicals, and an old castle. The occurrences were almost exclusively confined to a small house at 1 Byron Street, where John lived with his sister, Eileen Glynn; their grandfather, Sam Jones, a 68-year-old widower; Sam's sister-in-law, Lucy Jones; and another unidentified woman in her mid-50s, a spinster who was lodging at the home.

The story revolves around 17-year-old John, an apprentice drafts-man at the Imperial Chemical Industries, West Point Power Station. By all accounts, John was a well-behaved, slightly built youth with a quiet disposition. He was serious about studying to become a full-fledged draftsman and there was nothing to suggest he was about to be the focus of an alleged paranormal event.

The first disturbances began when the family received a visit for a week from Lucy Jones's son and his wife, who lived in North Wales. That made the house crowded and John had to share a double bed with his grandfather, Sam. Lucy and John's sister, Eileen, had to share another bed in the same room. When they had all climbed into bed and were trying to fall asleep, a dressing table in the room reportedly started to make noises. The mysterious sounds gradually grew louder, and the frightened occupants eventually left the bedroom. When they returned a short time later, the noises started up again. The family checked the dressing table but could find no reason for the occurrence.

The following night, the situation repeated itself with one new wrinkle—the dressing table was said to move about a foot away from the wall under its own power. By this time, John had become Suspect Number One, and other family members grilled him and checked him for strings or magic contrivances, but found none. To remove any doubt, four of John's relatives and friends sat on top of him as he lay on the bed, but the noises and rattlings of the dressing table continued despite his physical helplessness. Sam Jones had lived in the house for 35 years without any such problems; the old dressing table had remained quiet. When sitting atop John did not work, the family sealed the drawers of the dressing table with adhesive tape, but it reportedly continued to rattle and its mirror swung back and forth on its pivots.

Police officers could not solve the riddle. They set a trap for John, but they could not prove he had faked the occurrences. In fact, the police became victims of what they believed was an unseen force. According to the *Runcorn Guardian* newspaper, three burly officers were thrown off an empty chest in the hallway of the house, and soon realized they could not control the situation.

On one evening, it was estimated that a total of 14 people saw what they believed to be the paranormal movement of furniture and the smashing of china. A woman visiting from Sutton said that her husband's spectacle case was tossed across a room. As noises and furniture movements continued for 10 weeks, the *Guardian* closely followed the case and it eventually made it onto the wire services around the world. Sympathetic people wrote letters with offers of advice to get rid of what they thought was a poltergeist or demonic possession. Many of the writers recommended exorcism, and other well-wishers, along with curiosity-seekers, showed up at the Jones's house.

When nothing seemed to be working, the family called in a Spiritualist medium for a séance, but that only seemed to provoke more problems, as many objects starting flying about the bedroom, according to several witnesses: a picture book, a tin of ointment, a table cover, and two bibles.

Then, a member of the Society for Psychical Research in London, Reverend W.H. Stevens, a Methodist minister, was summoned. He came to the conclusion that the issue revolving around John Jones was not so much spiritual or demonic, but one of RSPK, believing that John suffered from a buildup of repressed energy, which manifested itself in an astonishing way. When it did, there was reduction of energy and a recuperation period before the disturbances started up again, Rev. Stevens said. The minister said there was no way that John was at the center of a hoax.

At one point, Rev. Stevens was hit on the head by a flying dictionary. On another occasion, another visitor, Mrs. E. Dowd, claimed she was hit in the face by a flying book. As the case dragged into the fall of 1952, it became more complex, and some occurrences raised suspicion that it had deteriorated into trickery: John Glynn and several friends, including a family friend, Thomas Barrow, spent four nights in John's home, and most of the time, the goings-on occurred only after the lights were turned out, which raised suspicions of tomfoolery. As soon as the light was turned off, Barrow said he was hit between the eyes by a book. Another night, two police officers sat on the single bed. As soon as the light was turned off, an old chest in the room lifted a few feet in the air and dropped to the floor, Barrow said. A short time later, when the lights were off again, the single bed on which the police officers were sitting lifted several feet off the floor—with the officers still on it—and crashed to the floor. "It lifted a couple of feet in the air and then dropped them down, after which they promptly departed," said Barrow, who was 18 at the time and on leave from the British Army. The officers did not charge anyone with a crime, he told me. "Whenever we'd shut the light off, the thing would go berserk," he added. "It upturned a huge, old-fashioned chest and it got ripped into small pieces. I was amazed at the destruction of such a solidly built piece of furniture. It would have taken two strong men to lift it upside down and a large axe to dismember what happened to it, all in the course of about 30 seconds...I got smacked on the arm and leg by flying pieces and I received a piece of timber in the middle of the back, which almost knocked me down the stairs, much to the two Johns' delight...it was amazing no one broke an arm or leg."

At no time did he see anyone throw anything, Barrow said, but he was surprised that John Glynn and John Berry seemed to treat the incidents in a light-hearted way, at least near the end of the case. Barrow said he couldn't believe that Glynn would deliberately damage his grandfather's home.

In an editorial, the *Guardian* said it believed the incidents were paranormal and not the result of fraud because so, many people—including its own reporter, two researchers, three ministers, and two police officers—witnessed the events.

Over 10 weeks, damage was estimated at about 20,000 pounds (more than $32,000) with all the broken items and a crack in the kitchen ceiling. In the 2003 book *Real Ghosts, Restless Spirits and Haunted Places* by Brad Steiger, there is a photograph of John Glynn Jones surveying some of the damage (on page 75) in his grandfather's house. It shows a rather bewildered-looking John, small-shouldered and clean cut, wearing a cardigan and tie, looking at the complete destruction of his bedroom, with mattress springs and pillow fluff everywhere and broken furniture flung upside-down. The story made the prestigious *Life* magazine on December 8, 1952, nearly two months after the occurrences had subsided.

"In the end, there was no satisfactory explanation as to the cause of all the trouble," said Mark Bevan, editor of the *Cheshire Magazine*, which has published stories about the case. "The SPR investigator, a local spiritualist organization and several independent psychic detectives could not agree on the origin of the phenomena, or on what an ordinary, quiet living family could have done to invite the attentions of some evil force to wreak its vengeance on their household and disturb their lives this way."[1]

After the disturbances at 1 Byron Street, John Glynn Jones reportedly settled into a normal life in northwest England, married, and had two children. He died in 1994.

all over england

The following list is just a sampling of some other cases reported in England throughout the years...

- A poltergeist case was reported in 1666 in Wiltshire, England, and recorded by Reverend Joseph Glanvill, who lived in a house at the present site of the Zouch Manor. He reported that two girls occupied a bedroom from which they said they heard strange drumming noises and saw levitations and flying objects. The girls became suspects, but were cleared by the minister, who could find no evidence of trickery.

- An 11-year-old boy, Gordon Parker, was said to be hospitalized from a nervous breakdown after he was suspected of being a poltergeist agent in a home in London in 1921. Police, ministers, a physician, and a journalist reported that coal buckets, irons, and burning coal danced in the presence of the boy.

- It's nice to have a normal poltergeist for a change. That's how Professor S. Ward of Wokingham described disturbances in 1926 in a thatched cottage in Finchampstead, England, occupied by a wheelwright/carpenter, George Goswell, and his two daughters, 14 and 16. For 15 years, things had been quiet, then a small bath reportedly overturned, chairs did somersaults, and pictures fell from walls, all in the daytime. Wokingham called it a mild case, sparked by the unconscious influence of one of the teenagers. However, he said the force was one unknown to science.

- A 7-year-old boy was said to unconsciously cause loud knocking nightly in a London home in 2000. Researchers Maurice Grosse and Mary Rose Barrington were confident the boy was not cheating. Some of the psychic tension building around the boy had to do with his mother's divorce and her alcoholism, Grosse said. The knockings lasted about three months. Grosse and Barrington counseled the family and, after the activity subsided, he received a telephone call from the estranged father, thanking him. The names were not released because the family was concerned about others finding out about their problems.

◉ A 34-year-old woman said she was driven out of her house on Mount Pleasant Road in Carlisle, England, in 2004. Carol Tuttle and her 9-year-old daughter went to stay with Carol's mother. "I won't live there again," Carol said. Her neighbor, Kevin Blythe, 37, was skeptical until he went into her house to get her cats out. "Two glasses flew right in front of me and smashed against the wall," he said. "There was a pepper pot flying in one direction and a wire basket flying in the other direction. "It was really powerful. You couldn't have caught it." Another neighbor said a perfume bottle flew towards her and a light bulb from a lamp shot into the ceiling. Tuttle had the house blessed by a priest, but she would not return.[3]

◉ In the English coastal town of South Shields in 2005-2006, chairs, beds, and drawers mysteriously moved in the home of a young couple, Marc and Marianne, and their 3-year-old son. Paranormal investigators Mike Hallowell and Darren Ritson say they witnessed disturbances, and photographed and filmed many of them, including a plastic water bottle that one of them saw—and photographed—balancing diagonally on the table, a quite unnatural position. The investigators, who wrote a book called *The South Shields Poltergeist: One Family's Fight Against an Invisible Intruder*, believe the poltergeist was an evil entity.

◉ China and tablecloths were reportedly moving on their own and telephones were ringing with no one at the other end in the George and Dragon Inn, near Canterbury, England, in 2006, psychic investigators said.

◉ A Horsham, England, teenager suspected that an evil force followed him home from a camping trip in 2008 and wreaked havoc in his home, causing doors to open and close on their own. The Sussex Paranormal Research Group investigated without finding anything. The teen's mother, a care worker, said she tended to be skeptical about such things, but that there was just no explanation for it.

Poltergeists in other parts of the uk and the world

- The widow Murphy and her family lived in a mountain cottage in 1913 near Brookborough, County Fermanagh, Ireland, where they were said to be plagued by flying pots and pans and clothes rising off a bed. A member of parliament, Cahir Healy, and a minister reportedly saw some of the events. The family had to leave, partly after being ostracized by superstitious neighbors. It was said that the poltergeist activity followed them for a boat ride to the United States. Some people refer to this case as the Coonian Ghost.

- An Irish family said they were forced from their home by a poltergeist or ghost. In 1997, Jackie Fahy and his wife, Esther, their two grown children, Michael and Martha, and their infant granddaughter, Sarah, lived in a home in Corrib Park, Galway. They complained of pictures flying off the mantelpiece, a baby's toys being tossed around, a toilet flushing on its own, a coffee table flipping over, and a porcelain dog exploding. One witness was Father Conan Garvey, a philosophy lecturer at University College in Galway, who said the incidents seemed genuine. The family believed a ghost was at work and they summoned a psychic, Sandra Ramdhanie, who performed a ritual with herbs and salts.

- At Hopfgarten, Austria, in 1921, Minna Sauerbrey was dying of cancer and was said to be so weak she could not move. However, there were strange knockings in her presence and movement of objects beyond her reach. Police reportedly saw a wash basin move under its own power. According to officers, her stepson, Otto, was a hypnotist, who had put Minna into a trance to help her deal with her pain. When she died, he was charged with shortening her life through hypnosis, but he was acquitted. And the strange occurrences died with her.

- A 13-year-old son of the mayor of Neudorf, Germany, was suspected as the poltergeist agent in his father's home in 1952. Parapsychologist Hans Bender said the boy was conflicted and confused, and highly charged with feelings of anger, anxiety, and fear. For a teenager, it's bad enough calling your father *Sir*, nevermind *Your Honor*.

- Think twice before inviting a poltergeist family over for a visit. In the summer of 1972 in Sorocaba, west of Sao Paulo City, Brazil, neighbors invited the Fernando Riberio family and their six children into their home because the family was allegedly suffering from strange noises and moving objects in their own house. But, according to the Brazilian Institute for Psycho-Biophysical Research, the occurrences followed them and the neighbors quickly became irritated as their house was ransacked. One of the neighbors said it looked as if a tractor had driven through the house. The Riberio family was sent packing and the events allegedly returned home with them.

- In 1974 in Timor, a small island in easternmost Indonesia, a young woman was suspected of creating psychic disturbances, including a series of loud rapping sounds, and making a table wobble and flip onto its side. She was a half-sister of two small boys, and was reportedly treated indifferently by her family because her skin was a different color.

- Can reports of a poltergeist stir up political tension? In 1998, cups and glasses were reportedly thrown around inside a house in Rangoon, Burma, which drew large crowds. Some area residents said it was the ghost of a police officer killed 10 years earlier. A BBC correspondent said Rangoon police tried to keep people away from the house because they were worried the scene would stir up anti-government feelings.

- In 2008–09 in Kolkata, India, Ratan Das, a court clerk, called the local police station to report household items toppling off shelves, flower vases trembling and a girl pushed hard from behind when there was seemingly no one there. The situation was a threat to lives, Das said. Police did not get to the bottom of the incidents, although they did suspect neighbors may have been behind the mischief.

hints of poltergeists in the u.s.

Last but not least, the following is a sampling of some tantalizing poltergeist stories popping up in the United States throughout the years that didn't furnish as many details as the other stories in this book.

- The Giddings case was famous in 1874 in Milwaukee. Servant girl Mary Spiegel, 14, was baking pies on a summer's night in the home of William Giddings when a trap door in the cellar allegedly opened by itself, and then dishes and silverware started to fly. Chairs and food reportedly floated in the air, followed by logs and pails, and the house was filled with a loud noise. Several witnesses saw more phenomena and soon crowds gathered. When the servant was fired, she attempted suicide by jumping into a river, but a bystander jumped in and saved her. A prominent Chicago physician took Mary under his wing and said she suffered from sleepwalking, was neurotic, and had been beaten by her father. Every time he took the girl back to the boarding house, objects began to levitate, he said. Psychical investigator Herbert Thurston called it a remarkable case. The house still stands as a private residence at the corner of Allis Street and Whitcomb Avenue.

- In 1957, goings-on were reported at the home of the James Mikulecky family in Rest Haven, Illinois, which included their 15-year-old granddaughter. *The Providence Evening Bulletin* reported that a crocheting needle floated out of a sewing box and across a room, and that chairs sometimes popped into the air, among other things.

- On a family farm in Hartville, Missouri, in 1958, 9-year-old Betty Ruth Ward was said to be the focus of poltergeist activity—objects moving and floating, and the sound of knocking.

Researchers from Duke University were witnesses to some of the action. The phenomena reportedly followed her to a store in Lebanon, Missouri. Also, when Betty Ruth visited her grandmother's home, walnuts apparently began flying around and bounced off the ceiling. When they fled to the Ward farm, things reportedly starting flying around as soon as they opened the front door. After two weeks, everything stopped.

No one was charged in a case in Indianapolis in 1962 because no suspect could be found after a police officer was struck by a flying glass in the home of Renate Beck, a 32-year-old Viennese-born restaurant operator. Incidents in the house began when a piece of crystal fell off the top of a bookcase onto the floor. For the next few days, figures, ash trays, vases, and goblets sailed through the air. Mrs. Beck; her 11-year-old daughter, Linda; and a friend, Lina Gemmecke, 61, all reported stinging pains in their arms and had small puncture wounds. Another friend, Emil Noseda, 60, and his wife were with Mrs. Gemmecke in the kitchen when a large clear glass vessel reportedly sailed completely around a corner and crashed at their feet. A police investigation solved nothing.

On December 19, 1976, at the home of widow Beulah Wilson in Pearisburg, Virginia, police were said to have seen a 200-pound kitchen cabinet floating through the air without any means of support. Other events reportedly involved the smashing of dishes, wooden chairs, and household items. The suspected poltergeist agent was a 9-year-old boy who had been placed into foster care with Mrs. Wilson. Parapsychologist Gaither Pratt believed it to be a case of genuine paranormal activity.

Some poltergeist cases are never resolved and leave investigators with an empty feeling. In 1987, investigative reporter Jim Henderson researched the case of Ron and Doretta Johnson, whose Marion, Indiana home was the stage for many unexplained events throughout the course of several years, including slices of bread that flew around the kitchen, strange noises, the appearance of shadowy apparitions, and electrical breakdowns. A parapsychologist believed that Doretta was responsible for projecting some of the occurrences from her mind. Henderson, who had won many awards for his newspaper stories, including those on race relations and the atomic legacy of the United States, believed there was a rational explanation for 80 percent of the events, but he was perplexed about the other 20 percent.

From all of these accounts we see that poltergeist activity is not confined to any one city, state, country, or continent. Quite the contrary: Paranormal phenomena has been reported throughout the decades and all throughout the world. In the following chapter, we will see that people's alleged ability to move things with their mind is equally widespread.

◉ PART V ◉

POLTERGEISTS IN POP CULTURE AND THE FUTURE

This final section ties up some loose ends, particularly revolving around this question: "If poltergeist activity really exists, can we learn to move things with our minds?"

In chapter 19, the believers and the skeptics check in, as well as a respected scientist, who believes he has been able to prove psychokinesis in laboratory conditions. Chapter 20 features a woman who says her RSPK acts up around her husband, but that she is able to turn it into PK by focusing on a pinwheel. Chapter 21 gives an overview of poltergeists in popular culture, and the last chapter is a look at how poltergeists can be lucrative, as well as damaging, for some pub owners and parapsychologists.

CHAPTER 20

The New Frontier: Tapping Psychokinesis

> "Whoever believes in psychokinesis, please raise my hand."
> *Stephen Wagner, paranormal researcher/writer, in*
> Your Guide to Paranormal Phenomena

We hear stories from time to time about gamblers in Las Vegas rolling lucky sevens just by focusing on the dice, or golfers like Tiger Woods helping the ball into the cup through sheer willpower or brain power. The alleged ability to consciously move things with your mind is psychokinesis (PK).

Most scientists are probably skeptical that PK even exists, never mind that we can tap into it. Statistical findings from controlled laboratory studies have resulted in contradictory results. Some experiments have been criticized for their methodologies, or tainted with accusations of fraud.

And yet, a respected academic journal, *Foundations of Physics*, published an analysis of 800 studies, conducted between 1959 and 1987, testing whether people can control micro-electronic machines with their mind. Their conclusion was that the odds were more than one trillion to one *against* the results being chance. In other words, they

207

concluded that some of the people tested did indeed affect machines with their minds. The effect was small and not automatic or easily controlled, but it showed that PK does exist.

This book is loaded with stories of suspected poltergeist activity, of people—mainly youths—purportedly moving things with their minds. Witnesses and parapsychologists lead us to believe that these so-called poltergeist agents summon a rare power called recurrent spontaneous psychokinesis (RSPK), in which they move kitchen utensils, chairs, and even heavy furniture with their minds, perhaps without even knowing they are doing it. RSPK differs from PK because is said to be harder to control, more spontaneous, and recurs repeatedly over time.

Throughout this book we ask the question, "Do poltergeist events exist?" Now come two follow-up questions—"Can we consciously move things with our minds?" and "Can anyone learn to do it?"

Throughout history, cases have been documented, however rare, in which people could reportedly move objects by focusing on them. Most of these people have been controversial and open to much skepticism, such as psychic Uri Geller, who claims to bend spoons with his mind or by gently stroking them.

nina kulagina

But there was a woman in the 20th century for whom usually skeptical Communist scientists had a great deal of respect. Nina Kulagina of Russia became so celebrated for her purported powers, the Soviet government wanted to keep her identity secret, so that her talents could not be studied by others during the Cold War with the West. And so she became known for a time under the pseudonym Nelya Mikhailova.

Her early life presented much challenge and trauma during the Second World War. Nina was 14 when the Nazis began the siege of Leningrad, and she joined the Red Army, for which she served on the front lines as a radio operator in a tank. She reached the rank of senior sergeant, but was seriously injured by artillery fire and her service ended. Nina recovered and went on to get married and to have a son. After the war, it was said she had unusual powers. Once, when she was angry in her apartment, a jug in a cupboard moved on a shelf, fell, and crashed to the floor, reportedly without anyone touching it. After that, many similar things took place, including lights going on and off by themselves.

Unlike many other suspected poltergeist agents, Nina said she knew that the power was coming from her and that she could control it, at least some of the time. The Soviet government, hardly known for embracing the paranormal or spiritual issues, went on to study her for three decades with its top scientists, 40 in all, including two Nobel laureates. They believed they had found a new force in nature and they wondered if it could be tapped.

Throughout those decades, not one of the scientists came forward to say that Nina used trickery or fraud. In some sessions, it seemed next to impossible for Nina to deceive anyone, because she was enclosed in a metal cage and surrounded by cameras, or forced to influence things from a distance in Plexiglas cubes.

But hers was an inexact skill. Nina said she could not always produce her powers on demand, and she often needed up to several hours of focus and preparation. She said she had to clear her mind of all other thoughts, and, when her concentration came to a peak, she would feel a sharp pain in her spine and her eyesight would become blurred. But that's when the miracles would allegedly start occurring: matchsticks would move, fountain pens would glide along a table, and compass needles would fluctuate.

The slow preparation time opened her up to criticism from skeptics, and one writer in the state newspaper, *Pravda*, called her a fraud, even though he had apparently never watched her in action. Soviet scientists believed in her powers, including biologist Edward Naumov, who claimed she moved matchsticks with her mind.

In 1970, some scientists and parapsychologists from the West were permitted to come to the Soviet Union to see for themselves. American paranormal researcher William A. McGary said he watched Nina move a wedding ring and the top of a condiment bottle across a dining room table. Parapsychologist Gaither Pratt said he saw Nina move small objects in tightly controlled experiments. The investigators said they always checked for concealed magnets or threads, and for further proof, 60 films were taken of the sessions.

A leading Czech scientist, Dr. Zdenek Rejdak of the Prague Military Institute, conducted his own testing on February 26, 1968, at the Kulagina family home, along with two physicians, Dr. J.S. Zverev and Dr. Sergeyev. After they were certain that no magnets, threads, or devices were available to Nina, Dr. Rejdak reported that she turned a compass needle more than 10 times, then the compass and its case, a matchbox and 20 matches at once. When he placed a cigarette in front of her, Nina moved that as well.

In another test by a group of celebrated physicists, filmed in Moscow, it was said that Nina moved several nonmagnetic objects, including matches, which had been placed inside a large Plexiglas cube, out of her reach. The objects reportedly danced from side to side. A ping-pong ball allegedly levitated in another experiment, and then, in 1970, it was said Nina was able to stop the heart of a frog, floating in solution, and then reactivate it.

A military physiologist, Dr. Genady Sergeyev, performed several years of research on Nina, studying the electrical potentials in her mind. He said her brain had very strong voltages and could expose undeveloped photos in a sealed envelope. The chairman of theoretical physics at Moscow University, Dr. Ya. Terletsky, said that Nina "displays a new and unknown form of energy."[1] With this focused energy, scientists said, she was able to move things as her pulse rate soared as high as 240 beats per minute.

Of course, many questions remained, and Nina was not always able to produce the phenomena. All of this attention and moving things with her mind apparently wore her down physically and sometimes emotionally, and in 1964 she suffered a nervous breakdown. She became exhausted, reportedly lost four pounds in one experiment, suffered an irregular heartbeat, and her endocrine system was disturbed—all apparently due to intense stress. She died in 1990, along with the state formerly known as the Soviet Union.

Today in Moscow, scientists and other investigators continue to look for ways to expand the abilities of the mind. According to Prof. Andrei Lee, head of the Moscow Neurological Clinic and the Poltergeist Emergency Service, researchers at the clinic have been able to move propellers under glass by intense concentration. He speculates whether it's possible to get poltergeist agents to do the same, but it is difficult to convince them to go to scientific settings. It might be also possible, he added, to redirect unpredictable RSPK into PK.

others with psi abilities

Throughout history, people have claimed to have PK they could control, at least partly, although they have not always claimed they knew how to do it. In the mid-1800s, medium Daniel Douglas Home put on demonstrations in which he seemed to levitate tables, a heavy piano, and even himself. Home, who had been the center of reported poltergeist activity as a teenager, submitted to tightly controlled laboratory tests by Sr. William Crookes, a Nobel Prize–winning physicist and president of England's leading scientific body. Crookes said he developed special devices to prevent fraud during the experiments. On one occasion, Home reportedly levitated himself right in front of Crookes, who said, "When he rose 18 inches off the ground, I passed my hands under his feet, round him and over his head when he was in the air."[2] Many other witnesses say they saw Home levitate objects under similar conditions, including magician Robert Houdin, after whom the famous magician Houdini named himself. Home and others who reportedly produced poltergeist-like effects were said to have had physical abnormalities (he suffered from consumption and eventually had to abandon his practices). In Chapter 8, we heard that some suspected poltergeist agents suffer from mental or physical maladies, including epilepsy, and their brains may be hardwired differently than are those of people who cannot perform paranormal feats.

In 1898, Eusapia Palladino was said to have stunned French scientist and Nobel Laureate Charles Richet and Nobel Laureates Pierre and Marie Curie with her PK feats of levitation. It was said she levitated a 48-pound table in Richet's driveway in broad daylight. After investigating Palladino, Pierre Curie said, "These phenomena exist for real, and I can't doubt it anymore."[3]

Austrian medium Maria Silbert (1866–1936) was apparently reluctant to develop what people called extraordinary talents, but her husband, a government official, put pressure on her. Author Adalbert Evian said he heard strange rappings when he was with her, and he "felt as if a hand were being laid on my knee. I distinctly saw the impressions of the five fingers." Then he said he saw a table levitate. Rappings became so loud, he said, "the blows came as if with an axe on the table, and the wood began to split."[4]

uri geller

The most controversial PK figure of modern times is Uri Geller, who began as a psychic and became celebrated for reportedly making spoons bend by stroking them, moving objects without touching them, and deflecting compass needles. Many scientists from around the world have studied Geller under laboratory conditions, and they say he often passes the test to prove PK is possible, but Geller has not always succeeded and has been labeled a fraud by skeptics, particularly James Randi.

In a test at Western Kentucky University, Dr. Thomas Coohill, of the physics department, declared, "There is no logical explanation for what Geller did here. But I don't think logic is what necessarily makes new inroads in science."[5] Geller said his power often could not be turned on and off. When he appeared on *The Tonight Show* with Johnny Carson, Geller was unable to produce any phenomena.

The late sociologist Marcello Truzzi, cofounder of the Committee for the Scientific Investigation of Claims of the Paranormal, now called the Committee for Skeptical Inquiry, said in 2001 that Geller "has not met the level of proof science properly requires to judge his psychic claims as valid. He has declined many invitations [for testing]... the burden of proof remains on him and not his critics."[6] However, parapsychologist William E. Cox, who organized a committee within the Society of American Magicians to investigate fraudulent claims of ESP, said that Geller had met the burden of proof under controlled conditions.

Many books have been written about Geller, who has dropped out of the public limelight in recent years. Through the 1990s and into present times, Geller has made a living as a private consultant and as a psychic geologist in search of precious metals buried in the earth. He says he also helps people develop their ESP abilities.

Bending Those Spoons

Spoon-bending is a controversial and unproven ability, yet best-selling author and medical doctor Michael Crichton said, in his 1988 book *Travels*, that he had a "successful experience" with PK at a spoon-bending party. Here are some of his observations:

- I bent a spoon, and I *knew* it wasn't a trick. I looked around the room and saw little children, 8 or 9 years old, bending large metal bars.

- Spoon-bending obviously must have some ordinary explanation, since a hundred people from all walks of life were doing it. And it was hard to feel any sort of mystery: You just rub the spoon for a while and pretty soon it gets soft, and it bends. And that's that. The only thing I noticed is that spoon-bending seemed to require a focused inattention. You had to try to get it to bend, and then you had to forget about it. Maybe talk to someone else while you rubbed the spoon. Or look around the room. Change your attention. That's when it was likely to bend.

- This seems to me to confirm the idea that so-called psychic or paranormal phenomena are misnamed. There's nothing abnormal about them. On the contrary, they're utterly normal. We've just forgotten we can do them. The minute we *do* do them, we recognize them for what they are and think, So what?"[7]

In general terms, Truzzi said he did not believe in the existence of extrasensory or psychic abilities. In a 2001 letter to the editor of *Parapsychology Press*, he wrote: "I scientifically take the view that parapsychology has not yet met the burden of proof for psi required by the general scientific community. Psi remains unproved, but not all evidence for it has been disproved. Evidence varies in degree, so I assert there is inadequate rather than no evidence for psi. Most evidence for psi, then, remains suggestive rather than convincing."[8]

Learning PK

Here is another question: Is it possible for someone who has shown no poltergeist powers to learn to tap into PK? Felicia Parise, an American hematologist, claimed she was able to develop PK in the 1970s after being inspired by watching old tapes of Kulagina in action. Parise said that if she got herself worked up to an intense level of concentration, she could move small plastic containers and pieces of aluminum foil across a table.

Sometimes it took an emotional event to get her started, such as the time she heard the news her grandmother was dying; when she then reached for a small bottle, it purportedly moved away from her hand. According to British paranormal investigator Colin Wilson, this emphasizes the point that PK is often performed better by the subconscious mind. "We are all split-brain patients," he said. "The logical self interferes with the natural operations of the right brain. This is why the artist has to wait for inspiration, for the left brain to relax and allow the right to take over."[9]

On one occasion, performed under controlled conditions at the Rhine parapsychology research lab in Durham, North Carolina, Parise reportedly deflected a compass needle 15 degrees and exposed film with her mind.

She said she gave up PK because it was too draining physically and emotionally, and it took her long periods of concentration to move something. Her confidence would start fleeting when the PK did not always happen, and she missed helping patients with her other work.

The Phillip Experiment

In 1973, eight members of the Toronto Society of Psychical Research tried to conjure up a ghost, using their minds. Instead, they reportedly summoned poltergeist activity.

Led by Dr. A.R.G. Owen, a psychic researcher and a member of the Department for Preventative Medicine and Biostatistics at the University of Toronto, they came up with an imaginary dead person, called him Phillip, and then held a séance for him. Instead of bringing out an apparition, they reportedly produced rapping sounds, flickering lights, and made a table move and flip over. They recorded the sounds.

Speculation was that the members had created a type of group consciousness, or perhaps a group hallucination.

They had suggestions for others considering their own experiment:

⊙ Use at least four people, who have good rapport with a common motivation.

⊙ Be open-minded.

⊙ Agree on the details and history of the imaginary person.

⊙ Make him or her a friendly entity.

⊙ Suspend your disbelief during the sessions.

⊙ Expect a miracle.

⊙ Be patient and enthusiastic.

matthew manning: from poltergeist to healer?

As an 11-year-old boy, Matthew Manning was said to be an agent for poltergeist activity in his family's home in Cambridge, England. Ornaments, chairs, and other objects were mysteriously moving, and so his father, Derek, an architect, called the police, and then the Cambridge Psychical Research Society.

When Matthew was 15, the headmaster at his boarding school and several other witnesses testified that he had been the agent for paranormal phenomena at the school. Manning's classmate, Jon Wills, who became a housemaster at another school, said that "things just started to happen. Water appeared from nowhere. My bed moved and there was nobody near it. One night, a pile of dinner plates came down, apparently out of thin air, and shattered on the floor. Matthew was frightened and I was bloody terrified. It was the sort of experience that, unless you've been through it, you can't begin to comprehend."[10]

Unlike many other suspected poltergeist agents, Manning was aware of his powers and he denied to critics that he had cheated. "The chances of an 11-year-old boy fooling all those adults is impossible," he said to me as an adult. "My feeling is that what I went through was caused by my own energy. It was nothing to do with spirits."

Manning decided to try to channel this energy into other areas. He started to practice automatic writing, which seemed to dissipate the energy he had to damage objects. By focusing on the names of dead artists, he was reportedly able to reproduce their drawings, particularly Albrecht Durer, Picasso, and Goya.

A 17-year-old Manning was tested in Toronto in 1972. Measurements of his brainwaves while he was allegedly bending cutlery suggested that he generated unusual patterns of electrical energy, emanating from his limbic system.

Manning has written several books, including *The Link* in 1974, a best-seller. He was interviewed by the eminent British broadcaster, Sir. David Frost, and appeared on many television shows, demonstrating his abilities and sometimes causing electrical problems in studios. Then Manning turned his energies to try to heal people. While standing on a Himalayan mountaintop, he had a thought: "At that moment, I realized if I could exert control over machinery and electrical products, perhaps then I could also help heal people...actually influence human bodies," he explained to me.

Now he claims that he can slow the rate of decay in red blood cells in a test tube, and also destroy cancer cells simply by the power of thought. Manning believes he has healed many people through the years, although the claim is difficult to prove. "He treats a lot of people, so statistically, it's likely some would have recovered anyway," said Richard Wiseman, professor of psychology at the University of Hertfordshire in England. "There is also the placebo effect; if we are in a positive frame of mind because we think we are going to get better, that undoubtably can help recovery."[11]

In his writings, Manning suggests that these types of psychic powers were once common to all mankind, but have been suppressed throughout the course of evolution.

american tests

In the West, some suspected poltergeist agents have been taken to laboratories to get them to perform PK feats, but the results have not been as conclusive as they were with Nina Kulagina in the Soviet

Union. If these people did indeed have paranormal abilities, in some cases they did not materialize, or they had weakened over time. Or perhaps the stresses in their household, which could have contributed to their RSPK in the first place, were not present away from home.

Julio Vasquez

But sometimes they came through. In the Miami warehouse case of 1967 (Chapter 6), shipping clerk Julio Vasquez was persuaded by parapsychologist William Roll to go back with him to the psychical research foundation in Durham, North Carolina. Under controlled conditions, researchers say they saw a bottle fall off a table while Vasquez was close by, and in another instance in a laboratory, a vase moved while he was standing with researchers. He was also tested with a dice-throwing machine and apparently showed better-than-chance averages, Roll said.

Tina Resch

In 1984, Roll was somewhat pleased with the tests he did with 14-year-old Tina Resch, the controversial poltergeist girl from Columbus, Ohio (Chapters 12 and 13). After many reported RSPK events in her home, Resch was brought for testing by Roll to the Institute of Parapsychology and to the Spring Creek Institute, both in North Carolina. According to Roll, a number of paranormal incidents took place at the institutes and at his home in Durham, but nothing was spectacular or conclusive. Later that year, while Resch's powers were dying down, according to Roll, she was back in North Carolina for more tests, to see if she could move objects with her mind on command. One day, Roll and two other researchers, neurobiologist Stephen Baumann and psychotherapist Jeannie Stewart, set up a table with a 12-inch socket wrench on it. Tina was not permitted near the table, and yet Baumann and Stewart said that the wrench had moved off the table and about 18 feet along the floor.

Also in North Carolina, psychotherapist Rebecca Zinn said Tina created a number of paranormal incidents. In one, Zinn said she led Tina down a hallway and a telephone struck the girl in the back. "There was no way anyone could have touched it, since we were the only ones in the office," Zinn said.[12] Resch then fell to the floor in pain and sobbing, Zinn said. At the time of the incident, Tina told Zinn she had been thinking of her mother and stepmother.

PEAR

As mentioned in Chapter 1, a respected scientist, Professor Robert Jahn, Dean Emeritus of the School of Engineering and Applied Sciences at Princeton University, and his colleagues believe they have proved that PK is a reality, that ordinary people they tested altered numbers and ping-pong balls just by thinking about them. Jahn and others at the Princeton Anomalies Research Laboratory (PEAR) claimed to have produced experimental data to support the existence of PK. They say some people have influenced small balls and pendulums through willpower and the force of their minds under laboratory conditions.

In the past, researchers used dice-tossing and coin-flipping to see if people could influence gravity, but now people are tested with high-tech machines called *random events generators* (REG). In one PEAR experiment, researchers dropped 9,000 polystrene balls down a network of pegs. They said that one of the experimenters was able to get more balls to go down one funnel of pegs by simply focusing on them. In addition, Jahn conducted more than five million tests of a pendulum, and he said that an experimenter got it to swing in certain directions with his mind "beyond chance...the effect was tiny, but real," Jahn told me.

The experimenters were not able to influence the tests every time, and they could not explain how they did it, and so testing for PK remains an inexact science open to criticism by skeptics. But the Princeton researchers suggested that athletes, just like people with paranormal powers, are not able to perform at the top of their game every night either, and that mood, confidence, pressure, and other conditions often affect results. "I know we're not quite there yet, but one day I hope we'll be able to show people how to influence things with their mind," Prof. Jahn told me.

The Princeton researchers tested ordinary people instead of psychics or mediums, Jahn said, because "psychics and those who claim to have unusual powers bring a lot of publicity with them; they come trailing in with TV cameras and you find yourself being misquoted." RSPK is even harder to prove than PK, Jahn told me, because "such effects are extraordinarily rare and irregular in their appearance, usually arise at locations far removed from the experimenter's home base, and tend to persist only for short periods." By the time the experimenter arrives, Jahn added, "he typically finds the site overrun by law enforcement officers, medical and psychological practitioners, the clergy, media, family members and skeptical representatives, who have so confounded and suppressed the effects that valid evidence is extremely difficult to obtain."

Robert M. Schoch, Ph.D., associate professor of Natural Science at Boston University, is a believer. "I do believe that some psychokinesis is real," he said, referring to the PEAR experiments and similar studies, and also to poltergeist cases. Prof. Schoch said he once saw a book "jumping off a shelf" while in a room where a female psychokineses agent was also present.[13]

When PEAR closed its doors in 2007, Jahn said, "For 28 years, we've done what we wanted to do, and there's no reason to stay and generate more of the same data."[14]

the death of pk research?

Other research groups have closed down as well. In fact, in the past 20 years, research into poltergeists specifically and parapsychology in general has decreased in the United States. Many university laboratories have closed, partly due to lack of acceptance by mainstream science. There has been opposition to such research from academics because early research into the paranormal has been considered inconclusive.

And yet, if there is such a thing as PK, it could be a tremendous force for good or evil on a broad scale, if controlled.

In 2004, the U.S. Air Force conducted a Teleportation Physics Study to review the research of real and hypothetical methods of teleportation, but it is still considered by scientists and the military as beyond the capabilities of modern science.

CHAPTER 21

The Poltergeist in Popular Culture

"The more civilized we get, the more we repress our sort of uncivilized nature. And one way to release that is through festival occasions, vicariously enjoying horror movies and all sorts of related things."

Leon Rappoport, professor of psychology at Kansas State University

Even if we do not believe in poltergeists, ghosts, and the paranormal, they certainly thrive in books, movies, and television. They've helped to make Stephen King (*Carrie*), William Peter Blatty (*The Exorcist*) and Steven Spielberg (*Poltergeist*) famous and quite wealthy. Through big-budget, lavish effects movies and detailed books, the public probably has the impression that poltergeists are spectacular monsters from other dimensions; however, if poltergeists truly exist, they are likely more subtle than that. But it seems we love to be scared out of our socks, and so writers and directors are glad to embellish scripts. We have made Blatty's 1971 book *The Exorcist* into a bestseller, and a movie by the same title in 1973 has become a cult flick, starring the head-spinning Linda Blair. Both were based on a reportedly true poltergeist/possession case.

Perhaps it is because we want to know more about the shadowy side of the universe—if there is one—or because we are bored in a mundane, controlled existence. Or perhaps we just want to get scared. "It goes all the way back to sitting around camp fires, telling ghost stories and folk tales," said Leon Rappoport, professor of psychology at Kansas State University. "It's a very prevalent, deep-seated, human characteristic to explore the boundaries where people can tolerate fear and anxiety, and then master that fear and anxiety by working through it. The more civilized we get, the more we repress our sort of uncivilized nature. And one way to release that is through festival occasions, vicariously enjoying horror movies and all sorts of related things."[1]

Rappoport says that poltergeist and horror flicks are particularly popular with teenagers, partly as a way of rebelling because their parents say such films are not fit for young minds.

the amityville horror

The Amityville Horror reappeared in 2005 with a remake of the famous movie by the same name in 1979. It is based on what was supposedly a true story, although controversy remains about the authenticity of some of the paranormal events surrounding it. In real life, the peaceful town of Amityville, New York, on Long Island's south shore, became known for what happened there in a three-story, Dutch Colonial home on Ocean Avenue. There, on November 13, 1974, the DeFeo family were slaughtered in their beds: Ronald DeFeo and his wife, Louise; their two sons, Mark and John; and their two daughters, Dawn and Allison. The killer was another son, Ronald Junior, who went from room to room with a high-powered rifle. Somehow, the victims never heard any of the shots. In his trial, DeFeo, who was on drugs, said an evil spirit in the house forced him to do it. He pleaded insanity, but the prosecution said he was just trying to cash in on six life insurance policies. DeFeo was sentenced to 150 years in prison.

About a year after the horrible crime, a young couple, George and Kathy Lutz, bought the home for $80,000 and they claimed it was a hotbed for paranormal events: strange noises, an unearthly presence, and locked doors and windows reportedly opening and closing by themselves. Following an exorcism by a Catholic priest, which apparently did not work, scratching sounds and thumping noises intensified, objects moved about mysteriously, telephone service malfunctioned, apparitions were seen outside, and Lutz, a former Marine, seemed to become possessed by an evil spirit. The Lutzes packed up and left. With the help of the Lutz family, author Jay Anson wrote the book *The Amityville Horror* in 1977.

But many people believe the paranormal events were fabricated, exaggerated, or a complete hoax. Another family that moved into the home after the Luztes reported no occurrences. And a skeptical author, Stephen Kaplan, wrote a book called *The Amityville Horror Conspiracy*. But it didn't seem to matter to the public, which remained enraptured with the story.

the exorcist

William Peter Blatty reportedly based *The Exorcist* on a story he read in the *Washington Post* on August 20, 1949, while he was a student at Georgetown University. The *Post* story described an alleged exorcism of a 13-year-old boy in nearby Mount Rainier, Maryland, who was apparently the only child of a dysfunctional family. But it is hard to pinpoint how accurate the real story is.

The boy's case took place in January, 1949, with bizarre noises coming from his bedroom walls, furniture moving, and objects moving about. A Lutheran minister reportedly saw a bed move and a chair flip the boy onto the floor. The boy apparently showed hysterical tendencies and, believing he was possessed, a team of priests performed a number of exorcisms, which apparently were unsuccessful, but the occurrences stopped after four months.

Some of the information for the real case was passed down from secondary sources because some of the priests refused to discuss it, and also from a 28-page diary kept by Father Raymond Bishop, who saw the second exorcism. Blatty also wrote the screenplay for *The Exorcist*, which starred a fictitious girl. Blatty's book sold more than six million copies.

the poltergeist trilogy

There were three films in the Poltergeist trilogy: *Poltergeist* (1982), *Poltergeist II* (1986), and *Poltergeist III* (1988). The series tells the story of a fictitious family, the Freelings, who lived in homes inhabited by spirits. Some of the events in the movies resembled several poltergeist investigations, including a 1972 case involving the Fischer family in Rothschild, Wisconsin. The family reported mysterious ringing bells, footsteps, electrical malfunctions, and strange shadows. They said they abandoned the home when a flying razor flew at Mrs. Fischer while she was in a bath.

Some people believe the series was cursed, because four of its actors died. Dominique Dunne, who played Dana Freeling in the original film, died at age 22 the same year the film was released, after being choked into a coma by her former boyfriend. Heather O'Rourke, who played Carol Anne Freeling in all three movies, died in 1988, before the third movie was released, of septic shock on an operating table after bacterial toxins got into her bloodstream. She was 12 years old.

Two others, who appeared only in *Poltergeist II*, suffered less dramatic fates. Julian Beck, the evil spirit Kane, died at 60 in 1985 after a long fight with stomach cancer. Will Sampson, who portrayed a medicine man, died at 53 in 1987 of post-operative kidney failure and fungal infection. Zelda Rubinstein, who played the psychic in all three movies, died of a heart attack at 76 in 2010.

other poltergeists on film

Here are three more widely seen examples of poltergeists in the movies and television:

◎ *The Entity*, a film starring Barbara Hershey, in 1983, loosely based on a 1974 case in Culver City, California. The real case was investigated by parapsychologist Kerry Gaynor, who was an advisor for the movie. As the story goes, a woman told Gaynor that a ghost had beaten and raped her. He was skeptical, but then he saw doors and pans moving under their own power, and also strange lights.

◎ A book and a television movie, both entitled *The Haunted*, were based on the middle-class lives of Jack and Janet Smurl, a couple in West Pittston, Pennsylvania, who claimed they were haunted throughout a 13-year period, from 1974 to 1987, by apparitions and poltergeist-like events—footsteps on stairs, unplugged radios blaring, a German Shepherd terrorized by an unseen force, and toilets flushing themselves. Several exorcisms apparently did not help, and some of their neighbors were skeptical about the claims of paranormal events. Demonic claims were not corroborated by independent observers. As for the movie, some viewers were skeptical of what they said were cheesy special effects, although it did get some good reviews.

◉ Television has not really embraced the poltergeist, although there have been some shows dealing with it on *The X-Files* and *Night Stalker*. The series *Poltergeist: The Legacy* (1996 to 1999, created by Richard Barton Lewis) was not about the *traditional* poltergeist, but a fictitious secret society that began many centuries ago to accumulate knowledge and artifacts to help fight against evil. John Edward's psychic show, *Crossing Over*, dealt with the afterlife.

the powerful and the paranormal

Many famous and influential people have believed in the paranormal, including:

◉ Abraham Lincoln consulted with spiritualists and mediums. His wife, Mary Todd Lincoln, often arranged séances for him. Of course, he was not without criticism; the Cleveland Plain Dealer said he "consulted spooks."

◉ Union general and U.S. President Ulysses S. Grant turned to Spiritualism later in life.

◉ Former U.S. President Ronald Reagan had an astrology advisor/

◉ Former President George W. Bush said God spoke to him and told him to invade Iraq in 2003.

Real-Life Experience

Veteran actor Brian Cox, who starred in the thriller *The Ring*, said he had a poltergeist experience at age 18 in his native Scotland. Cox said he rented a room in a house in Edinburgh and was lying in bed one night when he heard an unusual tapping noise. "It was a big room and I looked to the other side of the bed and there, by a big old Victorian dresser, was a chair," he said. "It was shaking; then it started to move. It moved along the room and then came in front of my bed. I was already gripping the sheet and when this happened. I pulled it over my head and passed out. It was scary."

The next morning, to make sure he had not been dreaming, Cox said he checked on the chair. It had indeed moved away from the dresser, and "there were scuff marks along the floor." Cox believes the incident may have been related to children with a family upstairs. "They say poltergeist activity often centers around young children," said the actor, who also appeared in *The Bourne Supremacy*, *Braveheart*, *Manhunter*, and *Zodiac*.[2]

CHAPTER 22

The Business of Poltergeists

"I thought about telling my story, but it's not worth the price."
A suspected poltergeist agent who wants to keep his story private

show me the money

I f poltergeists exist, they seem to cause a lot of damage and heartache. And yet there is apparently money to be made on things that go bump in the night—*and* day.

In 2008 in Easington, England, psychic Suzanne Hadwin earned 120 pounds (around $194) to rid a home of a poltergeist after tenant Sabrina Fallon reported objects moving on their own. Half of the money came from the town council, in charge of government housing for the family. Andrew Burnip, a manager for the council, said the family had been traumatized by the banging, which scared the two young children. Police investigated, but found nothing. A council spokesman said calling in the psychic was the most cost-effective solution because re-housing the family in temporary accommodation would have cost up to 40 pounds (around $65) a night. Ms. Hadwin said she was able to remove a restless spirit from the house, and the family returned.

Hollywood, of course, has raked in millions of dollars throughout the decades with poltergeist and ghost tales (mostly fiction), and perhaps thousands of books have been written about the subject.

"Everything today is for a buck," said a man suspected of being a poltergeist agent in a 1970 case in St. Catharines, Ontario (Chapters 2 and 3). At the time that objects and furniture were mysteriously being launched around his parents' apartment, some authors, museum officials, and even some of his old neighbors had tried to make money on the strange happenings, Mulvey told me. "I thought about telling my story, but it's not worth the price [to privacy]."

A photo or video of an alleged poltergeist can bring a pretty penny. Perhaps the most famous photo was taken in 1984 by Fred Shannon of the *Columbus Dispatch*, showing a telephone in flight across the lap of 14-year-old Tina Resch in Columbus, Ohio. It appeared on the front page of the *Dispatch* and was carried on wire services around the world. When I worked for the *Calgary Herald* in the mid-1990s, Shannon was still selling the photo for $500 to newspapers of medium-size circulation, and more for larger papers and magazines.

Eddie Brazil, a photographer who took photos of a poltergeist home in London, England, is asking 28 pounds for 12-by-16 black-and-white prints in the United Kingdom, and $45 outside the U.K., plus $15 for shipping. He charges the same price for photos of Borley Church in England, which is said to be haunted. Part of the money goes to the Borley Ghost Society and a church preservation fund.

Pub and store hauntings

On a different scale, no self-respecting English pub is without its ghost or poltergeist, and they are often advertised to attract business. There's Bob the Poltergeist at the Hobgoblin Public House in Maidenhead, Berkshire; supposed poltergeist activity at Shipman's Public House in Northhampton has been explained as the spirit of Harry Franklin, a former manager who committed suicide; and an exorcism was held to remove a stinky spirit at The Royal Oak in Huntingdonshire.

And yet, poltergeists may not necessarily always be good for the customers or staff at pubs and stores. In Scotland in December 2004, barmaids at the Castleview in Dundonald, Ayrshire, complained they were having their bums pinched by a poltergeist. "I won't even go to the toilet on my own because I'm scared he'll be there," said waitress

Tiffany Luxton, 18. "It's as if you're being stalked. You feel him brushing past you and touching you. It's really quite scary. You can hear footsteps, but there is nobody there." Pub manager Terry Quinn, 49, said that on one night, "12 huge water jugs sitting on a solid wooden gantry all flew off the shelf at once and smashed." In addition, Quinn added, "The CO_2 that powers the beer lines just turns itself off. What's going on is a mystery." Quinn summoned the Dunfermline Paranormal Research Fellowship, who said the pub was haunted.[1]

In September 2002, in a shop in Trowbridge, Wiltshire, a poltergeist named George allegedly tossed stock around the Millets Store. On one morning at 5:30, George was suspected of setting off a burglar alarm, when police could find no evidence of a break-in and nothing had been stolen. "His name is George and we think he's Victorian," said the store's assistant manager, Renate Parvin. "Some people get a strange vibe when they go into the stock room. None of us find it frightening... we're certainly not going to get an exorcist in."[2]

Paranormal investigators

There are many parapsychologists, ghostbusters, and psychics who investigate poltergeist cases for money—or for the love of it as volunteers through parapsychology organizations. Many are like William Roll—they are paid by universities to investigate paranormal claims and will come to a home free of charge. Others make cash by lecturing at conventions; I was offered $2,500 and expenses to give a workshop on poltergeists in Pennsylvania in 2010.

Some psychics and groups make a living off helping people with their paranormal abilities or problems. Their fees can range from several hundred dollars to $7,500 for an in-depth investigation. People who simply want to be tested for clairvoyance should expect to pay about $1,500, according to the International Society for Paranormal Research, based in Marina Del Rey, California.

Or, if you want to go with a psychic medium on a group paranormal investigation in England, UK Haunted, a team of mediums, photographers, and historians offers a commercial ghost-hunting venture. In

2005, they had an all-night vigil at Jerusalem Pub, beneath Nottingham Castle, for 99 pounds (about $160), which included, of course, a quality buffet meal. According to Nicola Froggett, cofounder and trainee medium, "We want the public to join us so they can see and experience what the team does. It adds credibility if unusual activity occurs."[3]

Many cities in Europe and the United States also have ghost tours. Be wary of other ventures, however. Just as the paranormal world does, its commercial side has its fakes. In New England, a man and wife said they had a poltergeist breaking dishes in their home, and they began charging admission for the public to see for themselves. A paranormal private investigator (PPI), Patrick Leonard, posed as a gullible tourist and discovered that the couple was hurling the dishes themselves when people were not looking.

Poltergeists in court

Some people have been accused of claiming to have poltergeists in order to get out of their council house. In 1995 in Rochdale, England, Jim and Vera Gardner said their council officials accused them of faking unusual water disturbances in their home so they would be moved to another council house. "That's ridiculous!" Vera said. "I've lived here 14 years and was perfectly settled until this started. Now I can't wait to leave."[4]

> In many countries, sellers of homes are required to tell prospective buyers if the home has a history of poltergeist or ghost activity. According to Peter MacDonald of www.homeloancenter.com, in the realty business they are referred to as *stigmatized homes*. That could also mean a home in which there has been an unusual death or murder or one which has been built atop a graveyard.

But proving the paranormal in court is another matter.

In 1999, an English couple, Josie and Andrew Smith, refused to pay the final installment of 3,000 pounds (more than $4,800) on their 44,000 pound ($71,000) cottage because they said it was inhabited by a spirit that caused objects to move and walls to weep. The couple ended up in Derby County Court. They explained to Judge Peter Stretton that they bought the house in Upper Mayfield, Staffordshire, in 1994, and were not informed by the previous owners, Susan Melbourne and Sandra Podmore, that it was haunted. A priest, Reverend Peter Mockford, who specializes in the paranormal, told the court he had been in the Smith house, which was also inhabited by the Smith's three children, and had felt a paranormal presence. But Judge Stretton ruled in favor of the previous owners. "I do not accept that it is haunted now or has been at any other time," the judge said.[5] A lawyer for the previous owners, Thomas Dillon, told the court that the Smiths invented the story to avoid paying the outstanding money.

In 1850 in Normandy, France, Felix Thorel reportedly sued his local priest, Father Tinel, for defamation, after the priest called Thorel a witch. The priest blamed Thorel for poltergeist activities in the parsonage of Cideville. Father Tinel said there were 34 witnesses to knockings, rappings of tunes, moving furniture, flying knives, risinga nd falling desks, rushing winds, and moving bedclothes. According to Sacheverel Sitwell's 1940 book *The Poltergeist*, the case was unsolved despite intensive investigation. There was no word on the defamation suit. Perhaps they settled out of court (lawyers thrived thence, as well).

Then, in Braintree, England, in 1971, a 13-year-old boy was accused of burning down his school. His lawyer in juvenile court, Peter Perrins, claimed that an evil poltergeist spirit also made the boy cause considerable damage in his home. Results of the court case were not made public.

Before Judge Sidney W. Kaufman in Lynwood, California criminal court in 1960, car lot manager Claude Monk testified that he saw rocks and stones do amazing things in damaging his garage and striking several police officers. In the jury trial, handyman Anthony Angelo was acquitted of obstructing police. A police captain absolved Angelo of any blame. The defense attorney put it down to "supernatural causes."

◉ A woman dubbed by the media as "The Nanny They Called a Witch" spent two and a half years in prison for being a poltergeist agent, parapsychologists said. Carole Compton, a 22-year-old from Scotland, was believed to be the center of spontaneous fires and moving objects in three homes in Italy in which she worked as a nanny in 1982. A court released her from a charge of attempted murder but convicted her of arson, even though some fire officials said there was no evidence that the fires had been deliberately set. Compton said she did not have paranormal powers, yet parapsychologists Guy Lyon Playfair, Hugh Pincott, and Hans Bender, who investigated, disagreed with her. In 1990, Compton published a book on her experiences, called *Superstition: The True Story of The Nanny They Called a Witch*, which became a feature film in 2003.

◉ In Barry, South Wales, a 40-year-old woman was jailed for 15 months in 2001 for setting fire to her own home. Adele Gallivan blamed a poltergeist or ghost for strange occurrences, including an apparition in her curtains. Gallivan admitted to setting fire to the house, causing $2,000 damage, and she told police she was never going back in the house because it was inhabited by a poltergeist.

Poltergeist insurance, anyone?

Believe it or not, there is insurance you can purchase to protect yourself against poltergeists and ghosts. An English pub landlord pays a premium of 500 pounds (around $800) annually for an insurance policy because he is worried that the "resident poltergeist" at his Royal Falcon Hotel in Lowestoft, Suffolk, will injure customers. "I saw glasses move across the bar one night and thought, "What happens if it does something to hurt somebody?'" pub landlord Terry Meggs said. "I never believed in ghosts before I came here."[6]

Some people believe that the pub is haunted by a monk who hanged himself after being caught having an affair with a pupil or teacher when the building was a school. "We get sounds of moving furniture, the glasses move, we get very loud banging, as if someone is banging with a hammer," said Meggs's wife, Shirley. "We get bells ringing and sounds of someone walking across the floor and things get moved to different places."[7] The couple has taken out the Spooksafe policy with the Ultraviolet insurance company, of Bristol, England, which says it will pay up to one million pounds ($1.6 million) if staff or customers are killed or permanently disabled by poltergeists, ghosts, or other paranormal phenomena.

Meanwhile, Ultraviolet said that in 2000, it paid 100,000 pounds ($161,000) on Spooksafe after investigators looking into the death of a woman, who had been thrown over the banisters at her home in the U.S., concluded that a ghost was responsible for the crime. "We had a specialist firm of investigators look into it and they were convinced," said Simon Burgess, chief underwriting officer, who did not identify the woman.

Ultraviolet said that it sold about 500 Spooksafe policies in 2004, mostly in California. The policy also covers damage reportedly committed by poltergeists.

heard of everything now?

Thought you've heard everything? Think again.

On December 6, 2004, a Hobart, Indiana woman sold her dead father's metal walking cane for $65,000 on the Internet in the hopes her son would believe his grandfather's ghost would leave their house with it.

When 6-year-old Colin Anderson refused to go anywhere in the house alone because he was afraid his grandfather's ghost might appear, his mother, Mary, put her father's ghost into an auction on eBay. She offered to give the winner her father's metal cane. It got 34 bids, including a high bid of $78. But then the media got hold of the story and an online casino, GoldenPalace.com, offered $65,000 for the cane.

Mary asked the casino to send her a letter explaining to her son that his grandfather's ghost had left their house. They did so.

Help for the Victims

How do you get rid of an alleged poltergeist?

- Most cases of RSPK seem to die a natural death after a few weeks or months, and sometimes it eases with the easing of stress in a household.

- Sometimes the occurrences end when the agent realizes he or she is the cause. Other times, psychotherapy seems to help.

- Exorcisms don't seem to work, but clergy and parapsychologists report some relief in the victims when they counsel the family.

- If the stress in a family is addressed, paranormal activity will often disappear, according to Alan Murdie, chairman of England's Ghost Club Society, which bills itself as the oldest organization in the world devoted to psychical research. In poltergeist cases, buildings are not haunted; people are, he said.

- "People who call up are often very upset about what's happening," says parapsychologist Maurice Grosse, the late chairman of the spontaneous cases committee for the Society of Psychical Research in England, who investigated paranormal phenomena for more than 60 years. "I reassure them that they won't be damaged by it, and sometimes this helps. Our role is partly being a social worker," he told me. Grosse advises people not to move out of their homes, because the paranormal activity will likely be dragged along with them. Rather, they should try to work out their problems and issues, he says.

- Stephen Mera says that his organization, Manchester's Association of Paranormal Investigators and Training (MAPIT), does not claim to be able to get rid of poltergeists. As he told me, "Most of all, our investigations help the family through the crisis, giving them information, support, and assistance, and we try to identify what is causing the occurrences."

◎ Sometimes encouragement is the way to go. In a case in Baltimore, parapsychologist Nathan Fodor suggested that suspected poltergeist agent Ted Pauls receive encouragement for his writing talent, which he was frustrated about. The family agreed and gave Ted praise and credit for his work. Not long after, the disturbances ended, Fodor said. Some of the youthful poltergeist agents pull out of their problems, others do not. "Some of them go on to normal lives," William Roll told me. "Some have psychological problems to begin with. When the phenomena stops, the problems continue."

◎ As strange as it sounds, a poltergeist case can be good for relieving tension in an unusual family situation, said British psychologist Dr. John Layard. "Poltergeists are not chance phenomena, but have a definite purpose...it is a curative one, having for its object the resolution of a psychological conflict," he said. Often, the poltergeist agent has no other way to relieve the unusual buildup of frustration or tension, whether it is psychological or sexual."[8]

Notes

Chapter 1

1. Zala, "Ramol Cops."
2. Ibid.
3. Kolodny, "When Apples Fall."
4. *Today Tonight*.
5. Colvin, "Acoustic Properties."

Chapter 2

1. Whitmarsh, "Relieving Frustrations."
2. From St. Catharines Police Department reports obtained by the author.
3. Ibid.
4. Ibid.
5. Whitmarsh, "Police, Doctors."

Chapter 4

1. Roll, *Poltergeist*, 4.
2. Kahn, "A Home's Bad Vibration."

Chapter 5

1. Tamayo, "Father Bill."
2. Quinlan and May, "Baffling Ghost."
3. Geller, "Haunted House or Hoax."
4. Ibid.
5. Patrick, "Demonic Doings."
6. Warren, Ed and Lorraine, "From the Case Files."
7. Geller, "Haunted House or Hoax."
8. Tamayo, "Father Bill."
9. Warren, Ed and Lorraine, "From the Case Files."
10. Geller, "All's Quiet."

Chapter 6

1. Houran and Lange, *Hauntings and Poltergeists*, 124.
2. Smith, *Prominent American Ghosts*, 173.
3. Ibid, 171.
4. Pratt and Roll, "The Miami Disturbances," 438.

Chapter 7

1. Roll, "Poltergeists, Electromagnetism."
2. Wagner, "Loyd Auerback on Ghosts."
3. Sokoloff, "Q and A."
4. Cheung, *Element Encyclopedia*, 45.
5. Barrington, "Finn Poltergeist."
6. Spencer, John and Anne, *Poltergeist Phenomenon*, 230.

Chapter 8

1. Beloff, "Modern Poltergeist."
2. Nichols, "A Water Poltergeist."
3. Budden , "Poltergeist Machine."

4. Allan, "Legacy."

Chapter 9

1. Bender, "An Investigation."
2. Ibid.
3. Nichols, Andrew, "Water Poltergeist."
4. Ibid.

Chapter 10

1. English, "Couple Claim Evil Spirit."
2. Brennan, "Team at Haunted House."
3. Ibid.
4. Hough, "Liquid Liability."
5. Leigh and Mera, "Rochdale Case."
6. Hough, "Liquid Liability."
7. Leigh and Mera, "Rochdale Case."
8. Price, *Poltergeist Over England*, 259.

Chapter 11

1. Driesch, *Psychical Research*, 2–3.
2. Kurtz, *Skeptic's Handbook*, 220.
3. Ibid., 221.

4. Taylor, "Mera Poltergeist."
5. Driesch, *Psychical Research*, 5.
6. Shermer, *Why People Believe*, 275–278.
7. Norman, "Poking Holes."
8. Sagan, "Does Truth Matter?"
9. Ibid.
10. Mayes, "Seeing Ghosts."

Chapter 12

* For the following two chapters, the author would like to thank William Roll for granting permission to use parts of his 1993 paper, "The Question of RSPK Versus Fraud in the Case of Tina Resch," Psychical Research Foundation and Parapsychological Services Institute, Atlanta, Georgia.

1. Roll and Storey, *Unleashed*, 63, 65.
2. Roll, "The Question of RSPK," 8.

Chapter 13

1. Widely reported in the media, including the *Columbus Dispatch* and the *Columbus Citizen-Journal* on March 9, 1984, from a press conference in the Resch home.
2. Ibid.
3. Ibid.
4. United Press International, "Giving Up the Ghost?"
5. Roll, *Unleashed*, 20.
6. Roll, "The Question of RSPK," 22.
7. Kurtz, "The Columbus Poltergeist."
8. Del Guercio, "Team Attempts."
9. Torpy, "From Celebrity to Cellblock."
10. Randi, "Two Tales Terminate."
11. Harden, "Girl Who Made Telephone Fly."
12. Review for *Unleashed* on Amazon.com, Aug. 17, 2004.

Chapter 14

1. Huler, "Ghost Hunter."
2. Randi, "It's Time for Science."
3. Nordenstam, "Skeptic Offers $1 Million."
4. Randi, "It's Time for

Science."

5. Nordenstam, "Skeptic Offers $1 Million."

6. Ibid.

7. Promotional material for Randi's biography in Speakers Platform Website, *www.speaking. com/speakers/jamesrandi. php.*

Chapter 15

1. From "The Enfield Poltergeist" on the now-defunct Paranormal Channel, UK, Dec. 8, 2008.

2. Ibid.

3. Spencer, *Poltergeist Phenomenon*, 59.

4. All notes made by Grosse about the case, as well as witness statements throughout the chapter, were provided to the author by Grosse in 2005.

5. Playfair, *This House Is Haunted*, 258.

6. Ibid., 51.

7. Ibid.

8. Ibid., 62.

Chapter 16

1. Author interview with Grosse in 2005.

2. Author interview with Manning in 2005.

3. "Interview With a Poltergeist," Channel 4.

Chapter 17

1. Spencer, John and Anne, *Poltergeist Phenomenon*, 44.

2. Allan, "Legacy."

3. Ibid.

4. Owen, *Can We Explain*, 163.

Chapter 18

1. Bevan, "Runcorn Poltergeist."

2. Wilson, "Poltergeist Terror."

Chapter 19

1. Terletsky, "An Unknown Form."

2. Schmicker, *Best Evidence*, 91.

3. Hurwic, *Pierre Curie*, 263–264

4. Nicholls, "Mediumship."

5. Uri Geller's Website, *www .urigeller.com/geller-effect/*

tge18.htm.

6. Truzzi and Lyons, *The Blue Sense*, 252.

7. Crichton, *Travels*, 319–320.

8. Truzzi, "Letter to the Editor."

9. Wilson, *Poltergeist!*, 25.

10. Chalmers, "Hands-On Approach."

11. Leafe, "Healer or Hoaxer."

12. Zinn, *Stardust*, 47–50.

13. Schoch, *Psychokinesis*, 42–43.

14. Odling-Smee, "The Lab," 10–11.

Chapter 20

1. This and the rest of the quotes from this chapter come from interviews by the author with Sarah (pseudonym), Michael Persinger, and William Roll in 2010.

Chapter 21

1. Rappoport, "Why We Like to Watch."

2. Fulton, "The Cox Files."

Chapter 22

1. Paterson, "Phantom Bumpincher."

2. Wiltshire Poltergeist, *www.ghosts-uk.net.*

3. Campling, "Ghost Hunters."

4. Hough, "Liquid Liability."

5. BBC News Online, "Haunted Houseowner."

6. BBC News Online, "Publican Insures."

7. Ibid.

8. Price, *Poltergeist Over England*, 387.

Bibliography

Allan, Brian. "The Legacy of the Sauchie Poltergeist; A Re-Investigation by Malcolm Robinson." Paranormal Encounters Group, 2000. *www.p-e-g.co.uk/Web/Articles/ARTICLESArticle23.htm* (accessed June 2010).

Auerbach, Loyd. *ESP, Hauntings and Poltergeists*. New York: Warner Books, 1986.

Barrington, Mary Rose. "The Finn Poltergeist Revisited." Presentation to the conference of The Society for Psychical Research. Bournemouth, England, August 31, 2002.

BBC News Online. No author. "Haunted House Owners Lose Case." January 18, 1999. *http://news.bbc.co.uk/2/hi/uk_news/257447.stm* (accessed May 2004).

BBC News Online. No author. "Publican Insures Against Ghost." April 5, 2002. *http://news.bbc.co.uk/2/hi/uk_news/england/1913960.stm* (accessed May 2004).

Beloff, John, ed. "Modern Poltergeist Research: A Plea for an Unprejudiced Approach." *New Directions in Parapsychology*. London: Elek Science, 1974, 142–43.

Bender, Hans. "An Investigation of Poltergeist Occurrences." *Proceedings of the Parapsychological Association* 5 (1968), 31–33.

Bevan, Mark. "The Runcorn Poltergeist: A Strange Twist." *Cheshire Magazine*. Unknown date. *www.cc-publishing.co.uk/Archives/twist.html*.

Branston, Brian. *Beyond Belief*. London: Weidenfeld and Nicolson, 1974.

Braude, S.E. *The Limits of Influence: Psychokinesis and the Philosophy of Science*. Landham, Md.: University Press of America, 1997.

Brennan, Claire. "Team at Haunted House." *The Mirror* (London), March 17, 2010.

Broughton, Richard. *Parapsychology: The Controversial Science*. New York: Ballantine, 1991.

Brovetto, Piero, and Vera Maxia. "Entropy Increase in Vacuum: A Conjecture About the Mechanism of Poltergeist Activity. *NeuroQuantology* 6, No. 2 (2008), 175–181.

Budden, Albert. "The Poltergeist Machine." *NEXUS* 4, No. 1 (December 1996–January 1997).

Campling, Katie. "Ghost Hunters Go on the Trail of Pub Spirits." *Huddersfield Examiner* (Huddersfield, England), September 6, 2004.

Chalmers, Robert. "Hands-On Approach." *Independent on Sunday* (London), December 1, 2002.

Chambers, Paul. *Paranormal People: The Famous, the Infamous and the Supernatural*. New York: Sterling Publishing, 1998.

Cheung, Theresa. *The Element Encyclopedia of Ghosts and Hauntings*. New York: Barnes and Noble Publishing, 2006.

Clarkson, Michael. *Intelligent Fear*. Toronto: Key Porter, 2002; New York: Marlowe and Co., 2002.

Cohen, Daniel. *The Encyclopedia of Ghosts*. New York: Dodd, Mead, 1985.

Colvin, Barrie. "The Acoustic Properties of Unexplained Rapping Sounds." *Journal of the Society for Psychical Research* 73.2 Number 899 (2010), 65–93.

Cook, Nick. *The Hunt for Zero Point: One Man's Journey to Discover the Biggest Secret Since the Invention of the Atom Bomb*. New York: Century Random House, 2001.

Cornell, Tony. *Investigating the Paranormal*. New York: Parapsychology Foundation, Inc., 2002.

Crichton, Michael. *Travels*. New York: Harper, 2002.

Crowe, Catherine. *The Night Side of Nature*. Hertfordshire, England: Wordsworth Editions, 1948.

Del Guercio, Gino. "Team Attempts to Solve Ohio Family's Mystery Floating Telephone." *Los Angeles Times*, April 28, 1985.

Dingwall, E. J., and T.H. Hall. *Four Modern Ghosts*. London: G. Duckworth and Co., 1958.

Driesch, Hans. *Psychical Research: The Science of the Super-Normal*. Manchester, N.H.: Ayer Co., 1975.

Ellison, Arthur. *The Paranormal: A Scientific Exploration of the Supernatural*. New York: Dodd, Mead, 1988.

"The Enfield Poltergeist." Shown on The Paranormal Channel, UK, December 8, 2008.

English, Eoin. "Couple Claim Evil Spirit Drove Them Out of Home." *Irish Examiner* (Dublin, Ireland), March 17, 2010. *www.examiner.ie/ireland/couple-claim-evil-spirit-drove-them-out-of-home-114712.html* (accessed September 2010).

Fodor, Nandor. *Between Two Worlds*. West Nyack, N.Y.: Parker Publishing, 1964.

———. *On the Trail of the Poltergeist*. New York: Citadel Press, 1958.

Fulton, Rick. "The Cox Files." *The Daily Record* (Glasgow). December 27, 2004.

Gault, Alan, and A.D. Cornell. *Poltergeists*. London and Boston: Routledge and Kegan Paul Ltd., 1979.

Geller, Herbert F. "Haunted House or Hoax at 966 Lindley Street?" *Bridgeport Post and Telegram*, March 2, 1975.

Geller, Herbert F. "All's Quiet With Goodins on Lindley But Who Knows?" *Bridgeport Post and Telegram*, January 18, 1976.

Gerding, Johan L.F., Rens Wezelman, and Dick J. Bierman. "The Druten Disturbances: Exploratory RSPK Research." A report given at the proceedings of the 40th Parapsychological Association convention in Brighton, England, in 1997, 146–161.

Goldman, Jane. "The Enfield Poltergeist." *Jane Goldman Investigates* (television show), October 19 , 2004.

Gris, Henry, and William Dick. *The New Soviet Psychic Discoveries*. New York: Warner, 1979.

Guiley, Rosemary Ellen. *Harper's Encyclopedia of Mystical and Paranormal Experiences*. San Francisco: Harper, 1991.

Harden, Mike. "Girl Who Made Telephone Fly Still in Prison." *The Columbus Dispatch*, June 27, 2004.

Henderson, Jim, and Doretta Johnson. *The People in the Attic*. New York: St. Martin's Press, 1995.

Hines, Terence. *Pseudoscience and the Paranormal*. New York: Prometheus Books, 2003.

Hough, Peter. "Liquid Liability." *Fate*, May 1, 1998.

Houran, James, and Rense Lange. *Hauntings and Poltergeists: Multidisciplinary Perspectives*. Jefferson, North Carolina: McFarland, 2001.

Hubbell, Walter. *The Great Amherst Mystery* (reprint). Charleston, S.C.: Nabu Press, 2010.

Huler, Scott. "Ghost Hunter Is a Hard-to-Please Believer." *The News and Observer* (Raleigh), September 12, 1995.

Hurwic, Ann. *Pierre Curie*. Paris: Flammarion, 1998.

"Interview With a Poltergeist." Channel 4 (UK), March 5, 2007.

Irwin, Harvey J., and Caroline Watt. *An Introduction to Parapsychology*. Jefferson, N.C.: McFarland, 2007.

Jahn, Robert G., and Brenda Dunne. *Margins of Reality: The Role of Consciousness in the Physical World*. San Diego: Harvest Books, 1989.

Kahn, David. "A Home's Bad Vibration." *Newsday*. December 1, 2004.

Kolodny, Lev. "When Apples Fall." *Moscow Pravda*. March 17, 1968.

Kurtz, Paul. "The Columbus Poltergeist Case." *The Skeptical Inquirer* 8 (Spring, 1985), 221–235.

———. *Skeptical Odysseys: Personal Accounts by the World's Leading Paranormal Inquirers*. Buffalo, N.Y.: Prometheus Books, 2001.

———. *A Skeptic's Handbook of Parapsychology*. Buffalo, N.Y.: Prometheus Books, 1985.

Leafe, David. "Healer or Hoaxer." *Daily Mail* (London). October 28, 2003.

Leigh, Alicia, and Steve Mera. "The Rochdale Case." From the Website of Manchester's Association of Paranormal Investigators and Training (MAPIT), but no longer available on the Internet (accessed in 2005).

Manning, Mathew. *The Link*. Austin, Texas: Holt, Rinehart and Winston, 1975.

Margolis, Jonathan. *Uri Geller: Magician or Mystic?* London: Orion Books, 1998.

Mayes, Tessa. "Seeing Ghosts: It's the Spirit of the Age." *London Sunday Times*. November 28, 2004. *www.timesonline.co.uk/tol/news/article396341.ece* (accessed December 2005).

Nicholls, David J. "The Mediumship of Maria Silbert." *Mediums and Spirit Guides*. *www.mediums-spiritguides.com/mariasiebert.htm* (accessed October 2010).

Nichols, Andrew. "A Water Poltergeist in Florida." Gainesville, Fl.: American Institute of Parapsychology and City College, 1998. *www.parapsychologylab.com/Articles/Water%20Poltergeist.doc* (accessed July 2005).

Nordenstam, Sven. "Skeptic Offers $1 Million in Paranormal Challenge." *Reuters*, December 3, 2004.

Norman, Michael. "Poking Holes in Hocus Pocus." *Cleveland Plain Dealer*. April 1, 1991.

Odling-Smee, Lucy. "The Lab That Asked the Wrong Questions." *Nature*. March 1, 2007. *www.nature.com/nature/journal/v446/n7131/full/446010a.html* (accessed August 2010).

Ostrander, Sheila, and Lynn Schroeder. *Psychic Discoveries: The Iron Curtain Lifted*. London: Souvenir Press, 1997.

Owen, A.R.G. *Can We Explain the Poltergeist?* New York: Garrett Publications, 1964.

Paterson, Billy. "Phantom Bumpincher." *Daily Record* (Glasgow). December 12, 2004. *www.thefreelibrary.com/Phantom+bumpincher%3B+Naughty+poltergeist+terrorises+barmaids.(News)-a0126045485* (accessed September 2005).

Patrick, Mike. "Demonic Doings Remain Haunting Two Decades Later." *Connecticut Post*. October 29, 1995.

Playfair, Guy Lyon. *This House Is Haunted*. New York: Stein and Day, 1980.

Pratt, J. Gaither. *ESP Research Today*. Metuchen, N.J.: Scarecrow Press, 1973.

Pratt, J. Gaither, and William Roll. "The Miami Disturbances." *Journal of the American Society for Psychical Research* 65, 409–454.

Price, Harry. *Poltergeist Over England*. Middlesex, England: Country Life, 1945.

Quinlan, James M., and Marsha May. "Baffling Ghost Wrecks a Home." *The National Enquirer*. January 14, 1975.

Radin, Dean, and Roger Nelson. "Evidence for Consciousness-Related Anomalies in Random Physical Systems." *Foundations of Physics*, 19, No. 12 (1989), 1499–1514.

Randi, James. "It's Time for Science to Take a Stand Against Popular Superstitions.' *Time*, April 13, 1992. *http://pw2.netcom.com/~cbell58/randi.htm* (accessed August 2004).

Randi, James. "Two Tales Terminate." The James Randi Hotline. *www.mindspring.com/~anson/randi-hotline/1994/0032.html* (accessed July 2005).

Rappoport, Leon. "Why We Like to Watch Scary Movies." Kansas State Media Relations and Marketing press release. October, 1997.

Rogo, D. Scott. *On the Track of the Poltergeist*. Englewood Cliffs, N.J.: Prentice-Hall, 1986.

———. *The Poltergeist Experience*. New York: Penguin, 1979.

Roll, William G. *The Poltergeist*. New York: New American Library, 1971. Special edition, New York: Paraview Books, 2004.

———. "Poltergeists, Electromagnetism and Consciousness." *Journal of Scientific Exploration* 17, No. 1 (2003), 75–86.

———. "The Question of RSPK Versus Fraud in the Case of Tina Resch." Psychical Research Foundation and Parapsychological Services Institute (Atlanta), 1993.

Roll, William G., and Valerie Storey. *Unleashed: Of Poltergeists and Murder—The Curious Story of Tina Resch*. New York: Paraview Books, 2004.

Sagan, Carl. "Does Truth Matter?" *Skeptical Inquirer* 20, No. 2 (March/April 1996), 28–33.

Schmicker, Michael. *Best Evidence: An Investigative Reporter's Three Year Quest to Uncover the Best Scientific Evidence for ESP, Psychokinesis, Mental Healing, Ghosts and Poltergeists, Dowsing, Mediums, Near Death Experiences, Reincarnation and Other Impossible Phenomena That Refuse to Disappear*. Lincoln, Nebraska: iUniverse, 2002.

Schoch, Robert M. "Psychokinesis: A Scientist Searches for the Reality Behind PK's Representations." *Atlantis Rising*, (January and February 2008), 42–43, 70–71.

Shermer, Michael. *Why People Believe in Weird Things*. New York: W.H. Freeman and Co., 1997.

Smith, Susy. *Prominent American Ghosts*. Cleveland and New York: The World Publishing Company, 1967.

Sokoloff, Alexandra. "Q and A with Alexandra Sokoloff." *Books on the House*. May 30, 2010. *http://paranormal.about.com/library/weekly/aa011303b.htm* (accessed August 2010).

Spencer, John and Anne. *The Poltergeist Phenomenon*. London: Headline Publishing, 1996.

Steiger, Brad. *Real Ghosts, Restless Spirits and Haunted Places*. Canton, Mich.: Visible Ink Press, 2003.

Talbot, Michael. *The Holographic Universe*. New York and London: Harper Perennial, 1992.

Tamayo, Juan. "Father Bill, Exorcist, Not Church-Sent." *United Press International*. November 26, 1974.

Taylor, Troy. *The Haunting of America*. Decatur, Illinoise: Whitechapel, 2001.

———. "The Mena Poltergeist." *Ghosts of the Prairie*, 2002. *www.prairieghosts.com/mena.html* (accessed July 2005).

Terletsky, Ya. "An Unknown Form of Energy." *Moscow Pravda*. March 17, 1968.

Torpy, Bill. "From Celebrity to Cellblock." *Atlanta Journal-Constitution.* October 25, 1994.

Truzzi, Marcello. "Letter to the Editor." *Parapsychology Press.* September 1, 2001.

Truzzi, Marcello, and Arthur Lyons. *The Blue Sense: Psychic Detective and Crime.* New York: The Mysterious Press, 1991.

United Press International. "Giving Up the Ghost?" *Philadelphia Daily News*, March 9, 1984,

Wagner, Stephen. "Loyd Auerbach on Ghosts." *About.Com*, 2002. *http:// paranormal.about.com/library/weekly/aa011303b.htm* (accessed August 2004).

Warren, Ed and Lorraine. "From the Case Files of the Warrens." *New England Society for Psychic Research*, December 31, 2004. *www.warrens .net/lindley.htm* (accessed September 2005).

Whitmarsh, Ron. "Police, Doctors Try to Spot Spirit Which Haunts Boy." *The St. Catharines Standard*, February 12, 1970.

———. "Relieving Frustrations, Pressures May Solve Boy's Ghost Problem." *The St. Catharines Standard*, February 21, 1970.

Wilson, Colin. *The Geller Phenomenon.* Menlo Park, Calif.: 1976; London: Aldus Books, 1976.

———. *Poltergeist! A Study in Destructive Haunting.* New York: Putnam, 1981.

Wilson, Natalie. "Poltergeist Terror." *The Cumberland News.* October 7, 2004. *www.cumberlandnews.co.uk/poltergeist-terror-1.445844?referrerPa th=home/2.3080* (accessed July 2005).

"Wiltshire Poltergeist." No author. Ghosts-uk.net. September 25, 2002. *http://ghosts-uk.net/modules/news/article.php?storyid=224* (accessed June 2004).

Zala, Vijay, Zahid Qureshi, and Ruturaj Jadar. "Ramol Cops Run Scared of Ghost." *The Ahmedabad Mirror*, December 25, 2008. *www .ahmedabadmirror.com/index.aspx?page=article&sectid=3&contentid=20 081225200812250305206262cf33524f&sectxslt=&pageno=1* (accessed June 2010).

Zinn, Rebecca. *Stardust.* Chapel Hill, N.C.: Providence Books, 1987.

Glossary

anecdotal Based solely on unscientific reports, descriptions, or observations.

ball lightning A rare type of lightning that takes the form of a luminous ball that is usually several inches across and close to the ground. The ball can be one of several different colors, may have an odor, and may be accompanied by a sound like a hiss. It will usually vanish quickly.

charlatan Someone who falsely claims to have special knowledge or power so as to deceive and take advantage of other people.

clairvoyance A special power or sense that can manifest as an ability to communicate with the dead, foresee the future, or obtain knowledge through means beyond ordinary senses or perception.

exorcism A ceremony performed to expel a demon or evil spirit from a possessed person, item, or location.

fight-or-flight Of or relating to the body's instinctive response to a stress-inducing experience, which prepares the body to either defend itself or run away.

geomagnetic storm A disturbance of the Earth's upper atmosphere—specifically its magnetosphere—that is caused by large magnetized plasma eruptions from the Sun's outer atmosphere.

inertia The property of an object to continue existing in its current state—either in rest or in motion in a straight line—until acted on by an external force.

levitation The lifting of objects through PK or RSPK.

out-of-body experience The feeling of being separate from one's body—often floating above the body or standing apart from it—and observing it from a different perspective.

parapsychology The study of general paranormal phenomena.

poltergeist A disturbance or energy with bizarre physical effects of paranormal origin that suggest mischievous or destructive intent, such as breaking or movement of objects and loud knocks or noises. The disturbance usually centers around an individual, often a young person going through puberty in a stressful house. The term is German, meaning "noisy ghost."

poltergeist agent A person, often an adolescent or teenager, around whom poltergeist activities seem to revolve.

psi A term used to encompass all paranormal abilities.

psychokinesis (PK) The power of the mind to consciously affect matter without physical contact.

recurrent spontaneous psychokinesis (RSPK) Bizarre movement of objects, noises, and other paranormal effects caused unconsciously by a person; otherwise known as poltergeist activity. Unlike PK, it occurs spontaneously and repeatedly throughout a period of time.

séance A gathering of individuals and often a medium in which they seek to make contact with the dead.

Spiritualism A movement in religion based on the belief that the souls of the dead can interact or communicate with the living, primarily by using a medium.

sublimation The psychological act of expressing a socially unacceptable emotion or feeling in a more acceptable way.

telekinesis Paranormal movement of objects. Psychokinesis is the modern term for this.

For More Information

The American Institute of Parapsychology (AIP)

Executive Center

4131 NW 13th Street, Suite 208

Gainesville, FL 32609

Website: http://parapsychologylab.com

The AIP performs research on all kinds of paranormal phenomena. Classes, workshops, and consultations for investigations of hauntings and other psychic phenomena are also offered.

The Canadian Haunting and Paranormal Society (CHAPS)

Website: http://www.chapsparanormal.ca/chaps/index.htm

Members of CHAPS investigate possible hauntings and paranormal activity in Ontario and other regions using scientific research and the latest technology and equipment available.

Ghost PRO

Website: http://ghostpro.org

Team members of Ghost PRO investigate reports of possible paranormal and unexplained activity in homes and business using observation, research, data collection, and analysis.

The James Randi Educational Foundation (JREF)

2941 Fairview Park Drive, Suite 105

Falls Church, VA 22042

Website: http://web.randi.org

Founded by skeptic James Randi in 1996, the aim of the JREF is to debunk pseudoscientific claims and promote scientific and critical thinking while exposing fraudulent claims of the paranormal. Scholarships and grants are offered to students who practice skepticism and investigative thinking.

Paranormal Research Organization (PRO)

Website: http://www.paranormal-research.org

The PRO supports paranormal investigators and researchers both in and out of the field. The organization sets ethical guidelines for psychic investigation and allows members to collaborate or share findings.

Paranormal Studies and Investigations Canada (PSICAN)

Website: http://psican.org/alpha

PSICAN explores paranormal phenomena—including ghosts, hauntings, and other subjects—in Canada, presenting articles, research, and more on its website.

Parapsychological Association, Inc.

P.O. Box 24173

Columbus, OH 43224

Website: http://www.parapsych.org

The Parapsychological Association provides professional support to scientists and scholars who study parapsychological phenomena and supports psi research and the development of research methodologies.

Parapsychology Foundation, Inc.

P.O. Box 1562

New York, NY 10021

(212) 628-1550

Website: http://www.parapsychology.org

The Parapsychology Foundation supports scientific and academic investigation of psychic phenomena and provides various resources to parapsychology professionals. It also educates the public through pamphlets, a journal, books, and more.

websites

Because of the changing nature of Internet links, Rosen Publishing has developed an online list of websites related to the subject of this book. This site is updated regularly. Please use this link to access this list:

http://www.rosenlinks.com/TTOT/Ghost

For Further Reading

Bailey, Diane. *Ghosts in America*. New York, NY: Rosen Publishing, 2012.

Belanger, Jeff. *Paranormal Encounters: A Look at the Evidence*. New York, NY: Rosen Publishing, 2012.

Belanger, Jeff. *Real-Life Ghost Encounters*. New York, NY: Rosen Publishing, 2013.

Belanger, Jeff. *World's Most Haunted Places*. New York, NY: Rosen Publishing, 2009.

Belanger, Michelle. *The Ghost Hunter's Survival Guide: Protection Techniques for Encounters With the Paranormal*. Woodbury, MN: Llewellyn Publications, 2009.

Breman, Billy. *Searching for Ghosts and Poltergeists*. New York, NY: Rosen Publishing, 2012.

Broome, Fiona. *101 Ghost Hunting Questions Answered*. Concord, NH: New Forest Books, 2014.

Broome, Fiona. *Ghosts: What They Are and What They Aren't*. Concord, NH: New Forest Books, 2014.

Broome, Fiona. *Is Your House Haunted?* Concord, NH: New Forest Books, 2013.

Clarke, Roger. *Ghosts: A Natural History: 500 Years of Searching for Proof*. New York, NY: St. Martin's Press, 2014.

Curran, Bob. *The Scariest Places in the World*. New York, NY: Rosen Publishing, 2013.

Ellis, Melissa Martin. *The Everything Ghost Hunting Book: Tips, Tools, and Techniques for Exploring the Supernatural World*. Avon, MA: F+W Media, 2014.

Ganeri, Anita. *Ghosts and Other Specters*. New York, NY: Rosen Publishing, 2011.

Groff, Nick, and Jeff Belanger. *Chasing Spirits: The Building of the Ghost Adventures Crew*. New York, NY: New American Library, 2012.

Haughton, Brian. *Famous Ghost Stories: Legends and Lore*. New York, NY: Rosen Publishing, 2012.

Hawes, Jason, and Grant Wilson. *Ghost Files: The Collected Cases from Ghost Hunting and Seeking Spirits*. New York, NY: Gallery Books, 2011.

Newman, Rich. *Ghost Hunting for Beginners: Everything You Need to Know to Get Started*. Woodbury, MN: Llewellyn Publications, 2011.

Pye, Michael, and Kirsten Dalley. *Ghosts, Specters, and Haunted Places*. New York, NY: Rosen Publishing, 2013.

Redfern, Nick. *The Most Mysterious Places on Earth*. New York, NY: Rosen Publishing, 2013.

Webb, Stuart. *Ghosts*. New York, NY: Rosen Publishing, 2013.

Recommended Paranormal Resources

Periodicals

Journal of the Society for Psychical Research
Journal of the American Society for Psychical Research
The Journal of Parapsychology
The Journal of Scientific Exploration
The European Journal of Parapsychology
The Skeptical Enquirer
Fate Magazine
The Fortean Times

Paranormal research groups

United States

- The Parapsychology Foundation: *www.parapsychology.org*.
- The American Society for Psychical Research (ASPR): *www. aspr.com*.
- Princeton Engineering Anomalies Research: *www.princeton. edu/~pear*.
- American Institute of Parapsychology: *www.parapsychologylab. com*.
- Rhine Research Center Institute for Paranormal: *www.rhine.org*.

255

- The American Ghost Society: *www.caiprs.com/Mission%20 Statement.htm.*
- Exceptional Human Experiences Network: *www.well.com/user/ bobby/ehe/eheorg.html.*
- The James Randi Educational Foundation: *www.randi.org.*
- Pacific Neuropsychiatric Institute: *www.pni.org and www.pni.org/research/anomalous.*
- Society for Scientific Exploration: *www.scientificexploration.org.*

United Kingdom

- Society for Psychical Research: *www.spr.ac.uk.*
- The Association for the Scientific Study of Anomalous Phenomena (ASSAP): *www.assap.org.*
- Manchester's Association of Paranormal Investigators and Training (MAPIT): *www.maxpages.com/mapit/home.*
- Parasearch: *www.parasearch.org.uk.* Investigates cases in the West Midlands of England.
- The Ghost Club: *www.ghostclub.org.uk.* Reportedly the oldest organization of its type
- Koestler Parapsychology Unit: *moebius.psy.ed.ac.uk.* A branch of the psychology department at the University of Edinburgh in Scotland.
- Scottish Society for Psychical Research (SSPR): *www.sspr.co.uk.*
- Institute of Paranormal Research: *www.iopr.org.uk.*
- Scottish Society for Psychical Research: *www.sspr.co.uk.*

International

- The Association for Skeptical Investigations: *www. skepticalinvestigations.org.*
- PRISMTEAM International (Australia): *free.hostultra. com/~adminprism.*

- Australian Institute of Parapsychological Research: *www.aiprinc.org*.
- Centre for Parapsychological Studies, Bologna: *digilander.libero .it/cspbologna*.
- Centre for Fundamental and Anomalies Research: *www.c-far.com*.
- Survival Research Institute of Canada: *www.islandnet.com/sric*.
- The Ontario Ghosts and Hauntings Research Society (Canada): *www.ghrs.org/Ashley/links1.html*.
- Psi Mart: *www.pst-mart.com*. Offers books, videos, and publications on parapsychology.
- Prairie Ghosts: *www.prairieghosts.com*.
- Haunted Places: *www.haunted-places.com*.

recommended reading on pk

Braude, S.E. *The Limits of Influence: Psychokinesis and the Philosophy of Science, Revised Edition*. Landham, Md.: University Press of America, 1997.

Jahn, Robert G., and Brenda Dunne. *Margins of Reality: The Role of Consciousness in the Physical World*. San Diego: Harvest Books, 1989.

other resources

- To test your psychic abilities, check the Web games at *www.gotpsi.org*.
- For Uri Geller's advice on how to develop paranormal abilities, check his Website at *www.uri-geller.com/howto.htm*.
- For more information on the Enfield case, check YouTube and these Internet sites: *paranormal.about.com/library/weekly/ aa080999.htm*; *www.mysteries.pwp.blueyonder.co.uk/1,5.htm*; *www.zurichmansion.org* (Haunted Mansions Around the World).

Index

About the Author

Michael Clarkson is an author and professional speaker who lives in Fort Erie, Ontario, Canada, with his wife of 37 years, Jennifer, after living many years in Toronto. His five previous nonfiction books have been largely based on fear and stress, including his latest on a famous pianist, *The Secret Life of Glenn Gould*.

During a career as an investigative newspaper reporter, he won a dozen national and international awards, including two National Newspaper Awards and two nominations for the Michener Award for public service in Canada for stories on police nepotism.

In 1980, Clarkson was nominated for a Pulitzer Prize for his rendezvous with reclusive author J.D. Salinger in New England.

While living in Calgary in 1994, Clarkson was a finalist for the U.S. Health Care Award for his investigation of a prescription drug scam, which had resulted in the deaths of 17 young women.

His books, including *Intelligent Fear* and *Quick Fixes for Everyday Fears*, have been translated into many languages.

Clarkson was the original researcher for the acclaimed 2009 documentary *Genius Within: The Inner Life of Glenn Gould*, nominated for a Gemini Award and a Director's Guild of Canada Award.

He is currently writing a screenplay with relationship therapist Rebecca Rosenblat.

Clarkson has two sons, Paul and Kevin, and a granddaughter, Skye.

Born in England, he has lived in Canada most of his life. His Website is *www.michaelclarkson.com*.